Renaissance in the Classroom

Arts Integration and Meaningful Learning

Renaissance in the Classroom

Arts Integration and Meaningful Learning

Edited by

Gail Burnaford

Arnold Aprill

Cynthia Weiss

and

CAPE
Chicago Arts Partnerships in Education

Routledge
Taylor & Francis Group

NEW YORK AND LONDON

The cover of this book shows children's self-portrait collages against a back-drop of a Renaissance map of the New World. We designed a cover image that would connect: the present with the future and the past, personal stories with social histories, and the self with the world. These are precisely the kinds of connections our students can make through the vehicle of arts integration.

We thank the students of Telpochcalli School: Edith Rivera, Diego Salgado and Rodolfo Castro, and artist/educator Guillermo Delgado, for creating such beautiful work and helping us to bring these ideas to life. Photo of art work: Scott Shigley

First published by

Lawrence Erlbaum Associates, Inc., Publishers
10 Industrial Avenue
Mahwah, NJ 07430

Reprinted 2009 by

Routledge   Routledge
Taylor & Francis Group   Taylor & Francis Group
711 Third Avenue,   2 Park Square, Milton Park,
New York, NY 10017   Abingdon, Oxon, OX14 4RN

Transferred to Digital Printing 2011

Library of Congress Cataloging-in-Publication Data

Renaissance in the classroom : Arts integration and meaningful learning /
   edited by Gail Burnaford, Arnold Aprill, Cynthia Weiss.
      p.   cm.
Includes bibliographical references and index.
ISBN 0-8058-3819-8 (pbk. : alk. paper)
1. Arts—Study and teaching (Elementary)   2. Arts—Study and teaching
   (Middle school)   I. Burnaford, Gail E.   II. Aprill, Arnold.   III. Weiss,
   Cynthia.
NX280 .R46   2001
700'.71'073—dc21
                                                    00-049028
                                                        CIP

The Sculpture group of the four Mende children who survived the horrors of the middle passage and the 1839 Revolt aboard the slave ship "La Amistad." Cast from Chicago school children, the sculpture piece was commissioned for the Museum's exhibition of the Amistad in which the famous Hale Woodruff Amistad murals of Talladega College were reproduced to scale as backdrop to the "Mende Children" by Rene Townsend. Rene Townsend, Sculptor. Photo courtesy of Ramon Price, curator, DuSable Museum of African American History.

Dedication

This book is dedicated to the loving memory of Rene Townsend, an artist and an educator who, by her life's example, constantly reminded us of our power to erase false divisions—between teaching and learning, between children and adults, between hearts and minds. A true artist and a true teacher, a live wire and a steady rock, she had a profound talent for sweetly challenging and warmly embracing at the same time. Everyone who knew her—students, teachers, parents, artists, friends—felt graced by her special attention, only to discover later that her spirit was so large that this personal, "exclusive" relationship included us all.

Not long before we lost her, the DuSable Museum of African American History honored Rene by commissioning her sculpture of the Amistad slave ship uprising. Rene chose to represent this historic struggle for freedom through an image of the children of the Amistad—children who survived captivity and grew up to make lives of their own choosing. The sculpture was cast directly from the bodies of students at Charles S. Brownell Elementary School. Their work with Rene connected them to their own history, their own freedom, and their own potential. It is in that spirit that this book is launched.

Contents

Arts Integration Snapshot   57
Art Is Not a Reward: Pitfalls and Promises of Arts Integration
by Andre LeMoine

Chapter 3   Moving Through the   63
            Curriculum: Doing
            the Work in Arts Integration

Appendixes

Author Index

Subject Index

Figures and Tables

Chapter 4

Arts Integration Snapshot

Chapter 6

Foreword

In most developed countries, the arts are at the margins of formal education. There are three reasons: They are seen as leisure activities, nonacademic, and irrelevant to employment or the economy. They are seen as separate from the main concerns of formal schooling, where the emphasis is on academic ability and especially literacy and numeracy. CAPE offers a powerful alternative vision of the arts and of education. This book says what this vision is and how it can be put into practice.

Education should be a social process. It must help young people engage with the cultural universes where they live and must make their way. It is through the arts that cultural values are most vividly expressed. Conventional academic education develops certain sorts of intellectual ability, especially verbal and mathematical reasoning and particular forms of critical thinking. These are very important, but they are not the whole of human intelligence. If they were, most of human culture would not have happened. There would be no music, no design, no feelings, dance, poetry, architecture, no love, relationships, or innovation. We often do need to think logically, but our deepest thoughts and judgments are also touched by values and feelings, by intuition and rapport, and by the very sensuousness of living. These are what the arts are about.

Education must enable young people to engage with themselves. It should help them recognize and develop their own unique capabilities. Human culture is so rich and diverse because human intelligence is so complex and dynamic. We can think about our experiences in all the ways we have them—visually, in sound, in movement, and in touch, as well as through words and numbers. All young people have academic abilities; for some, this is their real strength. But they also have other abilities, which may be expressed through music, art, sport, design, dance, and other ways. The arts offer many different ways to think and communicate—ways that have been the drivers of human culture and creativity down the ages. Too many young people never discover these abilities because education does not value or look hard enough for them. As a result, they often turn away from or against education altogether. CAPE has an impressive record of reengaging young people in education by rekindling their confidence in themselves and their real abilities.

The arts are important in themselves; they are also essential elements of a broad and dynamic curriculum. Motivation is born out of success. When young people find what they are good at in education, they tend to improve overall. Schools everywhere are under pressure to raise academic standards. Too often they think this means working within tightly defined subject boundaries, dropping the arts and humanities, and focusing only on conventional academic learning. This is entirely wrong. The sure way to undermine achievement is to focus on it in the wrong way.

The philosopher Michael Polanyi talks about two levels of awareness: focal and subsidiary. If you are driving a nail into a piece of wood with a hammer, you are aware of your actions on at least two levels. The focus of your attention is on the head of the nail. But you are also conscious in a subsidiary way of many other things—the weight of the hammer, the arc of your arm, the force of the drive. You must be aware of these in the right way to complete the task. If you focus on what your arm is doing, you are likely to miss the nail altogether. A pianist will be focally aware of the music and only tangentially aware of the movement of her hands in producing it. If she becomes focused on her hands, the music is likely to stop.

Similarly, in education, children often learn best by being absorbed in tasks that require the *incidental* use of skills and ideas, rather than *focusing* on them in a detached way. The arts provide powerful ways of doing this. There is growing evidence that standards of achievement rise through a broad and balanced curriculum that includes the arts, in which children are able to play to their strengths and to make connections with what they know.

CAPE illustrates these principles in practice. It is a vivid example of the educational power of the arts and of the arts in education. The tasks that face education are growing more complex and daunting by the day. They are compounded by the rate of social, economic, and technological change. Too often the arts are now being pushed to the edges of education at the very moment when what they offer is urgently needed at the center of it. CAPE is a beacon for all those who want to move forward. This book tells of its successes, its challenges, and its long-term hopes. It is written for practitioners and carries the tang of real people and real achievements in every chapter.

The example of CAPE is now being taken up in a growing number of cities beyond Chicago and beyond the United States and deservedly so. Archbishop Temple once said that the real challenge for education is "to help children to feel together and to think for themselves, instead of thinking together and feeling alone." I believe that task is becoming ever more urgent.

—*Ken Robinson*

Ken Robinson, Professor of Arts Education at the University of Warwick, England, is internationally recognized as an advocate for creative approaches to education and professional development. He recently chaired the British government's National Advisory Committee on Creative and Cultural Education, whose report, <u>All Our Futures: Creativity, Culture, and Education</u>, presented recommendations on new approaches to education and training in the context of rapid economic, technological, and social change.

Students at Mark Sheridan Elementary School send out their energy into the world through dance.
Photo courtesy of Dennis Wise.

Preface

Renaissance in the Classroom is, as its title suggests, a book about renewal. It is intended to provide a means for looking at how children learn through exploration that incorporates the arts. Our children bring with them a limitless array of intellectual, emotional, and social potential. As adult guides and teachers, we have the responsibility and opportunity to provide learning environments in which children are truly challenged, in which young learners will become capable, self-directed learners. We have the chance to provide them with the necessary opportunities to negotiate between the subjective self and the objective world, between what the Maori people call *dream time* and everyday life. This book is a record of brave experiments in realizing that potential, through what former Chancellor of the New York Public Schools, Rudy Crew, calls "that combustion of cognition that connects the world behind the learner's eyes to the world before the learner's eyes" (Crew, 1999).

Collectively, we must reclaim the value of the arts as powerful mediators between the subjective and the objective in our children's education and development. The book's six chapters and related stories provide teachers with a framework for incorporating visual art, dance, drama, and music into other subjects they teach. Such integration enhances learning and improves students' ability to think independently and solve problems. Yet we know that arts integration is a process that must be consistent with the ongoing concern for learning standards; we have tried to be mindful of our responsibility to connect to the realities of schools and incorporate strategies for directly addressing goals and outcomes of the traditional curriculum.

The book invites the reader to consider the possibilities for learning and growth when artists and arts educators come into a classroom and work with teachers. The power of introducing children to artists in and through the work of arts integration is repeatedly celebrated in *Renaissance in the Classroom*. The text is intended to be useful to administrators and parents, but is primarily directed toward K–12 classroom teachers, arts teachers, and visiting artists who are working or want to work with young people in schools.

A HUNDRED VOICES

When we decided to write a book that people could use to guide arts integration in other settings, we called together a group of representative teachers and artists from a network of arts education partnerships called the Chicago Arts Partnerships in Education (CAPE) to form a "Publications Advisory Board." These dedicated artists, teachers, and parents helped us to begin thinking about what such a book would look like and how it could be most useful to readers. We used a process of recording over 100 voices to tell the CAPE story and to write this book. We conducted individual interviews with artists, teachers, and principals. We held focus group sessions with students and parents. We also invited participants in arts integration in Chicago to write their own stories for this book. After this process of collecting data about how the partnerships worked, we faced a "network of hard and careful choices" as we planned the organization and content of this book (Wolf & Pistone, 1991, p. 6). We read hours of transcribed interviews, looked at photographs and student work samples, and poured over written curriculum materials. Originally, our goal was to serve as data collectors and preserve the individual voices of participants as cleanly as possible. We would simply arrange the ideas on the pages.

But as we began to look deeply at the data we collected, we began to push ourselves to say what arts integration really looked like. We began to move beyond the advocacy stories to the deeper questions of *how* arts integration might be described beyond the individual examples. We discovered that we were developing a theoretical account of the work as well as a practical outline of how participants had done it. It became apparent that there was an opportunity to develop a theory of practice through this research. We were aware that we, with much organizing, rethinking, and questioning, could describe just *how* arts integration occurs in classrooms and schools. We could detail what the teaching looked like in arts integration, and we could give rich examples to illustrate the framework that we were developing; we could give the reader the details of the furniture, but we could also describe the architecture of the building (Wolf & Pistone, 1991).

We returned to the data and looked for broad themes, processes, and concerns that cut across the individual perspectives of teachers, artists, principals, parents, and students. Then we developed a design for arts integration that seemed to capture much of what teachers, arts teachers in schools, and artists have actually experienced. We outlined a model that we believe is flexible enough to include the rich and welcome variability that we have tried to illustrate through the wonderful individual stories. We have suggested a process for doing arts integration supported by the examples and narratives available to us.

We also wondered whether we were moving too close to a template, suggesting that generalizations about arts integration can be made from case studies from one city. Although the processes we outline are based on the work that we witnessed in Chicago, we do not suggest that there is one way to integrate the arts. In fact, the more deeply we looked at the issues, the more complex we deemed the process. That said, we do believe that we have outlined the schemata for beginning arts integration from a set of criteria (see Appendix F: CAPE Checklist, chap. 1, and chap. 6). These criteria and descriptions of quality arts integration are intended to evoke dialogue across communities. They are a beginning, but we believe they are supported by the experiences artists, teachers, students, and parents have had here in Chicago.

We know that this process can be anything but neat and tidy, so we felt it was essential to include selected voices of real artists and teachers who express their own learning about the process and describe the work that their students and their whole school communities have produced in their own words. Those stories, called Arts Integration Snapshots, are inserted throughout the book. Although all of the book is based on the comments, suggestions, and passions of students, parents, teachers, artists, and school leaders, the snapshots are focused on a particular element of integration worth noting.

It is fitting that we tell this story in many voices because one of the arts' strengths and gifts to education is a special ability to unearth multiple perspectives on a given theme. Time and again, artists and teachers have talked about developing curriculum that uses multiple points of view as a way to get inside a text or as a means to open windows to another world, another culture, another person's life. Within the individual strands of stories, we found many common conclusions, each arrived at through separate processes of trial and error, experimentation and revision, across nine different arts partnerships. What has emerged is a theory of practice crafted through 6 years of dedication and hard work.

We as editors have combined our perspectives to bring together these 100 voices. Gail Burnaford is a teacher educator and former teacher who has worked with teachers and artists to explore how teaching and learning occurs in arts integration classrooms. Her voice has helped us clarify how the curriculum becomes renewed through a process that engages the arts. Arnold Aprill is the executive director of the Chicago Arts Partnerships in Education and the former artistic director of a theater company. His voice has helped us structure the organizational outline and see the big picture in this partnership work. Cynthia Weiss is a visual artist who has articulated what arts integration looks like from an artist's point of view. Her voice has opened up the possibilities for creativity and new ways of talking about school learning. We think the combination of our perspectives provides the reader with a rich portrait of this work.

Our diverse perspectives also helped us step out of the advocacy role and look deeply at what we were seeing as we visited classrooms, reviewed student work, and interviewed participants in arts integration. We questioned each other, challenged each other's perspectives, and pushed each other to say what it really looked like.

READING THIS BOOK

This is a book for teachers. If you teach in an elementary school, you can find teachers like yourself in these pages. If you teach middle or secondary school, you will hear from colleagues who work with students very similar to those you teach. This book describes in a very practical way just how curriculum is integrated with the arts. But it can also suggest how such curriculum integration may be possible in other areas as well. This book is about a process; it is also about a different way of thinking about one's classroom.

It is also a book for artists and arts teachers, especially those who work with children or who would like to do so in the future. For you, this book reveals the world of classrooms and how a guest in those classrooms can contribute to learning; it can open up worlds of possibility for young people. The book is about partnering with teachers, children, and the curriculum. It explains the process of integration; it also details the dynamics of being a partner for learning. For arts teachers, who often become isolated in their own schools, this book may suggest new roles for those who specialize in visual art, music, dance, drama, or media arts in the whole school curriculum.

OVERVIEW OF THE BOOK

This book is intended to be a guide to the nuts and bolts of arts integration. We do this by presenting a structure for planning and engaging students in arts integration and then surrounding this how-to explanation with rich curriculum examples and comments from people who have participated in this work. The Introduction and chapter 1 discuss a working structure for doing arts integration. Chapters 2 to 4 are the heart of that how-to explanation. Chapter 2, entitled *Getting Started With Arts Integration: Finding the Elegant Fit*, describes how teachers examine their curriculum and find meaningful teaching themes or *big ideas*. The process continues in chapter 3, *Moving Through the Curriculum: Doing The Work in Arts Integration*, which highlights what happens in and out of classrooms as arts integration is underway. Chapter 4, *Beyond the Unit: Assessment and the Learning Cycle*, provides illustrations of activities that engage students in collaborative projects and connect them to the larger community. Chapter 4 also includes some concrete examples of how arts integration can be an essential part of authentic assessment, and it describes evidence linking study of the arts with increased student achievement. These three chapters demonstrate how arts integration moves *into, through, and beyond* the classroom curriculum (Kucer, Silva, & Delgado-Larocca, 1995; see Table 1) Chapter 5 illustrates the *into, through, and beyond* by telling the stories of three science teachers who have integrated the arts in their curriculum. This chapter, *Science and Art: Lessons From Leonardo da Vinci?* reminds us how the text got its name; arts integration is an opportunity for a *Renaissance in the Classroom*.

The title of chapter 6, *You Don't Have to Do It Alone: Initiating and Sustaining Collaboration*, explains its context; there are strategies in this chapter to help individual teachers connect to others who are interested in learning through the arts. This chapter also demonstrates how whole schools can look at arts integration development over time, planning arts experiences for all children. Chapter 6 helps teachers see how they can explore the arts with the help of students and parents, even when they do not have access to an artist or an arts teacher. It describes how you can begin an arts integration approach in your classroom and, eventually, your school.

The description of how arts integration can happen is one that transcends any particular structure. The stories and curricular examples in this text illustrate how teaching–learning processes in schools can move from the linear instructional modes appropriate for a manufacturing economy to the hyperlinked, problem-based, project-based approaches appropriate for an information economy. When well planned and implemented, arts integration is one of the most effective ways for a wide range of students with a wide range of interests, aptitudes, styles, and experiences to form a community of active learners taking responsibility for and ownership of their own learning.

The resources and helpful hints in the appendixes at the end of the book provide an ongoing source of support for you. There are ideas for you to try, whether you

TABLE 1
Getting Started, Moving Through, and Going Beyond the Unit: What Arts Integration Looks Like

Getting Started: Finding the Elegant Fit	Moving Through the Curriculum	Going Beyond the Unit
◊ Building a team and a vision to do elegant work ◊ Learning from each other: the vocabulary of the arts ◊ Trying new skills: learning to dance and sing in class ◊ Finding problems and questions ◊ Brainstorming and planning together ◊ Planning shifts in teacher and artist roles ◊ Taking the time to do good work ◊ Finding and using access points	◊ Breaking ground: moving desks and opening minds ◊ Building teams of students ◊ Playing and exploring with art forms ◊ Warm-up exercises ◊ Deepening instruction: weaving parallel processes ◊ Translating across media ◊ Shedding new light on old material ◊ Coteaching and colearning ◊ Connecting to the community	◊ Traditional achievement measures ◊ Planning and doing as assessment ◊ Collaboration in assessment ◊ Revising ◊ Using rubrics ◊ Performance ◊ Exhibition ◊ Self-evaluation

work in one classroom by yourself or whether you have formed a community of artists, teachers, parents, and students interested in arts integration. The voices in this book help you find your own voice and bolster your own determination to bring the arts to educational communities in a meaningful way.

ACKNOWLEDGMENTS

This book is about meaningful learning through the arts and the kinds of partnerships that help make this learning possible. It is also a testament to the individual teachers, artists, parents, principals, partnership organizers, school liaisons, technical assistance providers, community leaders, and students who have invested their brains, bodies, and spirits in an ambitious experiment in making learning more meaningful. This book represents endless hours of their planning, dreaming, taking risks, arguing, laughing, writing, rewriting, researching, refining, rehearsing, dancing, singing, painting, cleaning up, moving desks, transporting materials, reporting, assessing, documenting, presenting, remembering, and reflecting.

All this hard work would never have coalesced into this book without the active participation of the CAPE Publications Advisory Board: Mary Cobb, Esther Grisham, Tara James, Kaja Overstreet, Jean Parisi, Thomas Park, Lara Pruitt, Tammy Steele, Victoria Turbov, Carolyn Washington, and David A. White. We also thank the CAPE staff, Associate Director Charles Twichell, Program Associate Kara Gebben, and Administrators Anna Mueller, Mignon Nance, Assistant Director and Editorial Assistant Marian Berger.

The CAPE Board of Directors has supported arts integration and the production of this book, and we thank them for their contributions: Francine Cabonargi, Kassie Davis, Harvey Daniels, Jill C. Darrow, Claudia Divis, Michael Dorf, Linda Ford, Olivia Gude, Judith Russi Kirshner, Susan Klonsky, Lee Koonce, Marcia Lipetz, Jobi Petersen, Celene Peurye, Debra Quentel, Nick Rabkin, Jean Rudd, Sarah Solotaroff, Nikki Stein, Encarnacion Teruel, Beverly Tunney, Laysha Ward, Rachel Weiss, Benna B. Wilde, and Angelique Williams. We continue to be grateful to the funders who have so graciously supported these endeavors. (See Appendix A for CAPE Funding Organizations.)

The partners in the CAPE Partnerships (listed in Table 2) have been true collaborative learners, exhibiting all the teamwork, integrity, perseverance, vision, and mutual respect we hope to see in our most effective classrooms. They have walked the walk.

The work of the Chicago Arts Partnerships in Education has been deepened by interaction with a national and international network of colleagues, including: the Armory Center for the Arts in Pasadena, the East Bay Community Foundation in Oakland, Arts Centered Educators in Detroit, the Philadelphia Education Foundation, the Center for Creative Education in Palm Beach County, the Center for Arts Education in Minneapolis, the Creative Arts Partnerships in Education in Leeds and Manchester, the London Education Arts Partnerships, the Scottish Arts Council, the British American Arts Association, the London International Festival of Theaters, Kids' Own Publishing in Sligo, Ireland, The Ark in Dublin, Ireland, the Arts Education Partnership in Washington, DC, the President's Committee on Arts and Humanities, the Illinois Arts Council, the National Endowment for the Arts, the Mississippi Arts Commission, the ICARE Program in Cleveland, the Calgary Arts Partnerships in Education Society, the Kenan Institute for the Arts in North Carolina, the National Writing Project, the GE Fund–MacArthur Foundation–U.S. Department of Education Champions of Change Initiative, Northwestern University, the Walloon Institute, the Center for City Schools at National-Louis University, Americans for the Arts, the Small Schools Workshop at the University of Illinois at Chicago, the University of Chicago—Chicago Public Schools Internet Project, the Imagination Project at UCLA, Grantmakers in the Arts, the Center for the Imagination at Columbia University in New York, the Illinois State Museum, and the Illinois Writing Project, the Metro History Education Center, and the Chicago Algebra Project through the DeWitt Wallace Readers' Digest Fund Students at the Center Initiative. ArtsVision in Rhinebeck, New York, played a central role in the design and development of the Chicago Arts Partnerships in Education.

REFERENCES

Crew, R. (1999, December). *Crossing boundaries: Arts and learning.* Presentation at Getty Museum, Los Angeles, CA.

Kucer, S., Silva, C., & Delgado-Larocco, E. (1995). *Curricular conversations: Themes in multilingual and monolingual classrooms.* York, ME: Stenhouse.

Wolf, D. P., & Pistone, N. (1991). *Taking full measure: Rethinking assessment through the arts.* New York: The College Board.

TABLE 2
Chicago Arts Partnerships in Education: Partner Schools and Arts/Community Organizations

Bridgeport, Armour Square, Near North Friends of the Arts

Healy School, Mark Sheridan Math and Science Academy, Chicago Moving Company, Creative Directions, Art Resources in Teaching, Hyde Park Art Center, Ogden School, Jackie Samuel, Terra Museum of American Art, Chicago Dance Medium, Pros Arts Studio, Donna Mandel/Dancer, Street Level Youth Media, Art and Design Department (Chicago State University)

ETA/Muntu Arts In Education Consortium

Brownell Elementary School, McCosh Elementary School, O'Keefe Elementary School, Metro/Crane High School, Parkside Academy, ETA Creative Arts Foundation, Muntu Dance Theatre, Community Film Workshop

Hawthorne/Agazssiz Arts Partnership

Agassiz Elementary School, Hawthorne Scholastic Academy, Lookingglass Theatre Company, Pool of Dancers and Visual Artists

Lakeview Education and Arts Partnerships (LEAP)

Audubon Elementary School, Lake View High School, Blaine Elementary School, Ravenswood Elementary School, Chicago Teachers Center (Northeastern Illinois University), Beacon Street Gallery and Theatre, Lakeview Chamber of Commerce, Sulzer Regional Library

Lincoln Park High School

Lincoln Park High School, Art Encounter, Hedwig Dances, Lookingglass Theater, IMPAACT, Old Town School of Folk Music, Betty Sitbon/Muralist, Textile Arts Center, Victory Gardens Theater

Tlahui Mexican Fine Arts Center Museum

Orozco Academy, Telpochcalli School, Mexican Fine Arts Center Museum

Pilsen Arts Partnership

Walsh School, Pros Arts Studio, Casa Aztlan, Dvorak Park

Southside Arts Partnership

Ray School, Murray School, Hyde Park Art Center, The Goodman Theatre, The Smart Museum of Art, The Chicago Children's Choir

West Town Arts Partnership

James Otis Elementary School, Elizabeth Peabody Elementary School, William H. Wells Community Academy, Sherwood Conservatory of Music, Northwestern University Settlement Association, Chicago Symphony Orchestra, The Goodman Theatre, Mordine Company Dance Theatre, The Marwen Foundation, Partners in Mime, Inc.

Arts Centered Educators (A.C.E.S.) Partnership

Pulaski Community Academy, Banneker Elementary School, Whirlwind Performance Company, Glenda Baker/Singer, Cynthia Weiss/Artist, Donna Mandel/Dancer, Coalition of Essential Schools.

Contributors

Connie Amon is the librarian and technology coordinator at Orozco School in Chicago. She is in her eighth year of teaching with Chicago Public Schools. Connie is married and the proud mother of a newborn son.

Andre LeMoine has been a teacher for the past 9 years in both parochial and public schools. He has often combined art and the study of literature and history. Andre has applied his love of painting and chess in various after school programs and has participated in the CAPE program for the past 2 years as a fourth-grade teacher at Orozco School.

Arnold Aprill is the executive director of the Chicago Arts Partnerships in Education (CAPE), a network of public schools, arts organizations, and community organizations committed to arts integration in Chicago. He comes from a background in professional theater as an award-winning director, producer, and playwright. He has taught at the University of Chicago, Columbia College, and the School of the Art Institute of Chicago. He is one of the writers of the musical *Sylvia's Real Good Advice* based on Nicole Hollander's nationally syndicated comic strip *Sylvia*.

Gail Burnaford is an associate professor and director of Schools/Research Partnerships and Undergraduate Teacher Education at Northwestern University in Evanston, Illinois. Her research interests, in addition to arts integration, include teacher action research and curriculum design. She is the author of *Teachers Doing Research: The Power of Action Through Inquiry* and *Images of Schoolteachers*, both also published by Lawrence Erlbaum Associates. Gail is a singer and has sung with Robert Shaw and the Atlanta Symphony Orchestra Chorus and Chamber Chorus, Basically Bach, and a variety of musical theater companies. She lives in Evanston, Illinois with her husband, David, and is the mother of two children, Maureen, a college student, and Brian, an actor.

Deb Diehl is one of the founders of Street Level Youth Media in Chicago, Illinois, and has been a leader in connecting media arts to school reform. She is currently teaching youth media for the Armory Center for the Arts in Pasadena, California.

Diane Deckert teaches fourth and fifth grade at Baker Demonstration School, a laboratory school affiliated with National-Louis University in Evanston, Illinois. Her interest in arts integration stems from her own experience working with poets, a choreographer, an actor, and visual artists to integrate art into her classroom teaching and from her work as a museum educator.

Charles Twichell developed an early love of the arts from his mother, an elementary school music teacher, and his father, a jazz aficionado. His 16 years of arts management experience has included serving in development and company management positions at Ford's Theatre in Washington, DC, as general manager of City Lit Theater in Chicago, and as associate director of the Chicago Arts Partnerships in Education from 1993 to 1997. He recently joined the staff of Prince Charitable Trusts in Chicago as a program officer.

Cynthia Weiss is the Director of Professional Development for the Chicago Arts Partnerships in Education. She has worked as an arts educator in the Chicago Public Schools for over 20 years, helping teachers to integrate the arts in their teaching practice. Cynthia is also an award-winning public artist, painter, and mosaicist. A member of the Chicago Public Art Group, she encourages community involvement in the art-making process and directs large-scale, public art projects throughout the city. She lives in Chicago with her husband, Nick, and two daughters, Emily and Claire.

Arts Integration is ...

A powerful vehicle to cross the boundaries of core subjects and arts concepts, affective and cognitive modes of expression, form and content, processes and products, the self and the world.

A process connected to a larger framework and history in which teachers have looked for connections across process and content.

Curriculum that is developed with artists and arts educators at the tables as peers with teachers in content fields.

A search for the rightness of fit between domains of knowledge across the boundaries of disciplines.

Arts learning that is deeply immersed in other content areas.

A strategy to move the arts off the sidelines of education.

A strategy for forging our way beyond false dichotomies.

A negotiation between the learner and the community.

A way of thinking about learning and teaching.

A way to teach beyond the standards.

Not an island.

Introduction

The Editors
with Charles Twichell

CHICAGO ARTS PARTNERSHIPS IN EDUCATION: HISTORY AND CONTEXT FOR LEARNING ABOUT ARTS INTEGRATION

The ideas and practices described in this book were developed inside a school improvement network called the Chicago Arts Partnerships in Education, (CAPE). CAPE was created in response to an identified need for a more coherent model for access to the arts in Chicago Public Schools. In the early 1990s, there was a high level of interest in the arts in Chicago schools, but the system of delivery could only be described as patchwork at best. Some schools had no arts teachers; most had a music teacher or a visual arts teacher, but not both, and almost none had access to dance, drama, or media arts. Arts specialists, where they existed, were often sorely overextended, serving as many as 1,400 students weekly, often having no regular work space, little equipment, few materials, and very little contact with the rest of the faculty—certainly no shared planning time. It was *art on a cart*.

At the same time, professional arts organizations were providing exposure programs (like student matinees and gallery tours), and organizations dedicated specifically to arts education were vending residencies to schools. There was very little assessment of how well these programs were actually serving schools, and access was inequitable and disorganized, both at the district level and inside individual schools. Although the quality of these exposure and residency programs was often quite high, there was something missing. They didn't *take* as part of school culture, and they didn't *catch* as curriculum.

The CAPE network was formulated as a model for making culture a true part of school culture by forging a clear connection between arts learning and the rest of the academic curriculum. This was to be done by insisting on the ongoing participation of classroom teachers and arts teachers in planning the role of the arts and visiting artists in CAPE schools, and by facilitating long-term partnership relationships between individual schools and arts organizations. CAPE was created to assist arts organizations in co-planning rigorous, innovative, sustainable curriculum with schools, rather than in delivering prepackaged and enjoyable, but transient, programs. CAPE provided technical assistance, professional development, and grants to jump-start school change.

There are six assumptions on which the CAPE partnerships are built, which also provide ways of looking at the projects described in this book. You see evidence of these tenets throughout *Renaissance in the Classroom*. We believe in:

- The integration of the arts (dance, theater, music, literary arts, media arts, visual arts) into other curricular areas (mathematics, science, social studies, language arts, physical education, foreign languages, etc.).
- The commitment of time for co-planning meaningful connections between arts learning and the rest of the curriculum.
- Long-term relationships among schools, arts organizations, and community organizations to form an ongoing professional community that reflects on and deepens the quality of instruction over time.
- A focus on the long-term professional development of teachers rather than the short-term provision of services to students.
- Attention to the development of arts education policy in whole schools.
- Democratic access to arts learning for all students, not just for the gifted and talented or just for students interested in the arts as a career choice.

CAPE was conceived of as a model for school improvement in which artists and educators co-plan integrated instruction, weaving exciting and challenging visual and performing arts learning into other academic disciplines to create more meaningful curriculum. The CAPE network supports whole schools in becoming places for artistic expression and creativity, involving and transforming parents, communities, and school leaders, as well as students, teachers, and artists. But arts integration can also occur in just one classroom, with just one teacher and one group of students.

For 6 years, CAPE functioned as a demonstration project, a living laboratory for generating new and innovative approaches to school improvement through arts integration. During this time, nine long-term partnerships were created involving 23 Chicago Public Schools, 33 professional arts organizations, and 11 community organizations (see Preface and Appendix B for partnership overviews). These partnerships have pioneered a body of work and a set of relationships demonstrating the feasibility of ongoing co-planning between artists and teachers and the value of integrating the arts across the curriculum. Partnerships like CAPE have slowly been making their mark in other urban areas. They have also begun to appear in midsize cities and small towns. Partnerships are a way of connecting communities to schools as they work together toward better educational opportunities for young people. (See the Learning Partnerships web site, *http://aep-arts.org*, for descriptions of arts education partnerships from across the United States. CAPE's website is *www.capeweb.org*.)

CAPE schools are culturally diverse; the arts organizations that have worked with them range from large regional institutions, such as a symphony orchestra, to small grass-roots organizations grounded in specific neighborhoods. They are assisted by community organizations that coordinate after-school and neighbor-hood-based programming that relates directly to in-school instruction. The partnerships are small enough to maintain a human scale of discourse. They are large enough to be inclusive of parents, children, and communities.

CAPE builds on the history of artist-in residence programs, but actively seeks to move arts learning beyond those time-limited encounters that are usually isolated from the rest of instruction in schools. The work we describe in this book investigates how the presence of an artist or arts specialist in the classroom can suggest new ways for both the teacher and students to interact with science, social studies, math, and the language arts curriculums.

CAPE not only supports the notion that arts organizations and community organizations have a civic duty to our schools, but also that schools need to take more initiative in accessing the cultural riches right there in their communities. The arts organizations have become informed enough about schools to be of real service. The classroom teachers have become comfortable enough with the arts to actually integrate the arts into their own teaching. Schools need to develop their own internal infrastructure for the arts. Outreach programs from arts organizations don't work if the schools don't know how to reach back and do *inreach* into the arts organizations. This is a dialogue, not a lecture.

THE ARTS IN AMERICAN PUBLIC EDUCATION: A BRIEF HISTORY

The arts in education have suffered an odd history in the United States. In the 1840's and 1850's, when the country was beginning to grow up and public education was taking shape, arts were largely absent from the "common" schools. Those schools- what we would now call elementary and middle schools- taught reading, writing, and arithmetic, the basic literacies and competencies considered adequate for the vast majority of working and voting adults.

When arts did begin to appear in schools around the turn of the century, they entered in a peculiar way. Music, theatre, and the visual arts, like the poetry that had filled the McGuffey readers for decades, were introduced to school children for purposes of teaching morals, enacting and celebrating the Protestant religion, enhancing patriotism, and developing habits of conformity. Arts education was also presented in schools as an extension of a "feminizing" set of abilities. It was an act of gentility to be able to sing and play the piano, draw and paint, as if these were no more than the niceties of social behavior. Young gentlemen took up pencils in their schools for the more practical endeavors of architecture and engineering that awaited them in a booming, industrializing America. (Sanchez-Purrington & Renyi, 1993, pp. 5–6)

From the earliest days of the country, the role of the arts in education was seen primarily as a refinement, not as something of value in itself. In 1844, Horace Mann, one of the chief architects of the public school system as we know it, lobbied the Massachusetts Board of Education to include music and drawing in schooling with the following words: "Drawing may well go hand in hand with music; etc. Every pure taste implanted in the youthful mind becomes a barrier to resist the allurements of sensuality" (Efland, 1988, p. 74).

Arts Education and the Public School Curriculum

From the 19th century to our current times, politics and commerce have, for good or ill, done much to shape arts education policy in this country. Ironically, in the latter decades of the 20th century, the fear of losing a competitive edge in global markets contributed to the exclusion of the arts from public school curricula in favor of a basic core curriculum. In the 1870s, it was this same fear that forced Massachusetts to become the first state to mandate the inclusion of the arts, specifically drawing, in the public schools.

The Paris Exposition of 1867 clearly showed New England textile products to be inferior to those from abroad and, if something was not done, local industry would not survive. The solution? Mandate the inclusion of drawing in all Massachusetts public schools in towns with populations of 10,000 or more. In the late 1800s, music programs also began to proliferate; Music teachers organized and began setting educational goals, the first set of graded music textbooks was published, and a serious effort began to train teachers in music through workshops and classes.

In 1882, the National Education Association, responding to a growing desire for stability and uniformity in the U.S. public education system, brought together leading educators to examine fundamental questions about education with the intention of creating a standardized curriculum for U.S. high schools. The resulting report argued for a focus on "observation, memory, expression, and reasoning" and an emphasis on "modern languages and science" as opposed to a "classical education grounded in Latin and Greek" (Sturm, 1998; cited in Efland, 1988, p. 163). The lengthy report made only scant reference to the arts, noting that "the omission of music, drawing, and elocution from the programmes offered by the committee was not intended to imply that these subjects ought to receive no systematic attention. It was merely thought best to leave it to local authorities to determine … how these subjects should be introduced" (Sturm, 1998; cited in Efland, 1998, p. 163). Although probably not the writers' intention, the report had a chilling effect on the development of arts education in public school systems for decades.

Progressive Education Theory: Arts Education as the Social, Common, and Public Aspects of Experience

Early in the 20th century, progressive education theories emerged that acknowledged the arts as an important part of all learning. John Dewey's writing, and his work at the University of Chicago's Laboratory School, signaled a major break with the traditions of the times, which were typified by authoritarian classrooms and an emphasis on the institution over the individuality of the child. Dewey saw education as "a matter of individual growth and development of the social, common, and public aspects of experience. Stress was placed on the interrelatedness of individual, school, and society" (Zimmerman, 1997, p. 3). Dewey espoused the belief that no subject "should be taught in isolation," and that the arts in particular are "not a segregated realm of endeavor but [are] a quality that makes certain experiences worthwhile" (Efland, 1988, p. 170).

In 1939, Leon Winslow (cited in Efland, 1988) published *The Integrated School Art Program*, where he described a model of education in which art—and all subject areas—are seamlessly stitched together to create a deeper, richer educational experience and are connected to the larger community outside the school walls. Winslow's book "strongly advocated creative expression but also maintained that art should be taught for broad cultural purposes, that in this capacity it can function as an important integrating agent in the curriculum" (Efland, 1988, p. 209). Harold Benjamin wrote the following introduction to *The Integrated School Art Program*:

> *Activities that have become divorced from community life and purposes are perhaps suitable or even indispensable for a school purporting to give a timeless culture for its own sake, but they are unsuitable for a school as a living community.... Arts as a cult, as an esoteric experience for privileged devotees, may be the art that is needed in a school of the first type. Art as a service to men living a common life, art as a means of attaining community goals, is certainly needed in the modern school.* (cited in Efland, 1988, p. 205)

The Suburbanization of Arts Education: An Emphasis on Self Expression

The years prior to World War II marked the appearance of a new middle class that began moving into newly created suburbs. This trend dramatically picked up speed in the postwar economic expansion. Part of the middle-class ideal of having *arrived* economically was investing in a broad palette of educational opportunities for middle-class children. This included attention to and resources for arts and physical education programs in suburban school systems, and it marked the beginning of increasingly stratified access to arts education in public schools in America.

This suburbanization of the arts coincided with new transience and mobility in American living patterns, the atomization of long-standing stable neighborhoods, and the rise of the nuclear family (as opposed to the extended family). In arts education, this was manifested as a shift from the emphasis during the progressive period on the arts as part of extended social networks and responsibilities to an emphasis on the arts as meeting individual, private needs for self-expression.

Curiously, during the 1950s, when the rest of education was adopting an increasingly conservative and antiprogressive stance, the arts education community refused to relinquish some aspects of progressive theory—specifically, its child-centered focus. Under the influence of prominent arts educator Viktor Lowenfeld, this emerged as a conception of arts education as personal expression. As cultural critic Karen Hamblen (1990) observed,

> Much of art education was embracing a theory of instructional noninterference for the sake of children's creative expressions.... Teacher autonomy, aesthetic problem solving, and student selection for content were integral to the assumptions of much of the field. Needless to say, none of these laissez-faire characteristics of the 1950's helped art education fit in with core curriculum subjects. (p. 28)

The legacy of an arts education focus on self-expression cuts two ways: creating both an enduring longing for space in schools unencumbered by the rigidities of high stakes testing, as well as an enduring image of arts education as frivolous and unable to distinguish between initial playful encounters with art media, and the rigorous, disciplined, reflective processes necessary for serious engagement with the arts.

Sputnik, the Cold War, and "Back to Basics"

In 1957, one act of technological wizardry on the part of the Soviet Union gave Americans their first full-scale inferiority complex in modern times and left an inedible mark on education and the arts: the launching of the spy satellite Sputnik. The U.S. government responded with an all-out push to increase its technological capabilities. Conservative forces in education quickly rallied, and "a counterrevolution against progressive education took place" with a call "for a return to 'basics' in the schoolroom" (Berube, 1999, p. 2). Sputnik was a watershed moment in the history of arts education, initiating decades of declining status as the U.S. government invested vast sums in "the mobilization of education to meet the pressing demands of national security and to maintain its competitive edge in math and science" (Fowler, 1996, p. 20).

Renewed Interest in Arts Education as Part of the New Social Contracts of the 1960s

President Kennedy's commitment to the arts and culture and President Johnson's vision of a "Great Society" ushered in a creative flowering of arts in education programs in America. The National Endowment for the Arts and the National Endowment for the Humanities were established. The Sputnik-era focus on academic excellence, especially for gifted students, gradually gave way to concerns about educational equity. Civil rights legislation and the investment of federal dollars in early intervention programs like Head Start, and in new educational development and research initiatives, laid the groundwork for a wide range of unprecedented arts education programming that attempted to address the needs of a wide range of American communities. A growing number of pioneering artists and educators began to reconceptualize the entire arts education framework and began experimenting on a wider scale with educational models in which the role and function of the arts were reenvisioned and retooled. New alliances began to form between the previously segregated arts disciplines and their professional associations to establish common goals and political constituencies. A new vocabulary began to emerge with terms like *comprehensive arts*, *artist-in-residence*, *aesthetic education*, and *arts infusion*. An arts education movement was born, and this movement continues to this day.

A National Report Relegates the Arts to Elective Status, Again

Beginning in the 1970s and picking up momentum in the 1980s, there again emerged a growing concern about America's capacity to compete in the global economy. Restoring excellence in education was on the minds of Americans, prompted by reports such as the oft-quoted A *Nation at Risk* prepared by the National Commission on Excellence in Education. *Accountability* was fast becoming a buzzword, and the groundwork for the current standards movement was laid. Art was again returned to the educational sidelines. The Getty Center for Education in the Arts was launched during this period, and its organizers attempted to demonstrate that creative expression and rigorous, discipline-based learning are not antithetical.

The Challenge of Moving Beyond False Dichotomies

The current and historical ambivalence toward arts education in America has been based on a series of false dichotomies:

- **A false split between the intellectual and the sensory**—a split that goes back to the belief systems of early American settlers. Studies by such researchers as Renate Nummela Caine and Geoffrey Caine (1991) and by Howard Gardner (1983) and his colleagues at Harvard challenge this polarity.

- **A false split among content, skills, and concepts**—a split that undergirds the pendulum swings between progressive education movements and back-to-basics movements. Quality arts integration stresses content, skills, and concepts, acknowledging both the importance of personal expression and of received knowledge.

- **A false split between the vocational skills needed by the economy and the intellectual and personal skills needed by individual learners.** The increased need for creativity, independent decision making, and flexibility called for in an information economy clearly argues for the importance of arts education in developing vocational skills for the 21st century. But it is worth remembering that the purpose of any economy and of any educational system is to be of service to its citizens and not the other way around. The citizenry *is* the economy. The nurturing of the citizenry's collective and individual aptitudes *is* the education system. Vocational, intellectual, and personal skills are all joined together in educational programs that develop and enact a wide range of student capacities.

- **A false split between the social and the personal, between the democratic and the elite.** Making and perceiving art has many different functions—some social and some personal, some democratic and some elite. "There is art that exists to maintain traditions. There is art that exists to break traditions. There is art that exists to individuate, there is art that exists to create cohesion. There is art that exists for exclusive connoisseur, and art that exists for democratic inclusion" (Aprill, 1998, p. 19). It is this very complexity and variability, this fluidity of functions, that makes the arts so valuable as an integrative force in education.

Arts integration is a strategy for forging our way beyond these false dichotomies by moving the arts from the sidelines of education into what arts educator and theoretician Jane Remer (1996) called "the muscle and sinew of the daily curriculum" (p. 3). Remer helped us summarize the history of arts education in this country in her book, *Beyond Enrichment: Building Effective Arts Partnerships With Schools and Your Community*, in which she quoted from the late arts education innovator Charles Fowler:

> *The goal is the utilization of the arts process as an integral part of basic education. One prerequisite to attainment of this goal is to treat all the arts, collectively, as a content area that has the same status and educational responsibility as other major departments. The first step to accomplishing this goal is to view the arts* **comprehensively**. *The comprehensive view is advantageous. It immediately helps to organize the segmented, varied arts offerings in a school into one cohesive area of curriculum with unified goals and evaluative procedures. Properly conceived, the arts constitute a great integrating force in the school curriculum. To achieve such an end they must be viewed as a component of every discipline, for their subject matter is as broad as life itself.* (Fowler; cited in Remer, 1996, p. 25)

ARTS EDUCATION AND SCHOOL REFORM: FINDING THE CONNECTIONS

There has been a surge of discussion in recent years about school reform. There has also been a renewed interest in the presence of the arts in classrooms in this country. According to the National Arts Education Association, the number of states requiring study of the arts for high school graduation has recently increased from 2 to 32 (Buchbinder, 1999). We see a clear connection between these two areas; arts education can play a key role in school improvement as policymakers and classroom teachers strive for excellence in education.

CAPE has consistently attempted to connect the work of the partnerships with that conversation about how to improve schools. For CAPE schools, **arts integration and school improvement go hand in hand**. Arts integration, however, does much more. For these teachers and these schools, arts integration is based on the notion of teaching beyond the standards.

The last decade has seen a boom in educational literature and research recognizing the importance of the arts in education. The same decade has seen a parallel boom in school reform practice and school improvement strategies. Unfortunately, like the proverbial two trains running on separate tracks, the arts education community and the school reform community have failed to combine their strengths in any ongoing or substantive way. Classroom teachers who want to implement their school improvement plans and simultaneously provide their students needed access to the arts often have to function in parallel universes that operate in contradictory ways.

Arts integration is an emergent strategy for school improvement. We are just beginning to understand its subtleties, promise, complexity, and limitations. We need more research that attends to what arts integration actually produces with respect to student learning, teachers' practice, and curriculum content. This book is a step in that process.

Renaissance in the Classroom is intended to be a thoughtful, well-documented portrait of the complex processes involved in arts integration, rather than merely an advocacy piece for arts integration as a monolithic entity. We are aware that some arts integration advocates unwittingly drift into a kind of boosterism that replaces nuanced attention to what the arts actually can and can't do for teaching and learning, with a generalized, undifferentiated enthusiasm. This sentimental approach often fails to distinguish between the particularities of the different art forms, doesn't attend to developmentally appropriate instruction, and takes early experimentation with art media and confuses the pleasures of that experience with the disciplined work needed for developed, finished art production. High quality arts integration values technical mastery and recognizes the creativity involved in all good teaching.

We are interested in contributing to a dialogue about how each art form contributes to learning and how the arts can enhance the literature and practice of good pedagogy in a larger sense. There are substantial connections between the teaching practices in arts integration classrooms and those in evidence in strong, well-conceived science inquiry classrooms or literature discussion classrooms. A dialogue about these practices and what connects them contributes to the larger effort to reform schools.

Similarly, there are aspects of arts education that are powerful models for how one could effectively teach other things. We need to continue our research to examine which art form is suited for which aspects of science content, literature discussion, or history interpretation. Because the arts have been so marginalized historically, some schools settle for any presence of the arts irrespective of quality. The bottom line remains; a good art program, regardless of whether it is integrative, is good for students, whereas a bad art program is not.

In this sense, this book is an attempt to cross the boundaries between school reform and the role that the arts can play in that reform. There is some compelling evidence that the arts can play a significant role in changing school environments and increasing student achievement. Our current work is to explore the more concrete implications for curriculum and instruction to provide more coherence to the discussion. The impact of arts experiences on learning was the focus of a recent research report, *Champions of Change*, released in October 1999 and funded by the G.E. Fund and the John D. and Catherine T. MacArthur Foundation. Seven teams of researchers from UCLA, Stanford, Columbia Teachers' College, North Central Regional Educational Laboratory (NCREL), University of Connecticut, Harvard's Project Zero, and Harvard's Graduate School of Education examined exemplary arts programs in schools (including CAPE) and in after-school settings. Although the researchers used different methodologies and presented their results independently, there was a remarkable consensus among their findings.

The Executive Summary by Edward B. Fiske reported the following across the projects:

The arts reach students who are not otherwise being reached.

The arts reach students in ways that they are not otherwise being reached.

The arts transform the environment for learning.

The arts provide learning opportunities for the adults in the lives of young people.

The arts connect students to themselves and each other.

The arts connect learning experiences to the world of real work.

The summary concludes:

These *Champions of Change* studies demonstrate how involvement with the arts provides unparalleled opportunities for learning, enabling young people to reach for and attain higher levels of achievement. The research provides both examples and evidence of why the arts should be more widely recognized for its current and potential contributions to the improvement of American education.

(See chap. 4 for more on the *Champions of Change*/UCLA's Imagination Project research on CAPE's impact in Chicago schools. The whole report, *Champions of Change: The Impact of the Arts on Learning*, is available on the Kennedy Center web page: *http://artsedge.Kennedy-Center.org*.)

Effective learning is a negotiation between received knowledge and original inquiry, between social consensus and individual expression. School improvement efforts sometimes get stuck focusing on just one or the other end of these negotiations. Arts integration gives aesthetic form to the negotiation.

The participants in this project have learned much about the arts as a pathway for meaningful learning. They have learned much about effectively addressing standards and state goals in and through arts goals. They have developed assessment strategies that are applicable across the curriculum and stretch our understanding of what students know and are able to do. Listen to their voices. They are the architects of this renaissance.

REFERENCES

Aprill, A. (1998, November). *Whole school improvement through the arts*. Presentation at Grantmakers in the Arts conference, Chicago.

Berube, M. (1999). Arts and education. *The Clearing House*, 72, 150–152.

Buchbinder, J. (1999). The arts step out from the wings. *Harvard Education Letter*, 15(6), 1–4.

Caine, R. N., & Caine, G. (1991). *Making connections: Teaching and the human brain*. Alexandria, VA: Association for Supervision and Curriculum Development.

Efland, A. D. (1988). *A history of art education: Intellectual and social currents in teaching the visual arts*. New York: Teachers College Press.

Fowler, C. (1996). *Strong arts, strong schools*. New York: Oxford University Press.

Gardner, H. (1983). *Frames of mind*. New York: Basic Books.

Hamblen, K. A. (1990). An art education future in two world views. *Design for Arts Education*, 91(3), 27–33.

Remer, J. (1990). *Changing schools through the arts: How to build on the power of an idea*. New York: ACA Books.

Remer, J. (1996). *Beyond enrichment: Building effective arts partnerships with schools and your community*. New York: ACA Books.

Sanchez-Purrington, S., & Renyi, J. (1993). *Arts and school reform*. New York: The National Coalition for Education in the Arts/The American Council for the Arts.

Sturm, C. A. (1998). Advocating music study in the United States: A colorful history with lessons for today's arts supporters. *American Music Teacher*, 47(4), 17–21.

Zimmerman, E. (1997). Excellence and equity issues in art education: Can we be excellent and equal too? *Arts Education Policy Review*, 98, 20–26.

Renaissance in the Classroom

Arts Integration and Meaningful Learning

1

Arts Integration:
What Is It and Why Do It?

Background

Curriculum Integration

- t   Finding problems and asking questions
- t   Negotiation between the learner and the community
- t   Deepening instruction
- t   Co-teaching and co-learning

Project-Based Learning

- t   Conceiving of a problem to solve or a question to answer
- t   Real tasks and real purposes
- t   Authentic audience
- t   Links between school learning and the real world

Multiple Intelligences

- t   Building on students' strengths
- t   Recognizing schools' dependence on logical/mathematical and linguistic intelligences
- t   Attending to students' capacities using their musical, spatial, bodily/kinesthetic, intrapersonal, and interpersonal intelligences

Arts Integration: The Elegant Fit

- t   Synergy between content areas
- t   Varied and connected ways to represent knowledge
- t   Means of committing concepts and content to memory
- t   Concrete evidence of learning
- t   Representation of history and culture

- t Means to reflect on contemporary life
- t Access to scientific and mathematical principles

Rationale for Arts Integration

- t The arts deepen instruction
- t The arts invite teachers and students to be co-teachers and co-learners
- t The arts help students connect their learning to the community and to the world

Arts Integration:
What Is It and
Why Do It?

Second-grade students at Pulaski Elementary had been studying ecology. They used recycled milk cartons to create a scale model of their school and its surrounding neighborhood. The students photographed actual homes in the area, reproduced accurate scale models, and designed communities on the computer program, "Sim City." Because the neighborhood is being gentrified, the homes were changing during the course of the project. This led to lengthy discussions about neighborhood planning and how to create communities that were the right scale for children. The project culminated in the presentation of the scale model to the principal and a discussion about the need for a school playground. Six months later, the school did indeed build a playground. (See photos)

p   p   p   f   f   f

Sophomores, juniors, and seniors in the Metro Program at Crane High School worked with filmmakers and video artists from the Community Film Workshop to dissect characters on TV. They analyzed African-American stereotypes in the media; examined what messages an image communicates through point of view, framing, lighting, focus, and color; determined their own messages; and then created their own story boards for filming. (See photo)

p   p   p   f   f   f

Third graders at Murray Language Academy studied birds, but they did much more than that. They took part in a multidimensional learning process that consisted of experiments (e.g., "What is inside an uncooked chicken egg?"); movement, dance, and role-playing (e.g., moving like penguins and eagles); origami and other visual arts; a visit to the zoo; research on migration patterns; reading both fiction and nonfiction books dealing with birds; and descriptive writing. Using the knowledge they gained through this multi faceted curriculum, the students created original illustrations of birds that were then laminated for bookmarks.

How is learning happening in each of the classrooms and schools described in these vignettes? How are children engaged? What seems to be the role of curiosity and imagination in each of these classroom stories? In other words, what's going on here?

Carol Navarro's second grade students at Pulaski Community
Academy build a scale model of their community in a lesson that
integrates math, social studies, and sculpture.
Photo: Cynthia Weiss

The Community Film Workshop teaches students how to view the world through a camera at Metro/Crane High School.
Photo: Jim Taylor, Community Film Workshop

For starters, each of these classrooms, as part of the Chicago Arts Partnerships in Education (CAPE) network, has access to painters, dancers, musicians, filmmakers, videographers, and others who think about the world as artists do. They also have day-to-day access to teachers who think creatively about how learning in their classrooms can go beyond the textbook and dip right into the real world. These teachers and the artists who work with them have been engaging in **arts integration**. These teachers believe that children not only need the arts in their daily lives, but also can benefit from arts learning that is deeply immersed in other curricular areas.

The teachers in those classroom stories are faced with the same challenge of meeting state goals and district standards as other teachers throughout the country. They are held accountable for students' test scores on a regular basis, and they feel the pressure of time to cover everything that a child should know by the time he or she moves on to the next grade level. Yet they have seen firsthand that none of those external goals can happen unless children participate actively, use their hands as well as their minds, and make connections between what they are learning and what they are living. These teachers see **arts integration** as one avenue for making these laudable goals into practical realities.

This chapter introduces the idea of **integration** as many of the teachers and artists in the CAPE network have come to know it. We describe how arts integration is embedded in the larger context of curriculum integration, which has a history in the field of education. The chapter also explores how arts integration is compatible with other engaged learning strategies such as problem-based learning and teaching with awareness of the multiple intelligences. Arts integration is not an island; this approach builds on the work of many other initiatives dedicated to making schooling more rigorous, real, and creative for young people.

Arts integration is a way of thinking about learning and teaching; it is not a formula, and it is not a strict structure that requires specific resources. Arts integration encourages individuals and groups of school people to stretch out a hand to community resources, whatever they may be, and make connections to the school curriculum. It encourages leaders of young learners to transfer knowledge from one area to another and to make connections between a unit in mathematics and a unit in social studies, or between a unit in science and a unit in language arts. This process shows students that such thinking is possible and actually done in the real world. That is what arts integration is all about.

CURRICULUM INTEGRATION: HISTORY AND CONTEXT

What does curriculum integration look like regardless of whether the arts are present? We felt it was important to take a step back and examine that question because arts integration is a process that is not unconnected to a larger framework and history in which teachers have looked for connections across processes and content.

As the vignettes at the opening of this chapter illustrate, curriculum integration often involves a structured inquiry process that encourages **finding problems and asking questions**. Students work from what they know and what they want to know, and they develop complex means to represent and present what they are learning. Even second graders can build a neighborhood architectural plan. The learning that they produce typically has value beyond their lives in classrooms; real-world people engage in that learning, see the performances, and share in many of the products that students develop. Then there is conscious and extensive reflection that helps adults and young learners figure out what they did and what it means during the arts integration experience. In other words, curriculum integration is a conscious **negotiation between the learner and the community**; it involves questions of personal meaning for the learner and questions of social responsibility for the learner as a citizen of the planet.

The history of curriculum integration suggests that we are talking about much more than simply joining one piece of content with another. Integration of content is really more of an educational philosophy than it is an instrument for *doing* something in the classroom. Jim Beane (1997) is an educator who has written and thought much about the meaning and purpose of curriculum integration in general. He noted that curriculum integration, when it is seen as a core precept of democratic education, "seeks connections in all directions."

What does that mean? **Integration deepens instruction** by bringing skills, media, subjects, methods, means of expression, people, concepts, and means of representation to the service of learning. Through integration, kids in schools have access to all these things. When the Civil War becomes a focus for integration, students have the opportunity to talk to real people outside the classroom about the meaning of the war; they find new ways to visually represent what the war might have meant to families in that time; they research the music that tells the tales of the war; they share their knowledge with people beyond the four walls of their classroom. Curriculum integration seeks connections in all directions.

Beane (1997) went a step further and contended that curriculum integration is really about social integration, claiming that "... teachers who use the approach make concerted efforts to create democratic communities within their classrooms" (p. 65). Arts integration classrooms also value this notion of democratic communities. The arts bring people together to work toward common goals and express key concepts and beliefs, as the stories in this book reveal. Integration of curriculum becomes a strategy for advocacy. Teachers and artists advocate for understanding, for knowledge across cultures, and for community building.

Curriculum integration reflects value systems about the purposes of teaching and learning. This adds yet another dimension to our understanding of curriculum integration—the aspect of integrating self and social interest. Curriculum integration is a methodology for assisting students in negotiating between their personal needs and their connection to the larger community. This negotiation is the basis of all meaningful learning.

The integration of two subjects—music and math, history and dance—is not an end in itself. Such connections invite integration of a continuum of skills, content, and concepts. Meaningful curriculum integration generates genuine exploration of concepts that stretch across disciplines while giving students opportunities to test their own skills (Whitin & Whitin, 1997). Integrative curriculum is more than a set of basic discrete skills that can easily be measured by standardized means. But such curriculum can engage students in learning and using those skills as they grapple with deeper concepts and themes that are not limited to one specific content field. Integration brings teachers and students together for **co-teaching and co-learning**. Curriculum integration is a means toward deeper instruction and meaningful learning, toward greater social understanding, and toward a more complex and more interesting view of the world.

Project-Based Learning: A Link to Curriculum Integration

Throughout this book, teachers, students, and artists discuss the projects they have done through arts integration. The term *project* has a long history in education, not unconnected to work in the arts. In 1918, William Heard Kilpatrick introduced the project method in educational circles (Hennes, 1921; Kilpatrick, 1918). Kilpatrick believed that children would learn more if they were engaged in some purposeful activity, rather than just completing tasks for the teacher to view and assess. If students had a purpose that was real and useful in the world, according to Kilpatrick, they would learn more and feel better about themselves. They would become thinkers as well as doers.

Sound familiar? Here in the advent of the 21st century, we are still working toward approaches in schools that link student work with real tasks and authentic purposes. Others initiatives in education, such as problem-centered learning (Casey & Tucker, 1994) and project-based learning (Wolk, 1994), take their cue from Kilpatrick's earlier methods, and so does arts integration. In all of these strategies, there are real products, with considerable input from students in the planning and conceiving of those products.

Students in project-based learning classrooms often collaboratively conceive of a question or an issue to explore. They see the inevitable links between what they are learning in school and what the community and the world have to contribute to that learning. What's more, they see what *they have to contribute back to that community and that world*. Students must solve problems and use strategies that they learn to work with others. The process of conceiving, designing, and following through on a plan of action becomes critical to students' success. As Eve Ewing, a seventh grader at Hawthorne School, put it, "Art changes people's minds." Action and reflection are both indicators of thoughtful integration. Art can, indeed, change people's minds … about social issues, about solving problems, and about how school children can be active agents in their communities.

Multiple Intelligences: More Awareness of the Value of Arts in Classrooms

One familiar movement in schools today is the alignment of curriculum with multiple intelligences. Howard Gardner's (1983) theory of multiple intelligences (MI), outlined in his book, *Frames of Mind*, has contributed to the increasing awareness of the value of the arts in children's learning and in schools today. Educators such as Thomas Armstrong (1994) and David Lazear (1991), have helped translate Gardner's theory, which is essentially a psychological framework, to the world of classroom teachers. Gardner suggested that there are at least seven intelligences that most people bring to learning. Of the seven, two (linguistic and logical/mathematical) seem to predominate in most classrooms, although many children have dominant intelligences in other domains. The theory, with respect to schooling, is that if we expanded the repertoire of teaching practices to include more attention to students' capacities to use their musical, spatial, intrapersonal, interpersonal, and bodily/kinesthetic intelligences, we may reach more children. Building on students' strengths through their more dominant intelligences equips them to learn more fully.

Teachers are attracted to this theory and have embraced the possibilities for their classrooms. They have attended workshops, conferences, and teacher development sessions that provide information on how these intelligences might actually be utilized as learning tools across the curriculum. As a consequence, we have seen more and more classrooms that include aspects of the arts in the curriculum.

What is the relationship between MI theory and arts integration? Can one inform the other? As with so many theories that educators borrow from other disciplines, it is important that practice-based strategies be developed to give form to theories about learning. Applying such complex theories about how the brain functions to classroom practice is a daunting task for teachers. Balancing the strengths of individual children and whole class curriculum goals requires attention to more than just one theory of learning. Teacher guidebooks invite teachers to design activities to *awaken intelligence, amplify intelligence, teach intelligence,* and *transfer intelligence* (Lazear, 1994). But what do those phrases mean in practical terms? Teachers who are not trained psychologists need opportunities to engage in arts activities to reflect on their value for children. They need to develop their own artistic awareness to design experiences with young people. They need to do more than apply theory; they must live it. David A. White (1983), philosopher and parent involved in arts integration in Chicago, commented:

> It has been suggested that the arts can be a rich assembly of interlocking intelligences. But, it may still be asked, why should the arts be considered as a source of principles and insights for reorganizing a purely academic curriculum? The practice of the arts will, by itself, not provide an increased understanding of academic content. Rather, it is necessary to _reflect_ on the practice of the arts in order to achieve this goal. (p. 1)

Arts integration begins with the strengths of the art forms. In arts integration, teachers and students practice that reflection deeply. The artist or arts teacher's presence and knowledge regarding each art form introduces teachers to other ways of knowing and reflecting on knowledge. Teachers are not designing lessons that have an arts option. Rather, the model is more of a multiple Venn diagram, with depth and breadth not just in the content field knowledge the **teacher** is bringing, but also in the art form that the **artist** or **arts teacher** is bringing. A psychological imperative to reinforce other content areas by tapping into other styles for learning does not, by itself, provide enough knowledge base in the arts to be of practical use to teachers and students.

MI theory has been a wonderful approach for teachers. Many have begun to realize that not all children learn in the same way, nor do they access information and ideas through the same conduits. Arts integration takes that initial insight and builds a real depth of knowledge and experience, coupled with reflection in the art form as well as the content field(s) that are studied in the classroom. Howard Gardner (1999) asserted that "every intelligence has the potential to be mobilized for the arts." That is what arts integration intends; its processes help create the environment necessary for learning to occur and for the brain to be engaged in a complex way.

Are these just fads or swings on the pendulum? There seem to be some undergirding themes here that persist no matter what approach is named. Arts integration is not a trend that will pass in time. It is a way of thinking about how children learn and think; it is a way of conceiving of teaching in classrooms that lets children be problem solvers, connoisseurs, and critics (Eisner, 1994).

THE ELEGANT FIT: NEW ROLES FOR THE ARTS IN SCHOOLS

Arts integration is teaching and learning, in which the arts play a key role in the development of learners' capacities to negotiate between multiple spheres—between the self and the world (between received knowledge and original inquiry, between social consensus and individual expression, between the learner and the community), between realms of experience (between thought, feeling, and action, between the adult world and the child's world, between life in school and life out of school), and between types of achievement (between processes and products, between academic skills and life skills, between content and concepts.) Arts integration gives aesthetic form to these negotiations. Because the arts give sensory representation to cognition, make learning palpable and visible, they are a powerful medium for learners knowing themselves as learners, recognizing when they are engaged in meaningful learning. Arts integration is a strategy for learners investing in their own development.

Arts integration is integrated curriculum that is developed with artists and arts educators at the table as peers with educators from other content areas. Even in schools that are committed to integrated curriculum, in which teachers from different content areas plan together, art and music teachers are often left out, and theater, dance, and media artists are rarely even considered as possible colleagues. Arts integration means that the artist provides a resource, not a recess, for teachers. Arts integration includes arts skills, concepts, and content as an integral part of instruction in all disciplines. This has particular benefits for the classroom.

Many art and music teachers have been given second-class status in schools, and many art and music rooms in such buildings have become invaluable safe havens for alienated youth. It is understandable and often useful for arts rooms to provide a sense of distance from the rest of the school. (Many high school students engaged in arts integration described their experiences in this way.) Nonetheless, arts integration initiatives tend to recognize the inherently social nature of the arts. Arts integration is not just about the arts deepening other learning in other areas; it is also about the rest of the curriculum deepening and enriching the making and understanding of the art. The word *aesthetic* originally referred to deep engagement with the sensory experience of the material world. Its meaning has been distorted to imply an ethereal sense of detachment to the detriment of art and learning (Buck-Morss, 1992).

🌀 **The arts produce a genuine synergy between content areas by engaging multiple models of inquiry.** Integrated teaching is not about studying diverse content all generated and represented in the same mode. Rather, integration is about engaging a rich array of skills and learning strategies so that the understandings of each content area is enriched and illumined by the presence of other content areas.

Example: *Students in Grades 4 through 6 at Ogden School participated in a Drama Integration Experience focusing on the Maya, Inca, and Aztec Cultures. (See Appendix D.) Teacher Martha Cerda worried about the amount of time devoted to this "playing" with drama and art. "After all, I had goals to meet accountability!"*

But when she began to analyze her arts integration efforts, she realized that her fourth graders did all of the following:

Participated in organizing and planning from start to finish

Researched information about the Aztec culture

Read and listened to stories of ancient cultures

Wrote their own scene scripts of cultural stories

Planned props, characters, setting, and chronological action for their scenes

Wrote dialogue

Used map-making skills

Used cooperative learning skills

Studied the interrelationships between geography and culture

Solved problems

Kept a drama journal

Drew, painted, and created

Ms. Cerda: *"When it was finished, I realized that the children had in fact done a great deal of reading, writing, social studies, as well as art."*

f   **The arts provide varied, connected, and increasingly challenging opportunities to generate and represent knowledge over time.** The arts, by providing a *variety* of connected learning opportunities, not only engage a variety of learners, but also demand higher order thinking of all learners as they *translate* between media (Gallas, 1994).

Example: *Visual artist Cynthia Weiss and classroom teacher Sue Shupe developed a social studies unit integrating visual arts and U.S. history. The unit introduced students to activities that provided multiple lenses for understanding both history and art making. The issues addressed in both content areas built on the preceding experiences and increased in sophistication over time. The big idea of the unit was that history is a timeline of competing points of view. The initial drawing and writing activities were focused on very concrete understandings of point of view from a visual arts perspective. Next, the students developed timelines based on their own family histories, bringing in family photographs from different periods in their lives. Students broke into groups and researched different historical periods from the point of view of different populations (such as conflicting concepts of land ownership from the point of view of Native Americans and settlers traveling west to homestead the land). They also discussed what each period must have been like from a child's point of view. The students created designs, transferred them onto large canvases, and painted banners to represent the conflicting points of view of different communities in each historical period. The students wrote about the historical content of each banner and made presentations to other classes.*

f   **The arts function as a way of committing concepts and content to memory.** Artists and teachers pose problems that require learners to actively engage concepts and content. This experience brings subjects alive for learn-

A fourth grade student in Martha Cerda's class at Ogden School models his costume based on the class research into Maya, Inca, and Aztec cultures. These costumes were worn in their performance of "The Flame of Peace" directed by Jean Parisi in a residency with Pros Arts Studio.

ers by incorporating a wide array of compelling visual, aural, tactile, and kinesthetic activities into the generation of new knowledge, thereby providing enough vivid sense memories to make new learning memorable (literally, able to be remembered). These indelible sensory images mark and organize information and concepts in a way that allows learners to access and apply new knowledge.

Example: *Eighth-grade students at Healy School, working with dancer Rosemary Doolas, developed an understanding of the underground railroad by choreographing a dance that moved through their entire school, transforming historical facts into living history. None of these students is likely to forget the concepts and content they have learned through this dance process.*

f   **The arts present concrete evidence of learning.** The walls and halls of arts partnership schools are full of murals, quilts, mosaics, videos, dioramas, theater pieces, as well as music concerts and dance performances representing student curricular knowledge. (See Color Insert C.a. and G.c.)

Example: *Students in the Lakeview Education Arts Partnership, working with artist Kim Salerno, designed and constructed a wardrobe full of unfolding panels arranged and painted to represent their understanding of the thematic structure of the C.S. Lewis classic novel, The Lion, The Witch, and the Wardrobe.*

Arts content, skills, and concepts deepen teaching and learning through a dynamic, functional relationship to the content, skills, and concepts in the other academic areas. Integrated curriculum often leverages new learning by drawing on the content of one area, the skills of another, and the concepts of yet another. This cross-disciplinary, interactive mix of content, skills, and concepts is what gives effective integrated curriculum its vitality. A focus on any one learning function in isolation (rote memorization of content, drill on skills, presentation of concepts ungrounded by information or technique) is insufficient to build learner capacity.

f   **Contemporary arts experiences represent history and culture in the curriculum.** Contemporary art forms help students construct their understanding of history. (See Color Insert A.b.)

Example: *Fourth-grade students at Brownell Elementary School, working with sculptor Rene Townsend, explored the uprising on the Amistad slave ship by making a sculpture representing the Amistad children cast from their own bodies. (This sculpture is on permanent display at the DuSable Museum of African American Art in Chicago. See Dedication.)*

Historical content becomes deepened and enriched by the presence of these art forms.

f   **Historical art forms help students reflect on contemporary life.** Studying, experiencing, reflecting on, and re-creating the arts of different periods are powerful ways to bring to life worldviews from other times and places.

Example: *Art specialist Miriam Socoloff at Lakeview High School has students paint fascinating self-portraits in the 17th century "Memento Mori" manner (stylized paintings full of symbolic objects representing the transience of life). New example: Seventh- and eighth-grade students at Orozco School, working with the Mexican Fine Arts Center Museum, study traditional "Retablos" (art installation, painted on tin or wood, offering thanks). Students create "new age retablos," documenting transformative moments in their own lives, working in both wood sculpture and painting on tin. (These student works are exhibited at local libraries, art galleries, and restaurants, and can be seen on Orozco's student designed website: www.orozco.cps.k12.il.us.)*

Students from Miriam Socoloff's art classes at Lakeview High School paint "Memento Mori" self portraits in the style of seventeenth century Dutch paintings that portray the fleeting nature of life.

f   **The arts help students understand scientific and mathematical principles and vc. vs.** When transferring mural designs to walls, timing sound recordings, or developing photographs, students use skills they learn in math or science classes. When preparing budgets or laying out literary publications, students need to become adept at such skills to make their art.

Example: *When students were designing silk textiles at Lincoln Park High School, they needed to become skilled at balancing the temperatures and the chemistry of their dyes to achieve the effects they needed. (See chap. 3 and Color Inserts E.a,b,c,d.)*

The reverse is also true. The arts can be a powerful medium for observing and recording data as students are learning about their world.

Example: *By applying the art processes of observation, drawing, and ceramic sculpture, upper grade students in the Hawthorne-Agassiz Partnership developed their understanding of ecosystems of Illinois wildlife. (See Color Insert C.b. and C.c.)*

Learning, like all dynamic systems, grows out of an interactive mix of functions. Integration's capacity to cut across disciplines, investigating the content of one discipline through the skills of another to develop cross-disciplinary concepts, in a living, shifting interaction of content engagement, skill application, and concept testing, is what gives integration its dynamism and vitality. Integration is itself an art, requiring responsive and balanced attention to the nuances of learning processes and products. Patterns have begun to emerge as to which mixes of content, skills, and concepts from specific arts disciplines and from specific other academic areas stimulate the most effective learning. Here are some of the patterns and relationships that have surfaced in the CAPE schools:

Experiential: Arts skills (often dance or drama) provide kinesthetic experience of academic content and concepts (often social studies, language arts, and science). *Examples: dancing the underground railroad, acting out a scene from a book about the civil rights movement, dancing weather systems.*

Representational and Presentational: Arts skills and concepts from all arts disciplines are applied to represent and demonstrate concepts and content from all academic areas. *Examples: composing and performing a song about math concepts, creating a banner about a period in American history, dancing the concept of biological interdependence, designing a sculpture to represent themes in a novel.*

Operational: Academic skills (often mathematics operations or science techniques) produce products embodying art skills and concepts (often music and visual arts). *Examples: timing the recording of a musical composition, figuring the proportions on a mural, preparing chemical dyes.*

Observational: Arts skills (often visual arts, dance, or theater) are applied to accurately observe and document academic content (often science and social studies). *Examples: making murals to observe wild-life, applying dance skills to document animal movement, applying character observation skills from the theater to record sociological data.*)

Historical/Cultural: Historical art content in all arts disciplines explored as a way of understanding the world-view contexting the historical content and concepts in all academic areas from other times and places. *Examples: Learning dances and music from the civil war period, recreating Leonardo's notebooks, studying the sculpture, politics, and mathematical systems of the Aztec Empire.*

There is no one way to integrate the arts. The more we engage in the process, the better we understand the rich and varied opportunities arts integration affords teachers and learners.

WHY INTEGRATE THE ARTS?

In chapter 3, we describe three ways that students *work through* content that reflect an arts integrated approach. We believe that these processes that students undertake also provide some excellent reasons why the arts can be so powerful in student learning. The more students participate in learning *through* arts integration, in other words, the more the rationale for this practice in classrooms becomes clear. In the following section, we describe what happens when quality arts integration occurs and when students are learning both the art form and the selected classroom content well. We have looked at many examples of arts integration units, classrooms, and verbal descriptions of the work. We have analyzed student work as artifacts to excavate what students do as they work through the content—of the art form and the subject matter. We have organized what we found into three rationale statements for doing this work: (a) Quality arts integration deepens instruction through the weaving of parallel processes, (b) quality arts integration involves co-teaching and co-learning, and (c) quality arts integration connects students and teachers to the larger community, thereby increasing the repertoire for learning.

Deepening Instruction

One occasion when this deepening happens is when *students experience and engage with text*. In his book, *You Gotta BE the Book*, educator Jeffrey Wilhelm (1997) described the frustration of his middle-school remedial readers who could not make sense of their reading. Out of necessity, he began to experiment with creating drama and visual arts experiences that helped his students visualize the characters, settings, and conflicts in the literature they were reading. He created a methodology for students to, in his words, *enter the story world*. When they manipulated cut paper characters and used them to describe the action of the story, Wilhelm wrote "Their reading was made visible, could be talked about, critiqued, manipulated and revised (p. 122)." The arts help make learning visible. "What these students revealed to me made me begin to believe that these students did not 'see' anything when they read, and that therefore they could not experience and think about what they had read. They had no ownership over the process, and no sense that it could work for them in personally meaningful ways" (p. 117). The drama and visual arts provided Wilhelm's students access to the text; they were the means for students to learn from their reading.

Instruction also deepens when the arts are present, *because art images help children think metaphorically*. Arnold Aprill, executive director of CAPE and theater director, has developed a writing exercise in which students describe themselves and family members through the objects that are important to them. The objects become metaphors for the family members.

One student writes, *Grandmother, you are the Chinese newspaper that falls off your lap when you sleep by the radio … you are the spicy egg rolls I smell cooking every morning … you are the spare change you give me to buy candy on the way home from school.* Another student writes, *I am the ants and frogs I find by the river … I am the animals I will study when become a scientist … I am the discoverer of something new.* And a third, *I am thunder, walking through lightning.*

The aesthetic experience provides children with access to metaphor and image. Metaphoric thinking, which reveals unexpected connections between seemingly disparate ideas, is central to the arts and to integrated curriculum. Art synthesizes. This shape-changing, form-inventing character of the arts is what makes the arts so useful in discovering new and surprising relationships.

The arts seem to deepen instruction authentically because they *invite intellectual depth*.

> *Authentic intellectual work involves original application of knowledge and skills (rather than just routine use of facts and procedures). It also entails disciplined inquiry into the details of a particular problem, and results in a product or presentation that has meaning or value beyond success in school.* (Newmann, Lopez, & Bryk, 1998, p. 6)

The key words that connect arts integration to this definition of intellectual work are *authentic* and *original*. These themes play a role in how classes get started, work through, and move beyond arts integrated lessons (chaps. 2, 3, 4). They stretch and challenge; they represent integrative approaches that help teachers and students do more than merely meet an external standard. Arts integration is concerned with intellectual work and with inquiry as ways to learn and grow. Students engaged in an art activity are expanding the repertoire of tools at their disposal to construct meaning. When they create a collage, choreograph a dance, block a dramatic scene, or develop a rhythm pattern, they are learning to think within the elements and vocabulary of that particular art form.

Quality integration requires quality instruction in all content areas being integrated. A dancer who gets students deeply committed to learning inaccurate scientific information is not advancing the learning of science content no matter how engaged the students are. Misinformation can be taught in any content area, and weak integration can occur in any content field. Simply engaging in the experience of making art is not enough for learning to occur, particularly over the longer term. Teachers who know content deeply and well are essential for the success of arts integration.

Some advocates of arts integration actually are only interested in art skills as tools to be used in enhancing other academic skills. These practitioners tend to be focused on isolated skills in both the arts arena and in the other academic content areas, with an emphasis on training teachers in specific activities and practices rather than on sharing practices while encouraging teachers to design their own approaches. This is not what CAPE means by arts integration for meaningful learning. Using art activities, such as graphic organizers or movement activities, no matter how charming or useful, is not the same thing as seriously engaging in the processes of art. When a utilitarian approach is taken, the other academic areas are often given short shrift as well. Yes, music uses half notes and quarter notes, but pointing out the existence of fractions in music doesn't make a lesson meaningful math instruction.

Art educator Elliot Eisner (1998) writes about the contribution of the arts to cognitive development. He notes … "the forms we use to represent what we think—literal language, visual images, number, poetry—impacts how we think and what we can think about" (p. 44). Eisner continues: "we ought to be interested in developing multiple forms of literacy. Why? Because each form of literacy has the capacity to provide unique forms of meaning, and it is in the pursuit of meaning that much of the good life is lived" (p. 52).

By working within each discrete art form, students are provided with a more articulated tool—a finer instrument—to describe complex ideas. The deeper the students understand and master both the elements of an art form and the core subject content, the better they can understand and communicate with nuance and depth.

Textile artist Eleanor Skydell said: I *have to teach my students the art principles of line, shape, movement, and surface design. They need to know about movement because a static design won't make for an interesting piece overall. We arrange the squares to suit how the eye will move through the whole piece. If you want to be elegant, you have to be able to move elegantly in your expression. When you have a complex idea, you can't draw stick figures.*

The arts integrate thought, feeling, and action.   Enduring myths of the artist as an exemplary sufferer, a legacy of the Romantic movement in 19th-century Europe, have led to the misperception that art is all (and only) about feelings. It just isn't so. Still, human beings are hard wired for the experience of translating sensory stimuli into cognitive symbols. This deeply engrained characteristic of the species means that art experiences tend to be engaging. This is good for learners. This does not mean that the arts should be trivialized into entertainment to lessen the boredom of uninspired teaching. It also does not suggest that arts learning, fun as it can be, does not also include frustration, disappointment, and just plain hard work. This is also, when appropriately mediated, good for learners. (See Andre LeMoine's Arts Integration Snapshot: Art Is Not a Reward.)

There is a growing understanding of the interrelatedness of thinking and feeling and a growing recognition that the best way to develop and retain knowledge is to put it to active use as it is generated. The arts require learners to bring together sensory processes with thinking processes to generate concrete representations of thought and feeling in the material world.

Playwright Jackie Murphy from the LEAP Partnership integrates thought with feeling through storytelling. I *love remembering the fact that the most natural thing in the world for a kid is to act out stories. The reason I use playwriting in the classroom is that it pro-vides the ability to create stories.*

Jackie works with Lakeview High School teacher, Elena Robles, on an integrated unit on genetics. The students begin their course of study by writing stories. Each student works on an imaginary scenario where a character is faced with some decision concerning defective genes. They struggle with moral dilemmas and make choices for their characters. The narratives that they create change the study of DNA from an abstract science concept to an experience of deep personal engagement. Their stories are the bridge that stimulates them to learn about genetics and gives them access into the science curriculum (see chap. 5).

Using the arts to teach content more deeply helps teachers understand how their students are thinking about the subject under investigation because **the arts reveal the internal logic of learners**. The arts reveal emergent meanings, messages, plans, themes, images, and intentions present but unexpressed by learners. Learners are not blank slates or disorganized chaos. The arts are an important medium for learners to discover, develop, and articulate their own understandings of the world, and to invent their own versions of and visions for the future. The arts are a primary venue for making public the internal logic of learners—not only for teachers, but also for the learners. Teachers ask, What do you know? How do you know that? The arts help learners respond. Students ask, Who am I? Where did I come from? Where am I going? The arts help learners chart their own course.

Co-Teaching and Co-Learning

The arts provide a tangible and concrete means for students to work with each other and to work with the adults in their world. The partnerships in Chicago have also noted the power of the arts to bring those adults together.

The arts open up dialogue among educators. The presence of the arts in in a school acts as a leveling force. It creates a space—a "demilitarized zone"—in which educators can reflect on their teaching practice, as well as a generative force, creating an *exotic terrain* in which educators can reconfigure their relationships. Teachers, principals, and parents in CAPE partnerships have consistently redefined their relationships and generated positive new associations with each other through their joint collaboration with artists.

The arts transform how learners are perceived by others. Arts integration consistently reveals unrecognized abilities in learners formerly perceived as a problem by teachers and other students. The arts provide useful difficulties to challenge difficult learners, and they carve out an educational space where young people can change how others perceive them.

The arts teach perseverance, tenacity, and the ability to withstand frustration. Artists persevere in the face of other people's judgment that they give give up. Students need to see adults in addition to their teachers that keep working even when they are daunted, bored, frustrated, misunderstood, or confused.

Teachers' constant encouragement to persevere is reinforced by the revising and rethinking process inherent in the arts. The arts provide compelling media for young learners to enact their perseverance.

That means that *they are taking risks*. Artists are researchers and problem seekers—they like to set challenging tasks for themselves. They are helpful in convening communities, but they are also good at modeling how one finds one's own path. What would this dance look like if all the movements were abrupt and angular? How would this play work if all the characters were exaggerated? What impact would this painting have if I limited the color palette? This is a type of organic inquiry inherent in the artistic process.

Just as when we speak we launch into an unrehearsed sentence with full confidence that we will end up saying something meaningful, the arts can teach children to have passionate faith in the generative capacity of their own creative impulses and questions. This is useful information for students and teachers. This sense of capacity makes the arts useful in encouraging the creativity and initiative in all teachers and students, not just the artistically gifted.

Connecting the Self to the Larger Community

The productive nature of the arts transforms learners' perceptions of themselves as productive citizens. Art production makes learners aware of themselves as capable learners and productive citizens. The arts give learners a sense of agency—of being able to make things that matter happen in the world. For students with damaged perceptions of their own abilities, arts experiences can be life saving. Because the arts provide another lens for learning, unexplored abilities pop into focus. (See Color Insert G.b.)

The arts invite access to resources outside the school. Arts partnerships leverage existing resources embedded in the community into use by schools, making the walls of the school more permeable, and crossing the false boundary between learning inside and outside the school building. This exactly parallels the negotiation between self and community that integrated curriculum provides to the individual learner.

Of course, with most arts integration initiatives, it is the artist who is the symbol of the outside world and/or the community. There is the implicit assumption that this is, in itself, good. Why artists? Artists are just one resource for schools that have tended to become isolated in many communities. They are perhaps less representative than other community members, but they open up worlds that, for many students, were not previously accessible. Artists are links to a different way of thinking about one's community. We have observed over and over that arts integration is often a venue for looking at issues of community activism, social justice, and individual integrity. Artists provide a lens for students to see themselves in the world.

The arts open up dialogue between students and parents. The parents we interviewed for this book revealed that the arts are among the most powerful avenues for them to develop a productive relationship with their children. One Lincoln Park High School father describes it like this:

> *You really want to take your kids to do as many things as they'll go to with you. We had opera tickets and my son and I would go every other time. He found opera interesting and he was more than happy to sit through five or six hours of one of the ring cycles or whatever! So I thought, "Hey, if he's interested in the fine arts, I'll take him to the Art Institute!" So I did. Having the arts in his school opened up that possibility for us as a family.*

When students, artists, and teachers are pursuing their own questions and exploring their own creativity, the arts become self-motivating. Art literally resonates in the body, keeping learners present and engaged. Because art springs from the mysteries of the learner's spirit, students have a stake in the outcomes of their art making. Students want to make quality artwork, not because the teacher says they should, but because the work is a piece of themselves. The teacher's task often becomes more about getting overexcited students past their fears of *messing up* than about getting students motivated to care about the work. Because the arts are self-motivating, they are extremely effective at reengaging alienated kids who have fallen through the cracks of the educational system.

p   p   p   f   f   f

All students have the right to equitable access to art in their lives and in their schools. The arts teach learners to know themselves as capable citizens in a democratic society, observing, creating, reflecting, making choices, and taking responsibility for actions in the world. Our children face a future that is much more mobile and shifting than the world we know. They need to be adept at crossing many more borders—real and virtual, social and geographic, intrapersonal and interpersonal—than we were prepared for in our education. The life-long employer, one-occupation career is over. Young people need flexibility, creativity, and a tolerance for ambiguity to successfully manage their emerging adulthoods and to become effective citizens.

The skills they will need to grow up well in the 21st century include the ability to: (a) plan with, negotiate with, and work well with diverse collaborators; (b) imagine alternate solutions to a problem and choose between options; (c) manage multiple, diverse, simultaneous projects; (d) self-monitor and adjust their work; (e) organize space and time; (f) convey information in diverse forms; and (g) synthesize information from diverse sources (U.S. Department of Labor, 1991). The arts offer opportunities to utilize many of these skills.

The adults of tomorrow will need to think outside the box because the box will not be there tomorrow. A curriculum with segregated subject areas may have made sense in a manufacturing economy based on the assembly line, but the emerging information economy calls for a more integrative approach to the curriculum.

At the beginning of this chapter, there is a series of vignettes that reveal what the work of learning through arts integration looks like. In the end, it's essential to return to those stories because they are the reason that this work is important. Definitions, theories, and explanations are beneficial, but the real value in arts integration lies in the students and what they give and bring to their own learning and growth through the arts. Students taking photos, creating story boards, or role-playing the movement patterns of birds ... these stories illustrate learning that is vital, alive, and engaging. These stories are the heart and soul of arts integration.

REFERENCES

Armstrong, T. (1994). *Multiple intelligences in the classroom*. Alexandria, VA: Association for Supervision and Curriculum Development.

Beane, J. A. (1997). *Curriculum integration: Designing the core of democratic education*. New York: Teachers College Press.

Buck-Morss, S. (1992). Aesthetics and anaesthetics. *October Magazine, 62*, 16–22.

Casey, M. B., & Tucker, E. C. (1994). Problem-centered classrooms: Creating lifelong learners. *Phi Delta Kappan, 72*(2), 139–143.

Eisner, E. W. (1994). *The educational imagination* (3rd ed.). New York: Macmillan.

Eisner, E. W. (1997). Cognition and representation: A way to pursue the American dream? In *The kind of schools we need: Personal essays* (pp. 44–53). Portsmouth, NH: Heinemann.

Gallas, K. (1994). *The languages of learning: How children talk, write, dance, draw, and sing their understanding of the world*. New York: Teachers College Press.

Gardner, H. (1983). *Frames of mind: The theory of multiple intelligences*. New York: Basic Books.

Gardner, H. (1999). The happy meeting of multiple intelligences and the arts. *Harvard Education Letter, 15*(6), 5.

Hennes, M. (1921). Project teaching in an advanced fifth grade. *Teachers College Record, 19*(2), 137–148.

Kilpatrick, W. H. (1918). The project method. *Teachers College Record, 19*(4), 319–335.

Lazear, D. (1991). *Seven ways of knowing: Teaching for multiple intelligences* (2nd ed.). Palatine, IL: IRI/Skylight.

Newmann, F. M., Lopez, G., & Bryk, A. S. (1998). *The quality of intellectual work in Chicago schools: A baseline report*. Chicago, IL: Consortium on Chicago School Research.

White, D. (1998). *The arts and the scope of knowledge: A philosophical justification of arts integration*. Unpublished manuscript.

Whitin, P., & Whitin, D. (1997). *Inquiry at the window: Pursuing the wonder of learners*. Portsmouth, NH: Heinemann.

Wilhelm, J.D. (1997). *"You gotta BE the book": Teaching engaged and reflective reading with adolescents*. New York: Teachers College Press.

Wolk, S. (1994, November). Project-based learning: Pursuits with a purpose. *Educational Leadership*, pp. 42–45.

U.S. Department of Labor. (1991). *What work requires of schools: A SCANS report for America 2000*. The Secretary's Commission on Achieving Necessary Skills.

Other descriptions of CAPE's *arts integrated approach can be found in these books*:

Daniels, H., & Bizar, M. (1998). *Methods that matter: Six structures for best practice classrooms*. York, ME: Stenhouse Publishers.

Remer, J. (1997). *Beyond enrichment: Building effective arts partnerships with schools and your community*. New York: American Council for the Arts.

Zemelman, S., Daniels, H., & Hyde, A. (1998). *Best practice: New standards for teaching and learning in America's schools* (2nd ed.). Portsmouth, NH: Heinemann.

2

Getting Started With Arts Integration: Finding the Elegant Fit

Building a Team and a Vision

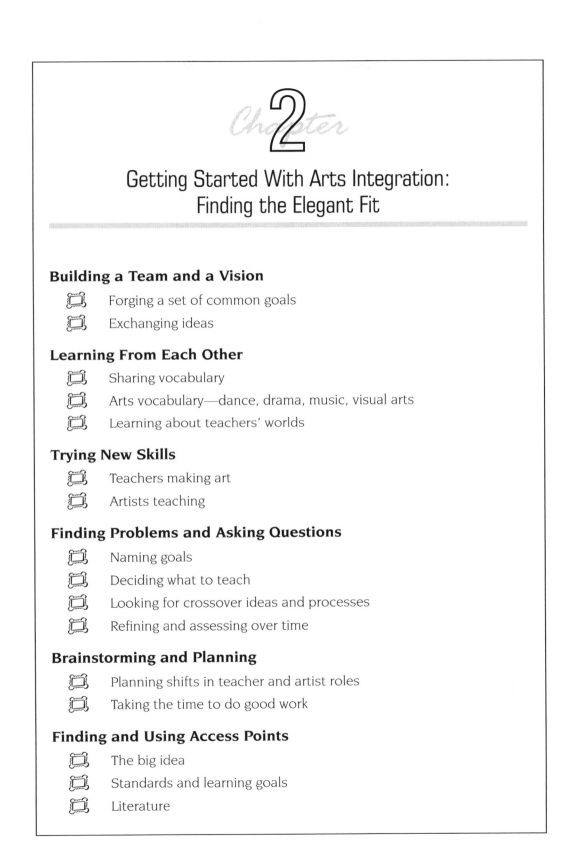 Forging a set of common goals

Exchanging ideas

Learning From Each Other

Sharing vocabulary

Arts vocabulary—dance, drama, music, visual arts

Learning about teachers' worlds

Trying New Skills

Teachers making art

Artists teaching

Finding Problems and Asking Questions

Naming goals

Deciding what to teach

Looking for crossover ideas and processes

Refining and assessing over time

Brainstorming and Planning

Planning shifts in teacher and artist roles

Taking the time to do good work

Finding and Using Access Points

The big idea

Standards and learning goals

Literature

- Prior knowledge/students' own questions
- Lessons you love and lessons you loathe
- Field trips
- Performance and exhibition

Getting Started
With Arts Integration:
Finding the Elegant Fit

It's a little bit scary to try new projects because a lot of them have failed. I have worked with teachers on units where the integration wasn't elegant; it was just a bumpy ride the whole way. The projects that were the most well integrated were the most successful. I worked with a teacher developing a science & video project. We did it for 4 years; we changed it and pushed forward the things that worked each year, but clearly the concepts we each brought were strong.

I really felt like I was able to accomplish my art skills, and she felt like she was really able to accomplish her science skills, and they worked very well together. The big picture idea was to compare the process of invention with the process of making videotape. The students came to think of themselves as both artists and inventors. It was really an elegant fit. (Deb Diehl)

This phrase, *elegant fit*, seems to be a wonderfully appropriate entree into the discussion of how arts integration works and what it looks like. Educational journals and books describe interdisciplinary curriculum, integrated subject areas, and strategies for teaching concepts and processes *across the curriculum* (Beane, 1997; Brazee & Capelluti, 1995; Gross, 1997; Jacobs, 1989). What is the goal of such initiatives in schools? What are we trying to achieve when we look for the links between math and science, between social studies and literature, or between an art form and writing? We are essentially searching for the elegant fit that takes learners to a more authentic understanding and a deeper way of knowing by offering connections between subject areas and bridges to the students' own lives.

An elegant fit implies that separate pieces of the curriculum have been brought together to create a new and more satisfying whole. The elegant fit occurs when teachers find the right forms and processes to deliver ideas and when students are engaged in the learning process. The arts are ideally suited for unifying curriculum because they help give a form and shape to knowledge.

Educator Elliot Eisner (1998) said: *Both the artist and the scientist create forms through which the world is viewed. Both artist and scientist make qualitative judgements about the fit, the coherence, the economy, 'the rightness,' of the forms they create* (p. 35). Arts integration begins then as a search for the rightness of fit between domains of knowledge and across the boundaries of disciplines. Arts integration is a powerful vehicle to cross these boundaries of core subjects and art concepts, affective and cognitive modes of expression, form and content, processes and products, the self and the world. A curricular fit works when the integration is not forced or artificial. It happens when teachers, artists, and children work hard and talk a lot about what they know, what they are doing, and why they are doing it. It is rigorous intellectual activity and it is exhilaratingly creative (Botstein, 1998).

The task of making something together encourages both sides to "think outside the box" to create new curricular work. As teachers and artists do this, they discover that the work of developing arts integration is an artistic process. When artists and teachers collaborate, they go through some of the same steps that artists follow to create new artwork. These steps, begun even before arts integration happens with the children, include:

1. **Building a team and a vision to do elegant work**
2. **Learning from each other**
3. **Trying new skills**
4. **Finding problems and asking questions**
5. **Brainstorming and planning together**
6. **Finding and using access points**

This chapter describes the beginning steps in a process that some Chicago educators have developed to find their own elegant fit with arts integration. These steps outline what you might do in and out of the classroom to successfully bring arts into the curriculum as a regular part of what happens in schools.

BUILDING A TEAM AND A VISION TO DO ELEGANT WORK

The first activity of our partnership was to decide our goals. This was a long process and many of us began to think that the heated discussions were destructive to the endeavor. We did not realize that we were working toward equal voices between artists and teachers, but the group unconsciously began to adopt that pattern of thinking. We began to know and respect each other. This allowed us to take risks that we might never have taken through our collective work. Robin Robinson, Drama Department Chair/Lincoln Park High School

Robin came together with her fellow teachers, artists, and art organizations to create a new arts integration venture at her high school. They formed a steering committee, guiding this process from the beginning, and forged a common set of principles that set the parameters for the work ahead.

In another part of the city, The Bridgeport-Armour Square/Near North Partnership was also forming a steering committee under the guidance of their coordinator, Tammy Steele, and an arts integration consultant, Karen Erickson. Tammy Steele said: *What was the vision the committee created? Students learn best when all five of their senses are involved, and arts integrated learning involves more of the senses more of the time. Our definition of arts integration was strict; integration does not occur unless both the art form and the other academic subject(s) are taught so the students learn more than if they learned them separately. When true integration happens, $1 + 1 > 2$.*

With those guiding principles in mind, the teachers, artists, and coordinators were ready to get going. But as Tammy, Karen, and Robin will attest, at the beginning of this work, it's crucial to form the **team**. The team may be no more than two interested teachers or one art teacher working with one classroom teacher, but the very nature of this work is *collaborative*. (See chap. 6: You Don't Have to Do It Alone.) The work truly begins with an early meeting of the minds.

The ETA/Muntu Arts in Education Consortium Partnership forged a set of common goals after they sat down and discussed what they hoped to accomplish across five schools. Here is what they wrote:

The ETA/Muntu Arts in Education Consortium facilitates integration of the arts disciplines and education to the end of enhancing the educational/academic achievement of the children by:

◎ providing a mechanism for mutual planning between educators and arts organizations to facilitate compliance with Illinois State Goals in the fundamental area of Fine Arts (Drama, Dance, Music, Visual Arts, and Writing);
◎ engaging the arts to assist schools in teaching all the academic subjects;
◎ assisting schools in the development of curriculum that integrates the arts in all subject areas;
◎ assisting in staff development that will enable teachers and artists to work collaboratively;
◎ increasing awareness in teachers, parents, and students of the impact of African and African-American art forms on all cultures;
◎ encouraging teachers to develop cultural proficiency in some aspect of the cultural arts;
◎ continuing cultural learning through home- and community-based arts activities;
◎ gaining and maintaining the support of Local School Councils in implementing the Illinois State Learning Goals in the Fine Arts;
◎ enhancing the competence of already proficient artists in working in school settings; and
◎ training artists to integrate their particular art forms into educational methodology.

Recent research on group processes indicates that working in teams is an important way to stimulate innovative thought in individual team members. *One consistent finding of the research on groups is that people working in groups generate new ideas. Not only do people bring different ideas to groups, something about the exchange of ideas in groups generates even more ideas* (Davis; cited in Hart, 1995, p. 81).

The exchange of ideas among classroom teachers, arts teachers, and artists is the special challenge and pleasure of arts integration work. These first discussions suggest new possibilities, define the terms of what good arts integration might be, and lay out a school structure to support the work. This structure provides a framework and begins the process of working toward elegant art integration practice.

The process described in the following pages brings classroom teachers together to work with artists and art teachers. Our practice has shown that the artist-educator's presence greatly enhances the depth of the art experience in the integration process. However, teachers *can* integrate the arts in their classroom without professional artists, and the principles described next are pertinent to anyone getting started with arts integration.

LEARNING FROM EACH OTHER: THE VOCABULARY OF THE ARTS

The first place to look for a *rightness of the fit* is between the participants on the team. These partners have to have the good will to talk across boundaries of training, practice, socialization, and experience. They need to understand each other's intentions and expectations.

Karen Erickson, an arts consultant to teachers and artists working in schools, explains: *The artists need to share their work and process with teachers. The teachers need to share their educational expertise with the artists. Each also needs to share the culture of their art form and their classroom with each other. Then they find the meeting points: the places where they can connect their work together. Both need to ask, "Where do we see our goals, objectives, processes, and activities coming together?" My role as a consultant is to say to the artists and teachers, "When you're done, what do you want to have achieved?" What they say, what their vision is for the end, informs the beginning. That's where they need to start in order to get to the final destination with the vision they have designed.*

Artists often work intuitively, drawing from an array of techniques and strategies in which they have been trained. Sometimes those strategies and ways of thinking seem foreign to classroom teachers whose training may have been very different. Some knowledge has become so second nature through use and experience that both teachers and artists have difficulty bringing basic operating procedures into conscious awareness.

Through the joint venture of arts integration, artists introduce teachers, and teachers introduce artists, to the techniques of their respective disciplines. Teachers and artists may need to spend time together after school, during introductory art-making workshops and summer institutes, where both communities can articulate to each other their different ways of learning, knowing, and doing. Teachers have the chance to learn the vocabulary and elements of an art form, as well as to actually experience such forms as improvisational drama, mask making, or story dance. They develop firsthand knowledge of thinking *through* an art form by participating in the kinds of activities their students will encounter (see Table 2.1).

Artists also need to learn the vocabulary and elements of classroom practice. They need to learn the teacher's hopes and expectations for their students and be informed about the academic goals, standards, and curriculum content. Universities, community arts organizations, and arts partnership initiatives are beginning to create opportunities for artists who wish to learn more about methods for teaching and about theories of child development. Artists as well as teachers have to engage new material and take some risks.

You start by learning what the teachers' needs are, what their styles are, what their interests are. You are trying to work that out, and she is trying to do that with you. I think it's a matter of letting go a little bit, and saying, "Okay, we'll make it work. We'll work something out, and this is going to be successful, and if we need to change things in the process, we'll change things, but let's sort of jump in anyway." The holding back is a fear of not being sure of how things are going to turn out. (Visual artist, Jackie Terrassa)

The first meetings begin the search for an *elegant fit* between art concepts and core curricular concepts, between teaching styles and rhythms, between distinct person-

TABLE 2.1

Selected Arts Vocabulary: Dance, Drama, Music, and Visual Arts

Dance	Drama	Music	Visual Arts
Space	Body	Timbre	Color
Shape	Shape	Orchestra	Hue
Level	Level	Choir	Chroma
Direction	Presence	Conductor	Value
Pathway	Statue	Instruments	Primary color
Warm up	Facial expression	(families)	Secondary color
Time	Focus	Voice	Tertiary color
Beat	Clarity of action	Warm up	Warm/cool
Tempo	Self-control	Rhythm	Analogous
Accent	Pantomime	Pattern	Complementary
Duration	Mirror	Beat	Composition
Rhythm	Warm up	Accent	Balance
Energy	Mind	Duration	Symmetry
Attack—	Focus	Fast	Asymmetry
sharp/smooth	Imagination	Slow	Variation
Weight—	Characterization	Tempo	Form—
Heavy/light	Visualization	Syncopation	3 Dimensional
Flow—free	Transformation	Dynamics	Mass
flowing/Bound	Voice	Levels/Volume	Weight
Strength—	Projection	Piano (soft)	Volume
Tight/loose	Cadence	Forte (loud)	Structure
Body	Volume	Mezzo (somewhat	Cone, cube
Inside parts	Rhythm	forte/piano)	Cylinder, sphere
Outside parts	Teamwork	Issimo (very)	Line
Axial Moves	Ensemble	Pitch (Intonation)	Contour
Stretch, bend,	Trust	Harmony	Continuous
swing, twist,	Improvisation	Tension	Flowing/broken
shake	Stage Picture	Sound	Thick/thin
Locomotor Moves	Up stage	Scale	Pattern
—Walk, run, leap,	Cheat out	Form/Style	Regular/irregular
hop, jump,	Lines	Verse	Tessellation
gallop, skip,	Script	Refrain (chorus)	Repetition
slide, crawl, roll	Character	Song	Decorative
Relationships	Plot	Quodlibet	Shape
Repetition	Setting	Melody	Geometric/
Contrast	Conflict	A Cappella	Organic
Unison	Resolution	Round	Simple/Complex
Canon		Lyric	Positive/Negative
Variety		Jazz	Texture
		Ballet	Rough/Smooth
		Opera	Value
		Program music	Contrast
		Absolute music	Shade

Note. Arts Vocabulary courtesy of: Hearne, S., (Ed.). (1996). *Art in the primary schools.* London, England: London Borough of Tower Hamlets Inspection and Advisory Services.

continued on next page

Table 2.1 *Note:* continued

Laughlin, M. K., & Street, T. P. (1992). Literature-based art & music: Children's books & activities to enrich the K-5 curriculum. Phoenix, AZ: Oryx Press.

Wachowiak, F., & Clements, R. (1993). Emphasis art: A qualitative art program for elementary and middle schools. New York: HarperCollins.

Whirlwind Basic Skills Through the Arts-ACES Resource Manual 1998. (Dance and Drama lists by Donna Mandel, Kathleen Maltese, Laura Sollmon-St. John, and Whirlwind artists.)

alities, and between clear and appropriate roles for both the artist and the teacher. The search happens over time, with much thinking and planning, trial and error, and a great deal of trust developed between the partnering artists and teachers.

TRYING NEW SKILLS: LEARNING TO DANCE AND SING IN CLASS

The teachers' familiarity with an art form develops through their personal participation in the art-making process and then deepens through creating, implementing, and revising arts integration practice in their classrooms over the years. Even parents notice when this happens: *It's exciting to watch some teachers who were just absolutely afraid of art, did not think that they could do anything with it, all of a sudden begin to experiment and grow, you know, personally* (a Ray Elementary School parent).

Middle-school teacher, Alfredo Nambo, recalled being skeptical about arts integration when he began with the project. Now after 5 years of working with dancers and actors, his colleagues joke with him. *Alfredo even _dances_ now. He was involved in a dance production with his students. The professional artists did not just create a project with kids, but they actually built a relationship around their work that was mutually compatible for everyone. They would think in ways that supported the strength of both the teacher and the artists in the collaboration.*

Third-grade teacher Andre LeMoine tells a similar story of learning more about the arts and understanding their power in his classroom. (See Arts Integration Snapshot: Art Is Not A Reward—Learning to Respect Art as an Integral Part of Education.) Artists need to learn about the constraints of time that teachers face each school day. They also can benefit from learning about the talents and strengths of partner teachers. Artists can learn much about what teachers bring to the team by watching and listening in a teacher's class for awhile before arts integration begins. Then the teacher and artist can discuss what the visitor saw and heard. In this way, the artist is allowed into the special world of teaching and learning—not as a performer at first, but as an observant adult who can absorb how children think and how one teacher thinks about her world.

Once the team members have taught each other a little about their separate worlds, they can begin to bring these worlds together. When a group of teachers meets to discuss integration, they are realizing their own goals for their subject field, but they are also seeing those goals as part of a larger vision for learning. When artists plan with classroom teachers, they too are searching for the common ground while advocating for the integrity of their disciplines.

FINDING PROBLEMS AND ASKING QUESTIONS

Scientists, like artists, formulate new and puzzling questions in order to enjoy the experience of creating answers to them (Elliot Eisner, 1998, p. 36).

Finding the problem is the necessary first step in creative teaching. The artist and teacher team is engaged in looking for ways to solve a problem together right from the start and in structuring an investigation. The problem they have to solve is how to develop a new methodology for teaching their material.

For my work, in the studio, I have a particular set of questions. There's a big idea that governs what I do. There are also lots of small directions I can take that may relate to the big idea. The one thing that is really important in relating what happens in the studio, to what happens in the classroom, is that as an artist, I know how to structure an investigation. I know how to ask what are the topics I'm interested in? What's the best vehicle and medium for exploring that topic, and what are the techniques that would really help me understand that? (Visual artist and architect, Kim Salerno)

Each of the CAPE partnerships has developed structures to use when planning curriculum. These structures have evolved over the 5 years of collaborative work after much trial and error. The partnerships created planning documents to bring to the table and help them achieve their goals. (See Appendix C for samples of planning documents.) The parameters begin differently in each collaborative project, but the goals of the investigations remain the same.

The deepest arts integration projects are the ones in which:

- the goals are carefully laid out,
- both sides decide what they want to teach,
- there is a crossover of ideas and processes that inform each other,
- there is an opportunity to refine and assess ideas over time.

If each partner brings problems or questions to the table, then common goals for the project can be formed.

BRAINSTORMING AND PLANNING TOGETHER

The search for the elegant fit between art concepts and core curricular concepts, and between diverse teaching styles and objectives, begins with brainstorming. The negotiations at the planning table give rise to deeper curriculum. The team usually begins by offering ideas and asking questions.

Wendee DeSent, kindergarten teacher, says: *Three kindergarten teachers are sitting around the table planning with the artists. First, we try to find the common ground. We search for the link across the subject areas in order to integrate. We began asking the question,* **Why is this important to teach?** *We keep asking it and asking it. The tension between the art form and the subjects comes from trying to find the common ground, you know, when you are searching for that link to try to integrate. Asking the big question eventually leads to the common ground. It's a richer curriculum because of the group planning. I couldn't do this kind of brainstorming by myself. I wouldn't push myself as hard to justify and clarify.* (See Appendix D for the Making Shape of Our Environment Kindergarten Unit that Wendee co-planned and implemented with her colleagues.)

Artist Kim Salerno asks her partner teachers, **What is it you really want your students to learn?** *As that discussion unfolds, some idea for the project emerges. It comes from brainstorming, and bringing together the teacher's desires with whatever I can do to help enable those desires. For the most part, neither of us really knows what's going to happen before we get together, which I like.* She adds that both the artist and teacher must bring teaching goals to the table. *If the teacher doesn't come with a clear academic goal, the project's a disaster.* This is not time away from the curriculum; goals and standards for learning are central to the process.

Dancer Michelle Kranicke elaborates: *Often times just by brainstorming together, the teacher and I will come up with an idea that maybe he or she has never used before. And then maybe they will go on using that idea in other parts of their curriculum. I think we learn about an alternative, about different ways to approach subjects. If teachers don't incorporate dance, per se, perhaps they'll continue to incorporate one of the supplementary activities that we discussed. I have had more experiences with teachers who tell me about the way their kids respond in ways that they never expect. They see different qualities come out in their own students that might change their approach in how they will deal with this kid in the future.*

Planning Shifts in Teacher and Artist Roles

In effective, long-term co-planning relationships, roles shift. When teachers and artists start working together, they should develop a timetable for when artists will model art activities, when teachers and artists will co-teach arts integrated instruction, and when artists will side-coach teachers as primary deliverers of arts integrated instruction. When classroom teachers have thoroughly integrated arts learning into their teaching, the artist role shifts to providing inspiration, quality control, authentic standards, side coaching, and collegial support. The artist can then help to develop increasingly challenging, exciting, and innovative arts programming in the school. The artist becomes a part of the school's ongoing growth and development.

Taking the Time to Do Good Work

Teachers are often concerned about the amount of time it takes to do arts integration and still cover their curriculum. There is no getting around the fact that students need to go through the process to create elegant work. Students and teachers need the time to work back and forth between different subject areas and media. This time demand encourages teachers and artists to develop working plans that cover multiple learning objectives and deeply engage students—all at the same time. How then do students and teachers spend their time? How *are* the constraints of time, the needs of students, and the demands of learning standards addressed? Integrative practices must be accountable and respond to these issues if the arts are to remain a viable part of schooling. Good documentation of effective planning can help teachers lobby for protected planning time in their schedules each year.

Sometimes teachers see planning as something that happens in the summer, when there is time and space without students to think globally and look at the whole of the curriculum. Recently, teachers have begun experimenting with ways to plan with students in their classrooms (Alexander, 1995; Beane, 1997; Burkhardt, 1994; Slesinger & Busching, 1995; Vatterott, 1995). Arts integration brings another dimension to planning; it brings people into the process who have not been there before. People outside the normal teacher–student domain of the classroom become involved—artists, museum docents, and others who have a contribution to make when schools want to deepen both teaching and learning.

This kind of planning process does not start and stop before students are in the room. It continues *through* the process—all the way to the culminating event or the concluding assessment. For the arts to become a meaningful part of a classroom, they must be integrated *intentionally* and *purposefully*. Artist and teacher together plan their involvement; they consider the learning goals they want to achieve, both independently and collaboratively. Jim Beane (1997) describes this work: *Our reach for help in this kind of curriculum is a purposeful and directed activity—we do not simply identify questions and concerns and then sit around and wait for enlightenment to come to us. Instead, we intentionally and contextually 'put knowledge to work'* (p. 40).

Textile artist Skydell affirms that there can never be too much planning. It seems that good co-teaching requires it. Who will do what? What are the learning objectives we have for today? For this week? For the whole unit? Skydell says: *There are always unexpected outcomes, objectives that you get, that you hadn't really intended. That is great - something to celebrate. But, one of the things that we forget is that these are really complex things that we're doing. Even if you think you have just two objectives that are very simple, they may turn out to be much more complex.*

Increasing complexity and achieving more outcomes than originally intended are familiar features in rich integration processes. Consider what happens when an actor and a French teacher collaborate. Actor Ralph Covert says: *I as the visiting artist mapped it out. I worked out warm-ups, exercises, and goals. Madame Breen had the curriculum standards to address. I had six drama skills to teach. We were very specific; they would be assessed on both drama skills AND the grammar skills in French. Each day they had a particular grammar skill and a particular drama skill to focus on.* (See Appendix D for unit plan.)

Teachers are under enormous pressure to address objectives purposefully and consistently. Yet in any classroom where learning is occurring, the unexpected happens. One day, Ralph Covert was in Madame Breen's French class. To prepare them for doing improvisation in the French language, he was doing an exercise with the students where he asked them to imagine going to a favorite place. Ralph then asked the students where they went in their minds during this imaginary journey. One girl said she was hiding in a cave. "*I was sitting there with my brother,*" she said. Ralph replied, "*What were you doing?*" The girl answered, "*We were just sitting there, talking, laughing, and holding each other.*" After class, Madame Breen told Ralph that this girl's brother had died several months before. That was the first time she had ever brought up the topic and that was a turning point for her in French class. She began to become more engaged with the rest of the students. She began to talk with others more openly about her tragic loss.

Not only is it important for teachers and artists to brainstorm during planning, but it is also important for teachers and artists to brainstorm with students as they get started together in the classroom. There are lots of ways and purposes for brainstorming with students: to help the class explore resources, materials, and subtopics within a unit of study, to help students access what they already know, to decide which information is important, and how to solve problems if and when they arrive. Perhaps the most important purpose is to engage students in their own learning from the very beginning.

FINDING AND USING ACCESS POINTS: EXPRESSIVE WAYS INTO THE CURRICULUM

In each arts integrated course of study, there is a need for a rich access point that invites students into the curriculum. The access point is the seed crystal—the hook on which to hang the project. It can be a novel, a quilt, a dance, a piece of music, or a work of art. Access points can also include affective experiences. Some schools have begun with the need for anger management, conflict resolution, and other such challenges. From there, arts skills are introduced. The students get hooked on a personal level and then become invested in managing their feelings. We have examined some of the various types of access points that teachers and artists have chosen in arts integration.

The Big Idea as Access Point

Integrated curriculum works when students can focus on skills and content through organizing concepts and processes that invite active engagement and inquiry. Artists and teachers search for compelling conceptual frames as they create arts integrated units of study. They look for the shared subtext between the disciplines being integrated to connect and deepen instruction. They are looking for organizing principles that can help bridge separate curricular areas and reach their students in intriguing new ways. We refer to this process as finding the "big idea."

One way to identify big ideas is to look at the content and ask: What questions does this information answer? What processes and relationships does it reveal? Some questions are *thinner* than others at stimulating inquiry. *Fat questions* invite deeper inquiry and more complex responses from students. Asking the *who* and *when* questions about the Great Migration of African Americans in the United States does not invite as much integrated curriculum development as asking why and how a major portion of the American population moved to another part of the country.

Here are two examples, with the same teacher, of how it works. Fourth-grade teacher Lissa Chaloff, from the Pulaski Community Academy in the A.C.E.S./Whirlwind Performance Co. Partnership, is preparing to teach a science unit about camouflage and animal adaptation. Artist Cynthia Weiss brings her knowledge of color theory to bear. Students closely study the color wheel, mixing paints to create complementary and analogous colors. Then they create paintings of camouflaged animals hidden in analogous-colored backgrounds. Color theory is brought to life. Students bring those tools of analysis to their science lessons and understand more deeply how the natural world uses both bright, warning colors as well as camouflage as means of adaptation. What is the big idea? What is the frame? The big idea becomes U*ses of Color in Art and Nature.*

This same fourth-grade teacher works with dancer Donna Mandel the following year. They now look to connect adaptation and the food chain with dance concepts. They arrive at an underlying theme of *Interdependence.* Their goal is to have the students understand this *big idea* in science, dance, and through the group work they use to collectively create their dances. Donna and Lissa want their students to learn how to listen, cooperate, and support each other as they solve problems together.

Dancer Donna Mandel teaches her students the dance principles of balance and counterbalance. Teacher Lissa Chaloff teaches the concepts of food chains and food webs. Each small group creates a dance where they physically support one another with connected and interdependent movements. They also write stories about interdependence in their families. The students experience these *big ideas* literally, metaphorically, emotionally, and kinesthetically. They bring their new understandings of interdependence to their science lessons and bring the material they learn in science to represent in their dance. This broader conceptual frame provides a vehicle for complex, multidimensional, and personal learning. (See photo).

A conceptual frame—or big idea—provides parameters for integrated teaching. The paradox about this work is that these parameters (these more focused views of the curriculum) end up being very expansive. With boundaries, learners have the freedom to deeply explore a train of thought. Within the frame of big ideas, parameters become clear and students can unleash their creativity. The arts provide a service in helping teachers to fashion lessons that move beyond the mundane. The elegant fit—between artists and teachers, between the artistic process and the classroom curricular planning process—is liberating.

One teacher explains: I *think that an ideal arts integration is when the educational goal, and your ability to conceptualize it through an art form, is real clear to you. When it has a lot of depth and a lot a of range, because then your limits are sort of boundless. It's kind of like how much magic you build into it. Then the students have a real freedom to explore both what the actual content area is, and what's your educational objective. They can sort of run with it. If the art form and the project allow for that, then it's great.*

Although certainly not the only approach to arts integration, the big idea approach is one that some CAPE partnerships have found extremely valuable in connecting separate subject areas. The big idea is an access point to find just where the links are between an art form and a subject, content field, or discipline. It is a powerful way to get started. Table 2.2 shows some elegant fits that have emerged by searching for and finding the big ideas (typically cross-disciplinary concepts) that connect art and classroom. These big ideas are discussed in various chapters in this book.

Standards/Learning Goals as Access Points

Some teachers and artists prefer to start with the big ideas and general concepts; others prefer to begin with specific objectives. Learning styles among teachers and artists are as varied as among their students, and good arts integration can begin at either end. Lourdes Valenzuela describes this process: I *usually put forward what I am trying to achieve educationally. That's my starting point. Here's where we are; here's the particular unit or the thing that I'm trying to accomplish, and how can we base it on your area of*

The balance Dance is a dance that shows we all depend on each other to hold us up. We all have to trust each other to hold each other up. We all count on each other. It's like a food chain. The earth and the sun, wind, water, fire, plants, and animals all depend on each other. And we can't waste any of our energy. This is a dance about interdependence.

Balance Dance

We are leaning on each other →

Drawing and writing by fourth-grade students documents the "InterdepenDance" Unit created by teacher Lissa Chaloff and dancer Donna Mandel at Pulaski Community Academy.

expertise to develop something. Sometimes I'll have an idea. For example, the artist and I decided to study the Civil War by having the students make a quilt. We connected the quilt making with the stories of real people we were reading about. We usually try to share our lessons in that way. The artist has an art form to teach, and I deal with the content issues.

Teachers work within the parameters of their own grade-level objectives, national and state standards, and the needs of their students. Specific learning goals

TABLE 2.2

Big Ideas Used as Access Points

Cross-Disciplinary Big Idea	Subject Area Topic	Art Form and Concept
Interdependence	Science animal adaptation	Dance (with partners) balance & counterbalance
The Elements in Me	Science chemical composition in the human body	Visual Arts figurative representation & life-size drawings
Physics in Everyday Life	Science Newton's Laws of Motion	Dance weight & counter- weight in choreography
Making Shape of Our Environment	Kindergarten curriculum shapes & mapping	Dance Levels; high, medium, & low Visual Arts shapes & birds-eye view
Going to Scale for a Liveable Community	Social Studies communities	Visual Arts scale & model building
Reconstructing History Through Archeology	Social Studies ancient civilizations & Literature selections	Visual Arts form, fragment & design in clay pottery
Jazz Poetry as an Expression of Historical Narrative	Social Studies migration	Music subject, tone & tempo spoken word poetry
Movement as an Expression of Freedom	Social Studies The Underground Railroad	Dance qualities of movement Visual Arts Adrinkra design & symbols
History as a Timeline of Competing Points-of-View	American History timelines & using primary sources	Visual Arts perspective & framing in banner painting
Displacement & Adjustment	Language Arts genre fiction; immigration stories	Drama voice, text, & subtext rhythm & timing
Translations & Adaptations	Literature Gabriel Garcia Marquez short story adaptation	Performance & Music found sounds, rhythm shadow puppets

are often a necessary starting point for teachers. Artists and art teachers must bring art objectives to the discussion as well.

Let's illustrate how the arts can make a standard come alive for children using a specific example. Here is the standard Dancer Dennis Wise examined to help develop an arts integrated unit at Healy School: *Students will be able to describe changes in political boundaries using historical maps.* (Chicago Public Schools, Grade 4-Social Studies Standard)

Dennis Wise:

I had no problem working with this standard because there was such a clear match with dance; **creating floor patterns is mapping.** *I asked the teachers what was important for them to teach about mapping. Their goals were to teach students how to (a) translate cardinal directions (North, South, East, West) from a map to real space, (b) interpret map keys, (c) group states by different geographical areas, and (d) recognize states by location.*

I knew what was important for me to teach too. I wanted students to learn how to (a) make and notate a dance floor pattern, (b) add level changes (high, medium, low), (c) add time elements (fast, slow), (d) change directions (forward, backward, and sideways), and (e) create expressive movements.

Dennis and his partner teachers created a dance-integrated unit that brought all of their goals together (Table 2.3). The students choreographed movements across the school gym and outside on a painted playground map in lessons that incorporated map-reading and map-making skills, dance concepts, personal interpretations, spatial relationships, and a kinesthetic understanding of mapping (see photos).

The friction between art and content area goals gives rise to new ideas on how to teach to the standards. In fact, arts integrated curriculum offers a way to *go beyond*

A Healy School fourth-grade student displays dance notation and the pathway drawn on a map of the United States in a unit that integrates mapping skills with dance concepts.

Dancer Dennis Wise helps students choreograph these movements across space outside on a playground map. This integrated curriculum was designed by Dennis Wise, with teachers, Denise Fitzgerald, Detra Torres, Patti Gausselin, and Margo Nakayama. Photos: Courtesy of Tammy Steele

the standards. In our criteria for good arts integration, we look for a balance among skills, concepts, and meaningful student engagement. With such comprehensive goals, the standards need not be antithetical to the artistic process, but rather are access points into creative curriculum.

Literature Selections as Access Points

Many partnerships have structured their arts integration work around literature. Literature is a wonderful starting place because the characters, setting, conflict, plot, and themes in a story can become the points of connection to other texts, other content areas, and students' own lives.

Walsh School works closely with the school's cross-disciplinary textbooks that include collections of short stories and excerpts from literature (see Color Insert F.b). The textbook series, Open Court's *Collection for Young Scholars* (Bereiter et al., 1995) has become the cornerstone for building drama, dance, and visual arts integration. One fifth- and sixth-grade unit at Walsh School focused on archaeology. The unit emerged from a textbook story on ancient civilizations and bloomed into an extensive historical, artistic, and literary unit. Students made replicas of pottery, which were ceremonially buried and broken in an archaeological dig site cre-

TABLE 2.3
Geographic Mapping and Dance Skills

Geographic Directions (North, South, East, West):

1. Have the students write North, South, East, and West on the edge of the map.

2. Have the students describe what directions they are moving (e.g., Northeast then South).

Map Keys:

1. Different symbols can represent different actions (e.g., An octagon represents stop).

2. Different line shapes can represent different actions (e.g., Squiggle line represents shaking).

3. Different line colors can represent different emotions (e.g., Red can represent an angry skip).

4. Different line colors can represent different actions (e.g., Green = slither; blue = evaporate).

5. Different line sizes can represent different tempos or movement size (e.g., Fast hops or little hops).

6. Different line textures can represent different actions (e.g., Dashed line = jump).

Coordinating with Maps of the United States:

1. Pick four different states and put them in an order. Follow your map. States can be chosen many different ways (e.g., Pull names out of a hat). Choose one from each geographic area (Northeast, etc.), those that have something in common such as produce similar products, or states that don't border each other.

2. Do actions that have something to do with the state (e.g., Drive out of Michigan which is known for auto production).

Add-on Maps: Put students in groups of four. Number them 1, 2, 3, 4. Have the group follow and learn Group 1's map. Then add on Group 2's map, etc. Have them start and stop in a group shape.

Map / Class Dance Performance: After the students have completed their small-group add-on map dances, number all of the groups. Have all of the groups pick an entering and exiting location. Overlap the groups so that Group 2 enters as Group 1 is exiting.

Visual Art Maps: Exaggerate the basic pattern of the map. Vary the colors, thicknesses, and textures of the lines. Try some repetitions.

Stories from Maps:

1. Write a story about the different states you traveled through on your map.

2. Write a report about the four states you selected.

Note. Start with a movement sequence and then draw the map. Have the students choose four different locations and how they are going to get there (floor pattern). Have them try it. Then sit down and draw a map of it. Table courtesy of Dennis Wise.

ated in the basement of the neighboring park district field house. Classroom projects included science experiments involving archaeology, a trip to the Field Museum of Natural History in Chicago, and the creation of the school's own Archaeology Museum, for which students acted as docents. (See photos)

Dani Kopoulos, Pros Arts Studio performing artist, explains: A *well-written story gets the imaginative juices flowing right from the start. Last spring we did a project with seventh graders around ecology and environmental studies. The teacher, Kendall Grigg, wanted to dramatize the novel* Seedfolks *by Paul Fleischman. The book was fabulous. It was about a community garden and 13 different people who lived in the neighborhood and worked the garden. Each one couldn't have been more different; some old, some young, Black, White, Mexican, Korean—a wide range of cultural and ethnic backgrounds. There were lots of different voices and different character motivations.*

This book was a wonderful access point because its theme and structure—the story of a community garden told from nine different perspectives—provided a framework for both the drama and environmental studies. Dani and Kendall invited their students to add new layers of meaning to the story. The students studied each character in the book, charting out viewpoints and circumstances, and developed a monologue for each of the narrators. Kendall focused on teaching ecology to her students, and Dani provided them with the tools they needed to improvise and develop characters. They brought all the pieces together in the creation of an original drama inspired by the novel.

The following four photos: Archaeology Unit at Walsh School, developed by Pros Arts Studio artist Kaja Overstreet, and 6th grade teachers, Nancy McDonough, Kristina Mondragon, and Thelma Strong. Photos courtesy of Pros Arts Studio/Pilsen Arts Partnership

A student's sketchbook drawing of an Anasazi Indian Village made at the Field Museum of Natural History.

Students reconstruct the village in a diorama for the Walsh School Archaeology Museum at Dvorak Park.

Students create their own design on pottery in the style of the Mimbres culture.

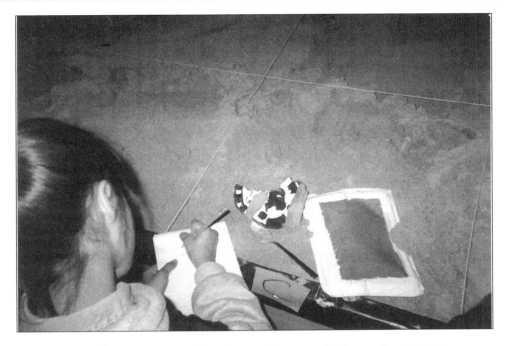

A student digs up pot shards and records her discovery.

Classroom teachers Nancy Geldermann, Sandy Carlson, and Kathleen Martin, and music teacher, Brian Santos in the Hawthorne/Agassiz Partnership used the novel *The Cay* by Theodore Taylor (1969) to help them frame an arts integration unit to explore biology, social discrimination, and interdependence in their fifth-grade classrooms. The novel raised these issues for the children by providing them with a context for two research questions that guided their reading and their artwork. The language arts question they pursued was one concerning social justice: What kinds of insights do people need to get past their prejudices? They also investigated a science research question: How do atolls form, and what sorts of flora and fauna inhabit this ecosystem? Because the novel was set in the Caribbean, the children were able to explore both subject areas through literature. They designed a coral reef quilt and a cloth book version of the coral reef images from the quilt to exhibit at their annual curriculum fair. They produced coral reef computer graphic images that were then transferred to tee shirts and caps for families. They also learned about discrimination, through literature, as well as through sharing stories with persons in their communities who faced prejudice in their own lives.

The point of this work is not just to create cool art projects, but rather to delve deeply into text through the arts. The students engaged in these literature arts integration projects were able to see, comprehend, remember, experience, connect with, and interpret the ideas they encountered in their reading. Literature is the starting point; deeply engaged readers and thinkers is the goal.

Prior Knowledge as Access Point: Starting with the Students' Own Questions

Another important access point can be the students' own questions. Jim Beane (1991, 1993, 1997) has written about the value of students learning to ask their own questions as frameworks for inquiry and as an organizing principle for integrated curriculum development. Others have examined how student questions can be utilized authentically in the classroom in which standards and state mandates must also be accommodated (Burkhardt, 1994). However teachers decide to utilize students' own genuine questions, it is clear that when learners want to know, they are motivated to go deeper and explore more fully.

As teachers begin a new unit of study or introduce a topic for student research, they might start with a simple KWL chart, asking students to state what they already KNOW about the topic, what they WANT TO LEARN, and then, as the unit progresses, what they have LEARNED (Ogle, 1986). Recently, Roger Passman expanded that familiar KWL strategy to the KWILT approach (1997; Table 2.4.). The KWILT provides even more room for student inquiry and engagement in demonstrating what they have learned for others.

Teachers may also begin a new unit or project with a mapping or outlining process that helps students, teachers, and artists plan collaboratively. Mapping may be a way to plan a timeline or calendar of events. It may also be a way for students to visually access the subsections of study and related areas of interest. Some teachers call these maps *graphic organizers* (Hawk, 1986; Katz & Kuby, 1998; see Fig.

TABLE 2.4
KWILT: An Inquiry Project Extension of K–W–L

❖ "**K**" What do I KNOW? The well-practiced process of activating preexisting knowledge. We ask students to brainstorm about what they know or think they know about a topic.

❖ "**W**" WHAT do I want to learn? The second step to K–W–L content area reading strategy. We ask students to focus on their own questions about the topic being discussed. This is where the students develop their "BIG" research questions.

❖ "**I**" How do I INTEND to learn? The first extension of K–W–L asks students to begin to think about the process of their own learning. Areas to be discussed include allocation of time, individual and group assignments, resources available, and how to process information once obtained.

❖ "**L**" What have I LEARNED? The reflective section of K–W–L where students are asked to reflect on what they learned, why what they learned is important, and how their conceptions have changed from the start of the project.

❖ "**T**" How will I TEACH what I have learned to others? The second extension of K–W–L recognizes the importance of an audience in helping students internalize their own learning. They have to decide how they will present their findings to a broader community than just their teacher. This is an accountability step, asking the students to be responsible for their own learning as well as the learning of others.

Note. Courtesy of Roger Passman.

2.1). These organizers may or may not be completed by students, although when learning is integrative, it is useful for all participants to play a role in planning how they will think and do the work.

Mapping or webbing is an excellent way to find out what students already know about a concept, topic, or art form. Examining prior knowledge is a time-honored way to begin. It entails listening as students remember what they may have studied last year or have been studying in their private music lessons outside of school. It is a place to begin that helps all students become engaged because all have had experiences they can bring to bear.

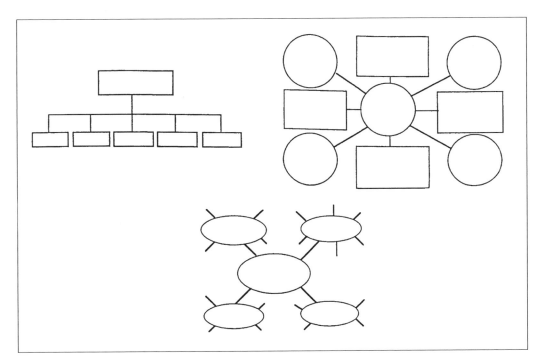

FIG. 2.1. Three graphic organizers.

Lessons You Love / Lessons You Loathe as Access Points

A good place to start developing arts integrated curriculum is where there is teacher energy—either the passion and enthusiasm they have for lessons they love or all the determination they need to bring to a lesson they loathe.

Lessons you love: Past successes provide a range and flexibility, a richness of anecdote and experience, and an integration of skills, content, and concepts for an artist or art teacher to resonate with and build on. The downside is that the artist's ideas may disrupt something that already works well for the teacher, and the loss may outweigh the growth. To avoid this, think about what you've always wanted to do next with it that you have never had the opportunity to do. An arts integration approach can perhaps make this extended goal possible.

Maybe the artist can interview former students to find out what they thought was most successful about the lesson or unit. (Their answers may be surprising.) Consider how the arts might help the students represent to others what they learn from a series of successful lessons. Share your passions. Articulate exactly what it is about the lesson that you love—what capacities it elicits in yourself and in the students.

Lessons you loathe: Getting started with arts integration is often about putting in a little extra work at the beginning to get a big payoff further down the road. Working on lessons you loathe can give you a payoff quickly. Because you are sharing a real problem with another creative adult, unloved lessons can encourage rapid artist–teacher bonding. The question of how to find a way into a subject that initially doesn't engage the teacher is often an authentic challenge for both artist and teacher. The artist gets to assume new roles, drawing on and demonstrating a wider range of real interests. The musician who adores World War I poetry or the dancer who knows intimately the profound antiwar sculptures of Kathe Kollwitz can be a breath of fresh air for a teacher who loves teaching about the Renaissance and is less enthusiastic about teaching the World Wars.

Field Trips as Access Points

Field trips are ventures out into the world where students collect sensory images and experiences. These experiences are access points that can bring the classroom curriculum to life.

A field trip to the Terra Museum of American Art was a wonderfully generative experience for an eighth-grade class from Healy School. Museum educator Scott Sikkema, Healy art teacher JoEllen Kerwin, dancer-in-residence Rosemary Doolas, and project coordinator Tammy Steele planned to connect an exhibit of Robert Capa's photographs with a unit on Character Education and a culminating dance performance (see Color Inserts A.c. and A.d).

The students came to study the photographs of Robert Capa, a *Life Magazine* war photographer. They observed the aesthetic qualities of the photographs, including compelling arrangements of space between figures and backgrounds, dramatic contrasts of lights and darks, and Capa's use of long shots and close-up views. They wrote responses while at the museum, imagining themselves to be inside the pictures, and they discussed the emotional qualities of the work.

This field trip led to many follow-up lessons. Students went on a photo shoot to take their own black and white pictures in the style of Robert Capa (see photos). Their assignment was to find and portray emotions in the structures they encountered. Their stunning photographs were projected and used as the backdrop for their culminating dance performance. The Robert Capa photographs also provided a model for the students' own paintings about foreground, middle ground, and background in art classes.

Using the same access point, Terra Museum educators worked with Ogden School teacher Eric Calderon and art teacher Ann Hallenberg to develop an entirely different unit of study. This team chose to explore one of the *subjects* of the Capa war photographs, the Spanish Civil War. In a project called A *Collaboration of Artists* (*Dear Pablo Project*), students looked at how three different artists—photographer Robert Capa, painter Pablo Picasso, and Chilean poet Pablo Neruda—responded to the same historical event.

The students studied the Spanish Civil War in social studies, read Neruda's poems about the war, and deciphered the composition and message of Picasso's antiwar mural, Guernica. They imagined themselves to be one of the two Pablos and

Photographs taken by eighth-grade students from Healy Elementary School in response to the Robert Capa exhibit at the Terra Museum of American Art. These photographs, expressing different emotions, were projected and used as the backdrop in a culminating dance performance entitled "Who We Are".

wrote imaginary letters from one Pablo to another. They also re-created a large-scale version of the Guernica painting for the lobby of their school.

Museum educator Scott Sikkema says: *It's wonderful when a field trip can become more than just a one-shot thing, when it becomes a multi-expansive experience that connects the museum to the classroom, and also to other sites and opportunities. When you see it as a real totality it makes such a difference. It's a learning experience for everybody, the teachers, the artist, the museum and the students.... It's so good for museum educators to roll up their sleeves, get out of their office, and actually work with teachers and students. It is both a reality check and an inspiration.*

The diversity and depth of responses to the same field trip speak to the creativity of the museums educators, the partnering teachers, artists and students, and the open-ended creativity used in the creation of arts integration work. Both field trips successfully became integral parts of larger units of study. Connections were made across the curriculum in reading, writing, painting, and dance. The energy that students felt out in the field informed their understanding of the artwork and inspired their classroom work for the duration of the projects.

Performance/Exhibition as Access Points

Artists often *see* the final production in their mind's eye when preparing for an upcoming exhibition or performance. They are accustomed to working backward when they begin their work. They have a sense about the qualities and messages they want to convey. There is a kind of wholeness at the beginning, and the artistic process becomes a search for the right forms that will express that imagined end. This image serves as an access point for an artist; the destination drives the process.

Although this may sound abstract, the work begins simply enough with a vision. Then the team goes about pulling together the parts that will lead to that vision. CAPE schools have begun units of study by heading toward final products such as ceramic and painted murals, Day of the Dead altars and parades, student-created web sites, quilts, thematic plays, dance performances, and concerts.

Kitty Conde, art specialist at Ravenswood Elementary School, says: *The mosaic wall on the school playground got started ten years ago in my head. When I lived in Madrid, I went to visit Barcelona and saw (the Spanish architect) Antonio Gaudi's mosaic benches. And I said, "Someday, when I have the hands and the money, I'm going to do this."*

The arts partnership gave Kitty the hands, money, and context to build the wall. Sixth-, seventh-, and eighth-grade students in her art classes created a mosaic timeline that celebrated artwork from the ancient past through the 20th century. Each glass mosaic piece marked a period of history that the students were studying in their social studies classes. Artist Eduardo Angulo Salas built the molds and poured the concrete for the wall on the playground. Kitty's original plan was shaped and changed by the participants as her individual vision evolved into a collaborative work of art (see Color Insert D.c and D.d).

Puppetry artist Frank Maugeri and art teachers Susana Erling and Jim Dee at Lakeview High School planned a shadow puppet performance based on an adaptation of a Gabriel Garcia Marquez story. They knew that Marquez' *magic realist* style of writing would translate well into the magic of shadow puppets, light, and music.

They knew the forms they chose would work well with the content. They didn't know exactly what the process would bring, but the anticipated performance gave them the direction they needed to plan the work with their students.

For teachers, the experience of preparing for school performances may not be so positive. There have been too many anxious rehearsals for school assemblies where the drive to create a good product cancels out the pleasure of the process. One solution may be to scale down the culminating event. A performance can be presented in the classroom for one other visiting class. An exhibition can be curated, organized, and hung by students who also act as docents for other students. Teachers can rely on the expertise of partnering artists to help structure an exhibition plan or performance schedule.

Most important, the process and product need to be seen as interconnected. The students will continually refine their work to present a product, but the product should be used as a way to shed light on the learning process. (See chap. 4: Beyond the Unit: Assessment and the Learning Cycle.) Then the joy of the performance comes full circle; the work begins with an imagined idea and ends with a completed one. There is great satisfaction for everyone involved in refining a form and approximating a desired product.

Creating real products for real purposes raises the stakes for learners. It makes their thinking visible in the concrete world. However, products are only meaningful when students are authentically engaged in the processes that produce them. Performances and exhibitions are meaningful when embedded in a whole series of valued learning experiences. The culminating event is not the purpose of learning; it is but an avenue for learning.

Getting started with the process of arts integration involves a search for the elegant fit between an art form and a content topic. It's also about finding the elegant fit between an artist and a teacher, each with a goal for learning and teaching. Elegant fits do not come without collaborative brainstorming, creative planning, and the sharing of common experiences.

But then there are the students. The next chapter describes what happens when the adults move arts integration into the classroom. In that space, the elegant fit expands and takes on new meaning.

REFERENCES

Alexander, W. M., with Carr. D., & McAvoy, K. (1995). *Student-oriented curriculum: Asking the right questions.* Columbus, OH: National Middle School Association.

Beane, J. A. (1991). The middle school: Natural home of integrated curriculum. *Educational Leadership,* 49(2), 9–13.

Beane, J. A. (1993). *A middle school curriculum: From rhetoric to reality.* Columbus, OH: National Middle School Association.

Beane, J. A. (1997). *Curriculum integration: Designing the core of democratic education.* New York: Teachers College Press.

Bereiter, C., Brown, A., Scardamalia, M., Anderson, V., & Campione, J. (1995). *Collections for young scholars.* Chicago/Peru, IL: Open Court Publishing Company.

Botstein, L. (1998). What role for the arts? In W.C. Ayers & J. L. Miller (Eds.), *A light in dark times: Maxine Greene and the unfinished conversation.* New York: Teachers College Press, 62–70.

Brazee, E., & Capelluti, J. (Eds.). (1995). *Dissolving boundaries: Toward an integrative curriculum.* Columbus, OH: National Middle School Association.

Burkhardt, R. M. (1994). *The inquiry process: Student-centered learning.* Loga, IA: Perfection Learning.

Eisner, E. (1998). *Aesthetic modes of knowing. The kinds of schools we need: Personal essays.* Portsmouth, NH: Heinemann.

Fleischman, P. (1997). *Seedfolks.* New York: HarperCollins.

Gross, P. A. (1997). *Joint curriculum design: Facilitating learning ownership and active participation in secondary classrooms.* Mahwah, NJ: Lawrence Erlbaum Associates.

Hart, W. I. (1995). Interdisciplinary team teaching: Help art lead educational reform. NASSP *Bulletin,* 82(597), 25–29.

Hawk, P.P. (1986). Using graphic organizers to increase achievement in middle school life science. *Science Education,* 70(1), 81–87.

Jacobs, H.H. (Ed.). (1989). *Interdisciplinary curriculum: Design and implementation.* Alexandria, VA: Association for Supervision and Curriculum Development.

Katz, C. A., & Kuby, S. A. (1998). Middle school confidential: The long gray good day. *Journal of Adolescent and Adult Literacy,* 41(6), 486–488.

Ogle, D. (1986). K-W-L: A teaching model that develops active reading of expository text. *Reading Teacher,* 39(6), 564–570.

Passman, R. (1997, March). *How do they do it? An inquiry into seventh and eighth grade research practices.* Invited paper presentation at annual meeting of the Illinois Reading Council, Springfield, IL. March.

Slesinger, B. A., & Busching, B. A. (1995). Practicing democracy through student-centered inquiry. *Middle School Journal,* 26(5), 50–56.

Taylor, T. (1969). *The cay.* New York: Avon Books.

Vatterott, C. (1995). Student-focused instruction: Balancing limits with freedom in the middle grades. *Middle School Journal,* 27(2), 26–38.

Arts Integration Snapshot

School Is Cool: Integrated Arts Programs and the High-Risk Child

by Deb Diehl

School

School is cool. But I'm a fool,
I could do beter. Or I could do werrs.
On my report card I got two F's.
I thait that I was faling. When I got to
my new class it wast the 5th grade.
When I got home I told my mom.
She was so prode of me. So was my dad.
They bought me a presant …
Evan D. age 11

I watched Evan fiddle with his newly pierced ear as he wrote this poem. From his self-selected seat in the far corner of the room, he furtively scratched away at this first draft, protecting any view of the paper with his arm and shoulder. Occasionally he glanced around to check the progress of the other kids or to monitor the proximity of the instructors. He bore down hard on his pencil, breaking the point. When I asked for it, he reluctantly handed over the paper without making eye contact. "You've written a poem, not committed a crime," I joked. He smiled and looked briefly in my face.

Evan continued avoiding contact with me and my co-instructor of this integrated media arts and literature project. He was aggressive and loud with boys his age, but diffident and shy when asked to give ideas for his team's poetry video. He showed enthusiasm for the video but declined to even touch the camera. Finally he was cajoled into shooting "just one shot." I told him I would spot him because he confessed fear of dropping the camera. He didn't. In fact, he showed a good eye and steady camera work. Clearly he had listened to instructions and knew the protocol. When his shots were critiqued favorably by his team, he punched his fist in the air. From then on, he was a confident camera person, eager to shoot and equally eager to offer his help to the others.

Flexing New Intelligence:
Creating Experiences to Help High-Risk Young People Identify Competencies

For the past 5 years, I've worked as an artist collaborating with classroom teachers on integrated arts curricula. During that time, I've worked with many children like Evan. They are often the *problems* in a class of 32 children. Sometimes they compose the entire class of 32. Some are hostile and depressed, others are charming and manipulative, and still others are barely visible shadows at the back of the room. They typically come from what are characterized as high-risk backgrounds. Shirley Brice Heath from Stanford University created a High-Risk Index to identify these children. They live in unsafe neighborhoods, attend schools where they do not feel safe, have gotten into physical fights at school, have families that have been recently divorced or moved, have fathers or mothers that have lost their jobs in the last 2 years, have families that have gone in and out of welfare in the past 2 years, have friends that have dropped out of school, and have been homeless in the past 2 years (Brice Heath, Soep, & Roach, 1998).

Reviewing this list, I am unable to identify a single youth from Evan's school on Chicago's West Side exempt from this category. Those of us who work with high-risk youths cannot possibly meet all of their needs. What we can provide them with are new experiences in which their diverse intelligences can be discovered and flexed. We can assist them in developing more positive, powerful images of themselves in their interactions with the world. As artists and educators, we can work to create the integrated arts projects that have been shown to be a strong method for doing so (Brice Heath, Soep, & Roach, 1998). By participating in the creation of art, problematic behavior can be transformed (at least for a short while) into more successful patterns. Like Evan, children can identify strengths they previously had not known that they possessed, and experience a shift in their own perceptions of themselves. Their own negative expectations of their ability or character are called into question when they experience success in a newly discovered area. Teachers, parents, and the youths have reported seeing untapped organizational, creative, and leadership skills in a young person who makes a video or designs a web site for the first time. As one 10-year-old wrote on a postevaluation, "Now I know that I am an artist even though I can't draw."

Making it Real: The Importance of Self-Direction and Responsibility

Integrated arts projects need to be seen as valuable by high-risk children. Only valued involvement leads young people to identify their unmined strengths. A primary way to make projects meaningful to children is by allowing them enough freedom to direct the content of the work. They need to have enough control to make what is real to them and does not reek of adult-driven agendas (Brice Heath, Soep, & Roach, 1998). Within safe parameters, children need space to experiment with the language, humor, and artistic techniques that will delight them and foster authentic work. Giving them input and decision-making power when real problems arise allows for alternative solutions that an individual instructor might never have conceived. Granting this freedom is not always feasible, but when it is, even the manner in which problems are addressed can add to the reality of the activity in the eyes of the youth participants.

This was best demonstrated to me during a literature and video arts integrated project in which one sixth-grade production team was inadvertently comprised of seven students infamous for their hostility and apathy. They named themselves the Power Crew and began work on a video with an antiviolence message. Because each had been involved in physical altercations at one time or another, this was meaningful content to them.

"Good, keep going," their teacher and I encouraged them, until they began to *rehearse* an intensely graphic beating. We intervened. Without making decisions for them, we introduced questions for them to discuss. How is your antiviolence message made stronger with a beating as opposed to one without it? Is it possible that younger people might be confused by your message? What things in your video have never been seen this way before? We hovered nearby as the animated group debated and reworked their course of action. They were completely immersed in making something important and *not phony*.

Ultimately, they changed their concept and worked together to create a video of which they were wildly proud. A year later, I was back at that school for a new program. One boy from the Power Crew greeted me in the hallway. "Remember me?" he asked. "I'm the Camera Guy. I'm gonna be a photographer when I'm grown."

Making it Good: The Challenges of Making High-Quality Products

Although process is and should be emphasized in integrated arts programs, it is product that is judged and gives a sense of satisfaction on completion. The submission of a piece of artwork for critique by one's peers is a powerful event. When the stakes of a project are heightened by the possibility of its creators appearing unprepared or of meeting a bad review, the instructor's goal to create the highest quality artwork becomes internalized by the children. When the critique includes suggestions and information from peers, not just adult authority figures, the experience takes on more salient meaning.

According to Brice Heath, over time, youth develop regard for their peers as "sources and subjects of critique allowing young people to recognize and take advantage of one another's unique areas of expertise" (Brice Heath, Soep, & Roach, 1998). The skills identified in one individual are reinforced by the group when they realize "that others' differences in the group are assets to be appreciated and used, not aberrations to be suppressed."

In after-school arts programs, Brice Heath and her colleagues (1998) found that greater numbers of high-risk youth self-selected to be involved in free after-school arts programs than other community programs. Among other factors, the high-risk youth were strongly attracted to the emphasis on divergent thinking, peer critique, and the opportunity for setting their own standards for achieving high-quality work.

With integrated arts projects, this process of involving young people in determining their project's standards of quality begins with the first day of the program. In one fourth-grade unit integrating science and media arts curricula, the teacher and I begin by showing the students samples of professional and youth-produced work. This frames a discussion on what makes some work of higher quality than another. Showing students examples of other work helps them develop the measurement standards against which their own work will be critiqued. An entire class can develop a tool, such as a rubric, in their own language ("Phat Audio" vs. "Garbage Audio"), giving their creative process real and concrete standards to guide their work.

With this last year's group, we heavily emphasized how both science and media rely on collaboration and focus because there were several children who literally had trouble sitting in their seats and many who were compulsive talkers. They were generally good-natured, but also extremely anxious and hyperactive. There were constant disputes and interpersonal problems.

Once they were arranged into groups, we helped them get started. In record time, one crew was in full-blown battle. One small girl commandeered the show and stood, hands on hips, barking orders at two angry looking teammates. They were arguing over shot composition. Another boy flatly refused to "put his name on it" because the ideas were "too lame" and the rest of the group would not take his suggestions. The teacher and I stepped in to consult, reviewing brainstorming and collaboration techniques. We made suggestions on how they might reorganize themselves, encouraged a couple of ideas, and moved away. The team finally decided to restructure an approach that they agreed was (and is) superior in creativity and clarity. They worked together through the storyboarding, rehearsing, and shooting—arguing until the very last take about camera placement and framing. Their arguments always reflected their concern for creating a good piece of work and, in the end, they had one. The commercial they created was a smashing success. Their peers voted to watch it twice. The piece was so well received that even suggestions for improvements were made and received enthusiastically.

Making it Feasible: Orchestrating Integrated Arts Projects

It really is a challenge to produce integrated arts projects in the public schools. Time and budgets are tight. Classrooms may be oversized and full of high-risk children. Collaborations between teachers and artists are sometimes awkward because it takes time to synchronize teaching styles, develop trust, and identify *elegant fit* of ideas. The list goes on. I've been involved in my share of bombs. Some projects were not well integrated, others lacked focus, and some were too tightly controlled. However, out of these disappointments, we as teachers and artists gained information that helped us create stronger new projects. By critiquing our own work, we are able to reinforce areas of strength and rework or discard areas of weakness. Through these self-evaluations, we have identified several targets to guide us in making our programs good and real for all concerned:

- Set youth up for success but allow for failure
- Try to be flexible and responsive to youth-driven ideas
- Make sure the emphasis is on a student self-evaluation and critique
- Don't cut planning time for teachers and artists
- Design projects that won't stress the time limits (or participants)
- Work toward the most elegant fit possible with the teacher's current curriculum

Moving beyond the difficulties is a challenge. In fact, it is a process parallel to the ones in which we endeavor to involve our youth. We try to make the projects real. We try to make them good. We continue to meet the challenges ourselves so that we can continue to provide new challenges for them because all children, but perhaps especially our high-risk youth, should have opportunities in which to discover those intelligences they hold.

Evan's Last Day

On the final day of our program, we critiqued the video poems and assembled the poetry *zine* (a desktop published magazine). We told the youth that if they wanted copies of their video, they would have to bring a tape to dub from home. Evan brought his tape 1 week earlier than the other children. We made the dubs, which each person carefully labeled. My co-instructor and I made it clear that each person would receive only one zine because we didn't have enough to give doubles. Then we passed out the "Grannies in the House Poetry Zine," which included the reworked and edited copy of Evan's poem "School." The class was dismissed and the young poets spilled out. As I packed up equipment, I felt someone behind me.

"I know you said only one, but can I have another?" I thought about it, gave him one, and told him he had done a good job. He nodded, tugging on his earring, then walked out with the videotape and two zines tucked under his arm.

References

Brice Heath, S., Soep, E., & Roach, A. (1998). Living the arts through language + learning: A report on community-based youth organizations. *Americans for the Arts Mongraphs*, 2(7).

Arts Integration Snapshot

Art Is Not a Reward: Pitfalls and Promises of Arts Integration

by Andre LeMoine

Art Is Not a Reward

When I looked up from helping Maria with the perspective of her drawing, I saw Felipe running across the room with purple paint all over the back of his crisp, white uniform. Anna was holding the guilty brushes while three students were sitting in the corner planning where to go shopping after school.

"Hold it!" I shouted over the din of creative seventh graders.

"Everybody in your seats. I warned you that if this happened, we wouldn't have art today. Take out your books and turn to page 35."

After reflecting on what I said, I realized that I had done the equivalent of saying to a rowdy reading class that they would be denied books for a week. The idea is absurd, but that is exactly what I had told my class. Although I value art and I paint on my own, I had just communicated to my students that art is not vital to learning; I was treating art as a reward for good behavior that can be taken away like recess. This event caused me to reflect more on student perceptions of art that are sometimes perpetuated by teachers and administrators.

The chaos that led to my bold and foolish decision to *take art away* was simply a matter of my reacting to poor classroom management. Normally I had an orderly classroom that was used to working independently as well as collaboratively. There were clear procedures, expectations, and consequences. But during art projects, self-control often deteriorated and time on task fell. It seemed I had allowed a second set of expectations to take over, which seemed to imply that students can't be creative and in control of themselves. Certainly a portion of the blame is on the faulty unconscious notion that creativity and art arise out of chaos, when in fact quite the opposite is true. Art is a skill that requires focus, discipline, and effort, just like reading or math. If problems arise, there have to be reasonable procedures and consequences. If I do not hold a student accountable for the project, I have reinforced the notion that the project was just a reward.

Art and Classroom Curriculum Must Connect

There are many reasons for the commonly held perception of art as reward and not a part of serious learning. In many of our schools, isolated art teachers are there to give teachers a 40-minute preparation period. These teachers have to see entire student populations and rarely have the chance to learn all their students' names. They have a difficult time completing an art project in a short time with students whom they barely know. The art projects or lessons often have no connection to the work the students do in their *regular* classrooms. In some high schools, students must attend summer school if they want to take a fine arts class as an elective because there is no room for such a class in their schedules. Arts integration works differently.

Art Time Must Be Flexible

"Why aren't we doing art today?" asked Marcos.
"We are going to be doing some reading today on the Maya," I replied. Several groans revealed the students' disappointment that we were not beginning a new art project that day.
"But today is Tuesday and we have art today!" Marcos persisted.
"Yes, it is Tuesday, but we don't have an art class. We have a humanities class where we blend art with learning about history."
"I hate history. We always do art on Tuesday."

This perception that art is a separate entity continues in the seventh grade even though we have been integrating the arts into the social studies program for 4 years. This problem arises when there are scheduled times when an art teacher comes to work with the social studies teacher to implement integrated projects. Being able to team-teach with an artist sounds like a dream come true, but this, too, can sometimes be a problem. When specific times are set aside for the art teacher to work with you, this distinction identifies art as a special time unrelated to the history class. Students see this difference and have a difficult time accepting that art is a vehicle for learning history.

This distinction also creates the tendency of doing art for art's sake. We sometimes feel compelled to start a project, even though we aren't ready, because that time has been structured into the day. Specific times for art can also create irritating problems of continuity. Instead of being able to focus on an art project, completing and critiquing it, there are often interrupting periods of days, which disrupts the flow of the arts integration. More flexible scheduling is needed in which art teachers can visit a class for several days until a project is completed before moving on to the next class. This would require an administration to be trusting enough to allow a teacher to set his or her own schedule with various teachers. We have done this with visiting artists who are able to focus on a few classes intensely, and the results have been more successful and less disruptive because the flow of learning is continuous and coherent. Art must be an integral component of the class, not just an add-on that an artist introduces. Every classroom teacher needs to feel confident and invested enough to involve art in the curriculum and to continue with an idea even if an artist is unable to be present in the classroom. Students then see that the classroom teacher really believes in the educational value of a particular art project.

High Expectations Are Important

"Teacher, I can't draw."
"What do you mean you can't draw?"
"I can't draw. I can't make it look like anything."
"It's O.K. It doesn't matter. Just do something."

I found myself having this conversation with a student one day. I wanted her to get started, but I was inadvertently validating her belief that art wasn't very important. Why did I say this? I wouldn't tell a reluctant writer that it didn't matter if his essay was unreadable. Why are expectations in art less? I have never seen a student fail art, yet many fail reading, math, and social studies. Does this mean that we have a world full of wonderful artists who can't succeed at anything else? More likely our expectations for art are often much lower than other subjects. For students to take arts integration seriously, we need higher expectations with clear rubrics and opportunity for students to reflect with teachers on their work. We can't just tell children, "Just do something." We need to show them the skills necessary to achieve what it is they want to do and not be afraid to say when a piece of art needs more effort or greater depth of thought. We don't accept careless writing, incorrect calculations, or poor reading, so there is no reason to accept effortless art.

Deadlines Are Important

"O.K, is everyone done with the project?" I asked several other teachers during a planning meeting.
"No. My class is still trying to finish it up."
"But haven't you been working on that for 3 weeks?"
"Yes, but the kids just don't seem to get it done."
"Why not? Haven't you set any deadlines?"
"No. They are just so animated, they just can't seem to focus on getting it done."

This little dialogue reveals another problem with treating art as a separate activity that requires unlimited time to develop. Just like any other class, students need to be given deadlines and clear expectations. Without them they will continue to eat up precious class time, delaying the completion of a project, because it is easier than starting something new. This doesn't mean that you need to rush a project, but you need to let students know in advance how much time they will have to complete a project. Often I was not sure how long an art project should take, so a project just seemed to drag until everyone was done, which left many students finished and restless. Those who spent a lot of time talking usually finished very little. I often grew frustrated when I realized how much class time we spent trying to teach a small amount of information. I realize now that it is important to set a time limit that is reasonable for the amount of learning that can be expected. If you only want to teach a few objectives through art, it is impractical to spend months on a project just so it looks good. The process is where the students are learning, and if there is a limited amount of time students will begin to realize they don't have it to squander.

Learning Goals Are Important

"What about that fun project that we did last week when we created the large Olmec heads. Wasn't that fun?"

"Yes. I really liked the pastels we worked with and the huge paper."

"O.K, now Felipe, can you tell me what you learned last week when we created the large Olmec heads?"

"Well, I learned they were really big and colorful."

"Yes, they were quite large, but nobody knows if they were colorful, since only a few paint fragments have ever been discovered. We just wanted you to use your imaginations to envision what they may have looked like. Can anyone else tell me what you learned about the Olmecs?"

A room full of silence told me I had fallen into one of the pitfalls of our humanities program; we hadn't thought about what it was that we wanted to teach through art. We knew we wanted students to learn and remember about the Olmec civilization, but we never sat down and detailed exactly what it was we wanted them to know other than that Olmec heads were large. We created beautiful 6-foot-high pastel drawings that dazzled visitors. This question however remained: Was it worth the weeks spent working on the project? It was positive that students negotiated working in groups and created beautiful pieces of art, yet had they learned much about history? To fix the problem, we decided to add a creative writing component in which students wrote and presented stories about the archeological discovery of their Olmec head. The stories had to incorporate information about time, location, and geography instead of just allowing free reign of creativity where opinion and fact can easily become one. Mixing mediums in a single project can often make an activity more meaningful and educational (see Color Insert G.a).

Clear Evaluative Criteria Are Important

To emphasize the seriousness of the art, my students also had to evaluate their group using a rubric that focused on the quality of the visuals as well the historical depth of information. This evaluation process can show whether the project is meaningful and worth students' effort. Often students receive an arbitrary grade on art assignments based on *gut reaction*, but with a rubric students see that there were specific attributes that were being evaluated. If you want to avoid those blank stares after completing an art project, first make a list of exactly what you want students to know. Then try a variety of strategies to achieve those goals. Finally, show students the evaluations with the goals so that they know what is expected before they begin.

PitfallsBut Promises Too

When you begin to incorporate more art into your curriculum, you will see the guilty paint brushes, talk with the stick figure artists, wish to see the mess of a project end, and see empty stares when you ask what was learned. But before you stop and shout that you are going to take art away, remember that art is not a reward, although it has been portrayed as frivolous. Art can be an integral learning process that draws on the often-unused talents and learning styles of many students. The process of arts integration is no easier or less demanding than any other skill learned in school, but it can make for vibrant, exciting, and memorable learning if you take the time to examine when it doesn't work the way you hoped.

Chapter

Moving Through the Curriculum: Doing the Work in Arts Integration

Breaking Ground

- Moving desks
- Building teams of students
- Playing and exploring with art forms

Warm-up Exercises

- Stretching muscles
- Finding voice
   Example: Framing the world with viewfinders

Deepening Instruction

- Parallel processes—Journal writing and sketchbooks
- Translating across media—The spiraling curriculum
- Shedding new light on old material
   Example: Retablos—Painting and personal stories

Co-Teaching and Co-Learning

- Arts as a lens for exploring equity and democracy
- Sharing adult interests with young people
- Teaming for collaborative teaching
   Example: Cross-high school playwriting
   Example: Working with color—High school chemistry and textile art

Connecting the Self to the Larger Community

- Presenting to the community
- Looking for audiences in the world
- Community organizations and arts in the schools
- Solving problems in schools through the arts
   Example: The school bus saga
   Example: Kindergartners make and see shapes in their environment

Moving Through the Curriculum: Doing the Work in Arts Integration

If reading, science, math, social studies, and language arts are radios, TVs, computers, and refrigerators, none of them is going to work for very long without an electrical current. Art could be that electricity; it's a spark that lights everything up. (Eve Ewing, seventh grade-student, Hawthorne School, Chicago, IL)

Eve's comment above reflects the obvious appeal of an arts approach to learning. Art can be the spark that engages students and draws them into learning. But usually just having the spark is not enough. There is genuine work involved in engaging the arts in a classroom. The process of integrating art takes revising, reversing, and reworking, as philosopher and parent David A. White (1998) describes:

> It is said that Mozart composed most of his great works in his mind and then more or less casually wrote them out just for the sake of a copyist, his income, and, we gratefully add, for posterity. But Mozart was blessed by some divine power; he was, in this respect, surely an exception. Much more typical was Beethoven, whose sketchbooks indicate that the feeling of inexorable power surging through so much of his music emanated from great art produced only after considerable writing, rewriting, revising, reversing, and all manner of process-related struggles and agonizing – plus, one suspects, no small amount of boiler room cursing when the pursuit of musical greatness wasn't going the way the deaf master intended. (p. 1)

This chapter discusses how teachers in classrooms have worked through the process of arts integration on a daily basis. Most children, teachers, and artists are not Mozarts; we are, in the main, Beethovens in the rough, working hard to achieve what we can and learning along the way. Working *through* the curriculum happens when the students arrive. First, there is the process of breaking ground and making classrooms look different. Then students and teachers learn to collaborate through the arts. As teachers, children, and artists work through the curriculum, they learn about the processes in the arts and processes in subject area disciplines. The glamor of finished products does not come without this day-to-day work. Understanding how those processes work together, on *parallel paths*, further informs arts integration in classrooms. They constitute the work of moving *through* the curriculum.

BREAKING GROUND:
MOVING DESKS AND OPENING MINDS

Artists bring the language of aesthetics into the schools. They work in the medium of the senses. In fact, art creates a language: It opens up possibilities for students and teachers to talk and make sense of their world together (Botstein, 1998). To do their work, artists literally change the shape and sensory landscape of the classroom. They push back desks to make room for dance or drama exercises. Musicians bring in drums, recorders, and boom boxes to focus on rhythm and music; video artists plug in equipment; and visual artists lay down plastic tarps to work with plaster, clay, and paint. Kids and teachers sense that the ground is being ploughed and broken up- that something new is about to happen.

Rosemary Doolas, a dancer working at Healy School, describes a performance about Harriet Tubman and the Underground Railroad. *I remember students telling their stories, and one Chinese student, who could hardly speak English, read her monologue, imagining life as a slave. We projected the kids' writing right over their bodies with an overhead projector, so you could see their written story while they read. It made it more effective. It looked so theatrical; it changed the shape of the library.*

This dissonance with everyday classroom routines can be a positive or negative disruption. Artists and teachers have to work hard to understand each other's intentions, respect each other's work styles, and make room for each other in their teaching. As in the best cross-cultural exchange programs, the teacher–artist dialogue can give rise to wonderful new ideas. This very dissonance leads to a synthesis of exciting new teaching practices.

BUILDING TEAMS OF STUDENTS

The thing I like about arts integration is it gets the kids working together toward a common goal. I mean, that's something that they're really going to need to learn later in high school and college. If they can see that it takes eight of them to accomplish one thing, and they know that everybody has a part, they learn that every part contributes to the whole thing. That's what I'm interested in about arts integration (parent comment).

Just as the adults involved in arts integration must build a way to collaborate and work together, so too must teambuilding occur with students. Bringing in different materials to work with in a classroom, introducing new people to the scene, and suggesting a different way of learning has great potential for chaos unless all participants see arts integration as an opportunity to bring people together to work for a common goal. Parents, students, principals, and others who have been involved with arts integration all mention how much young people learn by working together in small or large groups to accomplish something, produce a product, or perform. These events could not happen without the conscious building of a classroom community for learning. This means that the rules for the classroom must be considered and planned with students. Set up, clean up, proper use of materials, space allocation, and team assignments must be worked out. Proper attention to the working conditions pays off enormously later.

In most classrooms and schools where the arts play a vibrant and active role, you will see students working together (see Color Insert G.a). The project-based approach is one that lends itself to active learning in which students are talking to one another, sharing their work, and learning to critique each other in the interest of creating the best possible products. Arts integration almost inevitably provides a construct for students to team or collaborate with each other. Songwriter Amy Lowe remarks that music "solidifies a group—for a moment. There is a heightened awareness of each other."

The integration process is about integrating people with other people, just as much as it is about integrating content, subjects, or skills. This is true regardless of whether the arts are involved. Consequently, an integrative classroom is one in which you find small groups working, workshop approaches being implemented, and laboratory explorations occurring. It is the *doing* of the work that is being stressed here; it is a function of active learning in and through the arts, which is almost inevitably collaborative in nature.

Middle-school teacher John Nieciak has adapted the roles developed in the Literature Circles model for collaborative learning (Daniels, 1994) for his students to work effectively in arts integration groups. Students take the roles of Captain, Recorder, Spokesperson, Reflector, Planner, Optimist, Skeptic, Solver, Technology Specialist, and Spy (!) to work through the process of writing mystery stories and adapting them to video (see chap 4—Mystery Video Unit). The roles help his students understand the tasks that need to be done and to coordinate their efforts. The Spy, John tells the class, "is an information gatherer who is allowed to eavesdrop and observe other teams. The information gathered by the spy can help the team meet learning objectives, improve performance, or possibly clarify or reinforce something within the activity." Thus, groups also work with each other, not just in self-contained communities.

PLAYING AND EXPLORING WITH ART FORMS

Experimenting with materials is really playing with visualizing thought. You can actually see an idea and try it out, reject it, and manipulate it. If you just sat in a chair and thought about it, it wouldn't click in the same way because manipulating materials forces you to make an evaluation (Eleanor Skydell).

An important contribution that the arts bring to classroom process is their ability to give students the permission to experiment. Artists, students, and teachers need time to test out possibilities in their medium and improvise without passing judgment on their ideas. Play and exploration can lead to the most unexpected outcomes.

Dancers Kathleen Maltese and Donna Mandel teach a process they call *Story Dance*, where students create dance movements in response to text. The students may start experimenting with expressive hand gestures and then create shapes that extend throughout their entire bodies. They are encouraged to try movements at different levels, different tempos, and with different qualities, such as sharp and flowing, jagged, or smooth. Then they select sentences from the story and match the meanings of the words with corresponding movements. Some parts of their explorations will have particular resonance for them and will fit well with the stories. Through this process, students are able to create a new kind of sign language that deepens their understanding of the text. It is only by actually trying out ideas and playing with the possibilities that they develop a range of options to use in the creation of new work.

Experimentation is also a necessary part of developing arts integrated units. Teachers and artists plan out their teaching, but work with children often leads to new ideas and emergent curriculum. Exploring with new media and experimenting with the possibilities also help students and teachers understand how the concepts and the art to be produced in the classroom fit with the life of the student. Students need some autonomy to examine just how they will use what they are learning. Student choice and individual creativity become crucial even when that process is uncomfortable.

Dancer Kathleen Maltese says: *Things tend to come apart, to dissolve before your eyes before they really coalesce and become something. Art making is nearly always like that. It can be painful to be in the middle of creating a performance, and not know where to go next with it. Confusion and ambiguity are part and parcel of an artist's business, and though it's never easy to hang out there, it's important to remember that this is a normal (and healthy) process altogether. You encourage yourself (and your colleagues or your students) not to panic, not to give up, but to continue working with what you have and trust that something will develop.*

Textile artist Eleanor Skydell says: *To the degree that you can make your own choices and have ownership in what you are doing, you can be more committed, and you can feel more a part of it, instead of doing someone else's task. You are in the realm of being empowered as you struggle through it with your own choices.*

Teachers also need permission to experiment with art forms. A parent from Sheridan School puts it this way: *I think that what is available to the students should also be available to the teachers. Teachers need an outlet too.*

ESL/bilingual teacher Esther Lieber explains that teachers and artists first need to immerse each other in what they do. The artists need to spend some time as the teachers and the teachers as students. "It takes the mystery out of it," Lieber notes. Once this mystery about just what making art looks like is dissolved, teachers may feel they have permission to expand what they know as their job with students. Esther Lieber says: *My job is to know the kids, to translate, to deal with behavior, to facilitate the process. The artist in turn teaches me; I am her helper. I know bilingual kids. She knows the art form.*

This same exploration occurs with students. Lieber's ESL/bilingual students are repeatedly given permission for this exploration through the writing process. Expression of ideas becomes crucial as students communicate in more than one medium. Esther explains that students move from "I have to write a complete sentence" to "I have something to say." When an artist is not there to work with Esther's students, she continues to build this process of expression by laying the groundwork for the next visit, linking what they are doing in the class with what will happen the next time the artist comes, and building bridges with students between their own personal life experiences and the curriculum.

"You need an artist and a teacher who are ready to flow," Esther says. "Pull back as often as you can and see where the students are headed." Teaching becomes a process of creating images through drama, visual art, dance, and music. Those images are then a key to unlock the verbal images that are so necessary to communicative writing.

WARM-UP EXERCISES

Artists, athletes, and teachers understand the need for warm-up exercises. Warm-ups help stretch muscles, loosen fingers, and exercise vocal chords. They also focus seeing and get bodies and minds ready to be fully engaged in the present. The arts are a place where physical and spatial activities can have both literal and metaphoric meanings. Artists need to stretch to have the physical capacity to move more freely, and their freer movements give rise to new ideas.

Creative drama artist Jackie Samuel always starts her classes with voice and movement warm-ups. She has students practice "throwing their hellos" with their voices and their bodies across the room. Even the shyest students feel comfortable when projecting in unison within a group, coached by Jackie's encouraging instructions.

Jackie Samuel talks about the practical contribution that warm-ups provide to the classroom setting: *Warm-ups help you get the behavioral temperature of the moment. You know who is having a bad day, so that you can see who is going to be responsive when you're giving that lesson. You will know how to target that child and bring them out and back on track with the rest of the class. It's about preparing them.*

When students exercise their voices, they are discovering what their voices can do; they are preparing themselves for participation in their classroom community, and they are also warming up to have a voice in the world.

Theatre artist Dani Kopoulos says: *The need for warm-ups in drama is not immediately apparent. In ceramics, for example, no one would ever ask why it is important to pound the clay before molding it. When you get the clay it's full of air bubbles; it's important to roll it. In drama it's not any less integral to doing the work. Kids are basically told what to do in school, what to think, and how to think. Drama is so totally opposite of that; it gets them to speak their truth, speak their honesty, move that honesty, and to act from inside.*

Each of the different art forms does require students to warm up to the process. In the visual arts, warm-ups allow for a shift in focus and the opportunity to begin thinking **within** the medium of new materials.

Cardboard frames can be used as visual warm-up tools to focus students' attention (see photo). These pieces of cut cardboard are like a viewfinder in a camera; they force students to see their environment in sections at a time. Deb Diehl, videographer, explains: *We have an exercise where we take the students around with these little boxes that they look through, and we have them examine different things in the school from different perspectives. We want them to see things in new ways, and we can get to that in a very visual way through the arts.*

Cynthia Weiss, visual artist, says: *The students hold up viewfinders in the classroom. They look around the room to notice the teacher's messy desk, the ceiling tiles that don't quite match up, the buds on the tree branch out the window, trash blowing down the street, and a mother rushing her child across the street. The frame allows the students to take in one detail at a time, to discover and appreciate the parts, to bring them back to the whole, to notice their environment in a new way. The frame is a structure for wondering why: It is a tool for inquiry. The students may ask, " Why don't the ceiling tiles match up? Who built the ceiling in the first place? What better ceiling design could I make myself?"*

Both Deb and Cynthia use this visual exercise as a warm-up to help students think about complex ideas of perspective, cropped images, and point of view. It is a powerful warm-up exercise with many possible extensions. Teachers can adapt it for their own repertoire and uses.

Healy students frame the landscape to make drawings at the
Chicago River.

Video artist Deidre Searcy has students work in pairs: One student becomes the camera person and the other student becomes the video camera. The *cameras* must keep their heads straightforward—only seeing those things the camera persons point them toward. Their controlled fields of vision become their viewing frames.

The frame helps students literally notice things that they never saw before and to see the connections between the part and the whole. Figuratively, we can think of arts integration as a *curricular frame* to focus student learning so that everyone involved—teachers, artists, and students—has the opportunity to see subjects in fresh and unimagined new ways.

DEEPENING INSTRUCTION: WEAVING PARALLEL PROCESSES

Working through arts integration curriculum involves an explicit teaching of processes that transcend the art form and the content area concept, strategy, or skill. For example, the Writer's Workshop follows a process designed to help students learn how to write like writers. Artists, who take apart and teach the steps in their own creative process, are demonstrating how to paint like painters, make dances like choreographers, and direct like directors. When studio practice is brought into the classroom, parallel processes are revealed.

Lynette Emmons, writing consultant with the Illinois Writing Project, has worked closely with artists for many years. Also an accomplished artist, Lynette and visual artist Cynthia Weiss became interested in the ways that writing journals and artist sketchbooks could serve complementary ends. Writers' journals and artists' sketchbooks are parts of a process that lead to creative products. Lynette and Cynthia mapped out the parallel steps from each discipline:

Journal and Writing Process	Sketchbook and Art-Making Process
Record in journals	Record in sketchbooks
Brainstorm topics	Gather images and observational drawings
Read high-quality writing	Look at professional artwork and other artists' sketchbooks
Write first drafts	Make rough sketches, create storyboards
Research information	Research visual information
Share writing	Share sketches with peers
Revise and refine	Revise and refine
Write second drafts	Add details, color, background
Complete work	Complete work
Publish	Exhibit
Share work with an audience	Share work with an audience

Lynette brought together both processes by encouraging her students to keep a Writer's Sketchbook—an unlined sketchbook used to develop ideas in both image and text. Students could then move back and forth between words and pictures.

Both visual and verbal learners can excel with these sketchbooks as they move back and forth between writing and drawing. Exciting work has begun to emerge with teachers and artists using strategies from one creative discipline to reinforce and strengthen learning in another.

Merging Parallel Processes of Writing and Drawing in the "Retablos" Project

At Telpochcalli School, teachers Vicki Trinder, Erin Roche, and Alfredo Nambo have worked in tandem with visual artist Guillermo Delgado. As part of a unit on *Transformative Experiences*, the team planned lessons in the language arts classes to coincide with the lessons in the art room. Guillermo introduced the students to a "Retablos" project. Retablos, a Spanish tradition found throughout Latin America, are paintings created to give thanks for miracles. Although Retablos have a religious aspect to them, the teachers focused on them as documents of personal transformation. Vicki Trinder says: *We wanted our students to reflect not about something miraculous that happened to them in a passive way, but to think of themselves as active agents of change.*

The artist showed the students Retablos that he had made and shared his personal stories. He taught about the formal aspects of the work, the colors, compositions, and use of symbolic elements to tell a story. In writing classes, the teachers had the students create rough drafts of their stories on personal transformation. When they were in the middle of the writing process, they brought their ideas into the art room and began to find symbols that would represent their stories. The team worked back and forth, revising writing from the drawings and adding to the painting from the writing ideas.

The parallel process of writing and drawing began to merge in a sequence like this:

Introduced Retablos form and concept

Wrote second drafts after art session

Chose symbols for paintings from the writings

Created the painted Retablos

Wrote final drafts

Abstracted words from final drafts to paint onto the Retablos

Completed both pieces of work

Exhibited artwork and performed stories

Teacher Vicki Trinder says: *This is the way we are evolving our work at our school. But I don't think that the teachers or the kids can do this right away. You have to train your muscles first in each discipline. Once they are strong, you can fine tune them so that one can help the other. It's like being bilingual: When you have a strong formation in one language, it can help you in another.*

Translating Across Media

Much of the work of the world-famous early childhood education program in Reggio Emilia, Italy, is organized around developing higher order thinking skills by translating ideas from representation in one medium to another. Complex understandings are generated by visiting and revisiting the same subject matter through a variety of increasingly challenging media. To translate between media, students need to access visual, kinesthetic, musical, and spatial understandings of concepts.

Asking students to translate their work into different artistic genres requires both artistic and analytical skills as the learners abstract the *grammar* of the new genre. Mark Sheridan School teacher John Nieciak, working with Street Level Youth Media artists Deb Diehl and Deidre Searcy, has students translate the visual conventions of video into the literary conventions of mystery fiction (see chap. 4; see also Color Insert A.a). They explore the interconnections between making a video and writing a mystery. Their students first learn to use the tools available for video production: camera angles; long, medium, and close-up shots; fades and dissolves; sound effects; and lighting. Then they study the elements of the mystery genre, including setting, character, motive, plot, suspense, climax, and resolution. One area of expertise is used to inform another. A camera angle might give students ideas on how to advance the plot, and a suspenseful moment may call for a certain lighting effect. In the end, both areas of study have been deepened when studied through the lens of the other; parallel processes inform both disciplines.

Shedding New Light on Old Material

Arts integration is really a call for balance; a balanced curriculum is both deep and wide. Arts integration also sheds new light on old material. Walsh School Principal Dr. Clayton says: *Teachers have made some old fashioned, special reading materials we have in the building quite modern!* The exposure to other materials and resources helps teachers and students think beyond the textbook. Clayton continues: *The arts integration has helped teachers realize that you can learn things not necessarily in the book.*

High school history teacher Kyle Westbrook commented on this process when he, musician/actor Reggie Lawrence, and his students composed Jazz Poetry to study the Antebellum Period in American History (see Appendix D for unit plan). *We took basic scenarios of the Antebellum Period, such as the story of a runaway slave who is pregnant with the master's child. The students had to come up with a narrative that fit that particular story and then set it to music. I look for historical accuracy in these pieces so that we don't have a runaway slave jumping on the subway or into a Cadillac and driving away.*

Having an artist like Reggie come to my classroom really energizes me, and that usually happens when I need it the most. He comes in and he is like the X Factor. He would get the kids out of their shells. Then when he left, I would really try my best to keep them out ... keep them right out there in front. Some are resistant at first. They are so used to being told, "Sit down, shut up and listen to me," that by the time they are 16 or 17 years old, it's been drilled into them and they are very resistant of anything that gets them up and out of their seats.

Reggie teaches them to consider three things: subject, tone, and tempo. There have been students who put so much care and energy into their composing that we recommended they do it pro-

fessionally! I've thought a bit about how they can bring so much energy to this composing compared to that which they use to write a research paper. With Jazz Poetry, there is much more freedom to it. I, as a classroom teacher, am pretty rigid. I'm a stickler for details. What I think they learned from this process is that, together, Reggie and I gave the freedom to explore.

Having an artist in the classroom brought a new perspective to the study of American History for Westbrook's students. Jazz Poetry was the avenue for bringing the Antebellum Period to life. The structured techniques of music, creative writing, and drama paradoxically allowed these high school students the freedom to learn history.

CO-TEACHING AND CO-LEARNING: EXPANDING THE CIRCLE OF EXPERTISE

Drama artist and teacher Jackie Murphy, English teacher Ken Mularski, and history/sociology teacher Diane Fashingbauer have been working on a student collaboration that teaches us something about the power of kids working with kids (see Table 3.1, 3.2). For the past 5 years, they have brought students from suburban Glenbrook North High School and Chicago's Lakeview High School together to learn about themselves, each other, and the art of writing plays. The process of playwriting has afforded these high school students an opportunity to move out of themselves, if only for a few moments, to learn about students beyond their own neighborhoods. They have had to work together in small groups composed of students from both schools to **make something**—to produce a play that they can then perform, discuss, perform again, and discuss.

The three teachers describe the process as it appears in Table 3.1. First students collaborate with others in their own class. There, in the security of their own school buildings, they learn the process of discussing the literature, writing, improvising, and then producing a play. Then students and teachers go beyond their own classroom and into a more complex process of collaboration. They must take the risks inherent in writing coupled with the risks inherent in crossing boundaries of culture, race, and social class (see Appendix D for unit plan).

What can this process of collaboration teach us? In these instances, the artist has introduced a way to approach the art and craft of writing, which opens up possibilities for students. The arts serve to clarify and intensify the experience for these students (Jackson, 1998). The playwriting is a way in; it is also a way out. Playwriting is a way into a student's thoughts and ideas that are waiting to be expressed. The venue of improvisation in a group is a safe mechanism for students to blend verbal and written language. Jackie reminds them, *You are not responsible for what you say, but your character is*. These are important pedagogical precursors to articulate and meaningful writing. They are learning about point of view, clarity, and audience.

Students are also learning about much bigger issues than a traditional school scope and sequence focused on writing could provide. The arts integration has provided a means of looking at issues of equity and democracy. It has opened up questions of identity and stereotyping. This arts integration has led to other initiatives that have benefited both schools. Students have taken days to shadow those from the partner school; they have discussed the value of meeting and knowing

TABLE 3.1

Cross-School Cooperative Learning: Playwriting in the City and the Suburbs (Comments by Drama Artist/Teacher Jackie Murphy)

(This process occurs first in separate classrooms/separate schools, then once again when urban and suburban classes come together for playwriting)
Begin with a poem. Example: "Mother To Son" by Langston Hughes (see Fig. 3.1) "It's like stepping inside a poem first. We distill the poem down to something small, then look at all the possibilities."
Find the possibilities in the poem–characters, setting, plot. "At the beginning of writing, there is only possibility."
Begin writing the poem as a play. "When the curtain opens, write down the first words said on the stage."
Begin a 2-minute dialogue from that first word among two characters from the poem. "Now that you have heard that voice, listen now to how everyone else responds and let these two people talk for 2 minutes."
One student donates her or his 2-minute dialogue to the group for improvisation. "You are not responsible for what you say, but your character is."

Well, son, I'll tell you:
Life for me ain't been no crystal stair.
It's had tacks in it,
And splinters,
And boards torn up,
And places with no carpet on the floor–
Bare.
But all the time
I'se been a-climbin' on,
And reachin' landin's
And turnin' corners,
And sometimes goin' in the dark
Where there ain't been no light.
So, Boy, don't you turn back.
Don't you set down on the steps
'Cause you finds it's kinder hard.
Don't you fall now–
For I'se still goin', honey,
I'se still climbin',
And life for me ain't been no crystal stair.

(Hughes & Bontemps, 1970)

FIG. 3.1. Mother to SonPoem by Langston Hughes (used in Cross-School Playwriting).

those who look different or come from different parts of the community. They have found commonalities among each other. The schools have implemented two ACT test preparation programs that focus on Chicago and Glenbrook students. The initiative has begun collecting data on how students' writing has improved and how this process is affecting test scores. The collaboration has worked.

Community artist Myrna Alvarez reminds us: *Everything we learn cannot fit on one piece of paper.* Arts integration does not allow the content to remain where it began. Indeed, the content grows as the process continues. Objectives are set in place for both the art form and the teacher's curriculum content. Then, as many teachers report, the teaching becomes influenced by the artist's approach, and the artist learns to complement the teaching style. Maureen Breen's French class was forever changed because of the imaginary journey that a dramatist brought. The classroom dynamic was changed, and one student became engaged. That outcome was not defined in a predetermined objective, but it happened nonetheless.

Artists talk about *mirroring* what the teachers do. Reflecting back when students are working really helps teachers see more deeply what is going on in their teaching. The preplanning affords all parties to get started. But then the actual work in the classroom begins to reshape how and what students learn … and how the adults in the classroom teach. Even parents can notice the difference. One artist says it like this: *It has happened to me where the teachers actually said, "Oh you know, I could teach that in a different way.… It would be great if the students started research groups." So the teachers now have the kids working in these research groups*!

The structure that worked well for the artist suddenly works well for getting the work done in the classroom curriculum as well. Research and planning ends up squarely in the center of the classroom activity. A high school chemistry project, portrayed in Table 3.2, outlines this active research and planning (see Color Insert Photos E.a—E.d).

Ms. Pat Riley takes 1 week of her class to present the unit in the chemistry textbook for high school sophomores focusing on acids and bases. Ms. Skydell then comes to the chemistry class for 16 consecutive days; 5 of those days focus on the art form, which is textile geometric art. Pat doesn't formally teach during those 5 days, but she does circulate among the students while they work on their pattern block designs. When the actual lab experiment work begins, both teacher and artist are needed to, as Eleanor puts it, *Save the students from themselves!*

They get confused or they may not realize how important it is to have various members of the team functioning on different tasks simultaneously in order for them to accomplish the final goal. We don't give them their hypotheses; we don't prove anything in their labs for them; we don't do their journals; we give them a skeleton and then this is their work.

Riley and Skydell's arts integration unit on acids and bases includes time for the artist to share her work. "Here's what I do" brings a new definition of the term *teacher* into the classroom. Good teachers know that they succeed most when they can build relationships with their students. Classrooms where the personality and individual presence of the teacher is felt are places where we want to be. The teacher who has family photos on her desk or a piece of artwork that she created on the wall takes a step closer to forming a relationship on which learning can be framed.

When the artists share their lives with students, they open up new ideas for what one does in the world as an adult. Students report that this factor has tremendous impact on them; teachers indicate that just seeing the arts as a career path is new

TABLE 3.2

Acids and Bases Meet Value, Line, and Hue: The Chemistry of Color

Chemistry Teacher Pat Riley	Artist Eleanor Skydell
1. Teacher divides class into teams. They are given the task and directed to keep journals on their process.	1. Students learn about value—minilesson. Artist introduces textile art and shares some of her own work.
2. Teams design a laboratory experiment.	2. Students design small pattern blocks.
3. Teams develop a hypothesis.	3. Artist photocopies students' pattern blocks.
4. Teams develop an experiment to test the effect pH has on color/on dye.	4. Students manipulate the pattern blocks to make a composition that shows an understanding of line.
5. Teams dye pieces of silk (see Color Insert—Silk Baths).	5. Teams produce a larger pattern block collaboratively (see Color Insert—Measuring Board).
6. Teams discuss observations about time, temperature, and pH effects. Change the pH and repeat experiment.	6. Students manipulate color of pattern pieces using the experimental procedure designed by the teacher to produce quality final product (see Color Insert—Assigning Hues and Values/Placing Design on Board).

to most of their students, and they relish the option, imagining themselves doing that work someday. Some artists bring classes to their studios where they can see what happens there. *We got to go to see a real kiln—where he actually bakes the pots!*, one youngster informs a visitor who is observing a clay artist teach about clay as self-expression. Other performing artists perform for their young charges. They play their guitars or sing their songs for classes before ever suggesting the students' involvement in the art.

A visitor went into a classroom at Ray School where arts integration is a regular and vibrant occurrence. She asked the students, *I'm not a dancer. Could I come in and teach you how to dance?* Without missing a beat, one eighth-grade student spoke up: *What do you love to do? You could come in and teach us that.* Integrative teaching involves revealing an integrated adult self to students. Part of working **through** an integrative curriculum process is showing what the adults in the classroom know, love, and can do.

In the chemistry class described previously, the team of artist and teacher is teaching the students how to team by being a team themselves. The teams of students in Ms. Riley's high school chemistry class take the team of adults seriously. The pair is introduced as co-teachers from the very beginning, each on parity with the other. What the artist brings to the topic is valued from the start.

French teacher Maureen Breen and actor Ralph Covert report a similar kind of collaborative teaching. Ralph says, *We would pass the baton back and forth whether it was co-teaching drama or language. It was kind of like childrearing. The thing about having two parents that's key is not necessarily that it has to be 50–50. You get that 10 minutes in the hour and then the other 50 seems manageable.*

Principal Dr. Ron Clayton describes the process at Walsh School in Chicago: *Teachers identify their relationship with the art activities. I've said to teachers: "If, during the art activity, you view yourself as working directly with the artist, then you both could work as a team with the whole class. If you don't see yourself as part of the art activity, then you might send half of the class to work with the artist, while you, the teacher, works with the other half."* Dr. Clayton's comments reveal that co-teaching with two adults in the room at the same time doesn't just magically happen. Orozco Principal Rebecca de los Reyes echoes Dr. Clayton's view: *We've got teachers who freak out over glitter. So how do the teacher and artist work together so that the artist knows this? The artist needs to be careful when planning to work within the realm of this teacher's comfort level.* The comfort level of both artist and teacher is at issue; the familiarity and ease with the art form is also a key point. The solutions offered by these two perceptive school leaders allow for more individualized attention for students; time is not lost, and students continue to learn—from two adults.

CONNECTING THE SELF TO THE LARGER COMMUNITY

CAPE partnerships have taken the time to think about the role of parents as well as the involvement of community-based and after-school programming in conjunction with arts integration. Some of the CAPE partnerships require a parent component in every arts integrated unit. All of the partnerships make formal presentations of their arts integrated curriculum to their parents and their communities—through parades, parent–child workshops, performances, exhibitions, and enthusiastically attended curriculum fairs. Thinking beyond the classroom expands learning opportunities for young people beyond the school sites, acquaints them more fully with the resources in their communities, and invites the larger world to get involved with education.

Whirlwind ACES artist Glenda Baker and Banneker Elementary School teacher Bettye R. Hinton worked with their fourth-grade students to trace the migration of their African-Americans families from the South to Chicago. Students began by reading the book, *The Great Migration*, by artist Jacob Lawrence and watching a performance by *In The Spirit* storytellers, Baker and Emily Hooper Lansana. The students collected oral histories from their parents and grandparents, shared family heirlooms, graphed the number of families from each southern state, and turned the graph into a rhythm exercise. Glenda taught the students traditional African-American work songs and ballads, and how to write their own songs. A culminating student-written musical performance told the story of moving north and the living conditions, jobs, and life that their families found and made for themselves in Chicago.

Looking for audiences and collaborators beyond the four walls of a classroom is one option for working through an integrative curriculum process. *It's about ideas, it's about worlds, it's about cultures, it's about different settings*, says Myrna Alvarez, a community arts organizer. Working through the arts integration curriculum means really understanding how learning involves more than a single classroom or even a single school.

Community arts organizations, such as orchestras or theater ensembles, provide another way for students to connect with their world. The Chicago Symphony Orchestra has developed a Learning Center in which students can participate in a variety of musical experiences designed around five themes: Celebrations in Time, Links, Sounds and Silences, Teams, and Mapping/Recording. Teachers can learn to serve as guides in such an experience; they take their students out of the classroom to resources and performances that are not possible within the school building. Then what? How can we justify those ventures? How can we see what students are learning? The themes that the Chicago Symphony has created suggest the way to move back and forth—from performance, to community learning center, to classroom. Global themes that are broader than any one subject area raise the possibilities of reinforcing concepts and skills mandated in a classroom curriculum. They open up avenues for teaching history (Celebrations in Time), science (Sounds and Silences), or geography (Mapping/Recording). Students see that the map drawings with colored pencils that they complete in social studies have application in other venues. One maps music through a series of notes and rests; one charts the course of a scientific method through a series of carefully labeled steps; one maps a quadratic equation through a series of signs and symbols. Students encounter varying means of representation and expression through these experiences. Music and classroom content are both embraced; larger conceptual frameworks are the umbrellas.

The School Bus Saga: A Classroom Story of Connecting the Self and the Larger Community

Picture this. Up in the observation tower of the John Hancock Building, there are 25 kindergartners craning their necks to see the city of Chicago far below. They are armed with sketchpads and pencils. Each of them is searching—searching for the bright yellow schoolbus that brought them to the John Hancock right by Lake Michigan. They also see the lake, of course, and many, many buildings in the big city below. Their teacher, Wendee DeSent, describes what happened:

It was goosebumpy to walk around and hear the different children talking about what they were seeing and recognizing.

"Hey! There's our school bus!"

"That's not the same bus!"

"Sure it is. It's the same color, the same shape."

"But you can't see the windows. How do you know it's a school bus?"

"Well, I can tell because it's a rectangle. And that's what it would look like if you were on top of the school bus, standing on top of it looking down."

We knew they were going to see the lake. We discussed how they would see swimming pools on top of buildings. We knew we were going to show them all those kinds of shapes. But the idea that our school bus, the one that we rode, was the connection—the ah-ha.... That I would never have been able to plan for. It happened, and it proved to me that what we were doing was working. That school bus taught what we wanted to teach.

Twenty-five kindergarten children have just made a big discovery about their world. They have just made the connection between what they have been studying about maps, geography, and space with the real world. They have learned that drawing representations of the world requires a shift in perspective; maps typically make shapes of things the way they are seen from above.

For the past few weeks, Wendee's class had been studying this phenomenon in their own smaller worlds. They did Shape Hunts in their classroom; they drew corners of the classroom, complete with the multiple shapes that were naturally found there. They looked at photographs, searching for shapes (see Appendix D for unit plan, Making Shape of Our Environment).

They had been standing on desks, looking at books, recognizing shapes in the school, and mapping their bedrooms at home (see photos). Working with a dancer, they had been using their bodies to make shapes, too. They were beginning to understand shapes in different ways—painting them, representing them in mathematics, and dancing them.

Wendee says: *By representing a concept in multiple ways, at different times during the week, I have a better chance of getting it inside them, of getting it internalized.* This challenge of internalizing learning is the real stuff of working through an arts integrated curriculum. How can we know what children are learning while they are in the process of learning it? How can we understand what they perceive? Wendee's kindergarten unit seems to move us closer to the means of capturing their conceptions and misconceptions. If teachers and artists have more of a sense of what children are learning and knowing, they can continue to adapt, reteach, reinforce, and move students forward.

The teachers and artists at Hawthorne School went through such a process to plan their work with shapes in the kindergarten classrooms. The children learned first about different levels they could use when looking at their environment. The visual artist taught them how to paint on paper at high, medium, and low levels. The dancer had the children dance at high, medium, and low levels. They worked with the attribute blocks in mathematics, making basic and complex shapes using the blocks, and eliminating the blocks that were not useful to make a given shape. They learned words such as *high, medium,* and *low,* as well as attributes such as open, closed, smooth, and angular. For example, the children were asked to dance a high-level, open circle shape. In other words, the task required them to transfer what they had learned with the math blocks and represent that learning in their physical movements.

The children moved back and forth from the outside physical world to their own bodies and their own artistic creations. They learned about permanent and nonpermanent shapes in their worlds. They began to think about mapping those shapes and how such maps might look. Maps in dance are called choreography, and the students ventured there next. They learned that a floor plan could be acted out.

They created a dance that had to contain two shapes. They then had to connect the two shapes with either a smooth or a sharp line. Then they had to exit from the dance somehow. The children had to write this movement plan—this choreography —on a card and then dance the shapes and the lines in the appropriate area of the room. Wendee says: *We asked the children when we presented this challenge, "Can you do this?" And they would just do it, no hesitation.*

It's a basic kindergarten unit—shapes. Every teacher does it. But this is taking it to another level. I used to use books to do this unit. I used to use books that have shapes in them. But they have shapes all over their environment and they can make shapes with their bodies! We are teaching them to represent shapes they have actually observed. It's no longer just a worksheet picture of a circle that says, "What am I?" Instead, we used the ME Syndrome. It's perfect for kindergarten. Children know best what they feel and what they do with their own minds and their own bodies.

This Shapes Unit does indeed take learning to another level. Wendee DeSent's kindergarten experience demonstrates how an integrative approach begins and ends ultimately with how individual students connect to the subject. That connection to self extends to a wider look at the concept or theme in the larger world. Looking at shapes in one's body through dance, in one's bedroom through visual art, and then on the top of a skyscraper deepens the concept of shape in these children's thinking.

Working *through* the curriculum is a process of doing. It involves an ongoing cycle of research, planning, collaboration, connecting, and balancing. Teachers—and their artist partners—are engaged with students in the learning of both skills and concepts. Arts integration is action and thinking. One parent helps us see just how this looks in this letter to Ms. DeSent, the kindergarten teacher who worked with shapes and the environment:

Dear Ms. DeSent,

We were a little confused on the visual arts project, so sorry it's late. Nevertheless, what a great project. Jake knew exactly how to approach the medium level concept and seemed to understand the difference between angles. He told me about ovals, and rectangles, and he explained that his racecar bed was a free-form shape. This is a thought process and appreciation never taught to me, and I'm sure my perspective of certain things or, more appropriately, my lack thereof reflects it! Great job. Keep up the creativity. You're teaching some parents too.

We have looked at what arts integration looks like in classrooms, acknowledging how important it is for students to also be collaborators and assist in the planning for arts integration. We have examined the value of warm-up exercises as students prepare to roll up their sleeves and learn. As arts integration continues, teachers deepen their teaching by engaging students in parallel processes that cut across an art form and a content area concept, strategy, or skill. Students learn to translate across art forms and media; they bring new eyes to material they read in their textbooks; they learn from each other; and they teach each other as they learn and relearn what is now an arts-and-content project. Students find means to share their learning beyond their classroom; they search for audiences, and they reach out to their community and the world. This is what it means to *work through the curriculum in an arts integrated classroom.*

Making Shape of Our Environment: Kindergarten
students from the Hawthorne Elementary School
make birds-eye view maps and draw elevations of
their classroom and bedrooms.

(this page and facing page)

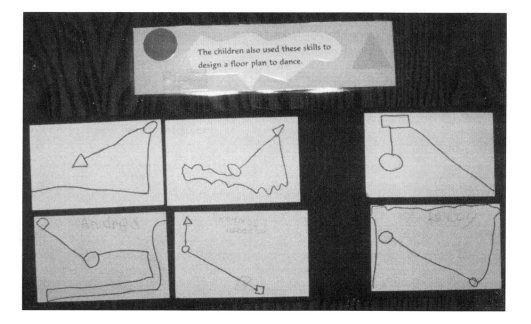

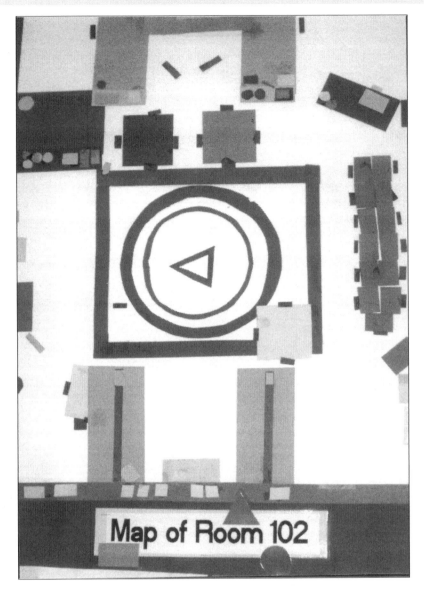

Map of Room 102

REFERENCES

Botstein, L. (1998). What role for the arts? In W. C. Ayers & J. L. Miller (Eds.), A *light in dark times: Maxine Green and the unfinished conversation* (pp. 62–70). New York: Teachers College Press.

Daniels, H. (1994). *Literature circles: Voice and choice in the student-centered classroom.* York, ME: Stenhouse.

Hughes, L., & Bontemps, A. (1970). *The poetry of the Negro 1746–1970.* New York: Doubleday.

Jackson, P. W. (1998). *John Dewey and the lessons of art.* New Haven, CT: Yale University Press.

Lawrence, J. (1993). *The great migration.* New York: The Museum of Modern Art.

White, D. (1998). *The arts and the scope of knowledge: A philosophical justification of arts-integration.* Unpublished manuscript.

Chapter **4**

Beyond the Unit: Assessment and the Learning Cycle

Standardized Assessments and the Arts

- Research on arts programming and student achievement
- The arts and reading scores
- The arts and math scores
- The arts and personal/social skills

Beyond Standardized Tests (the #2 pencil)

- Presentation and the development of understanding
- "Re-searching": Assessment as a process of inquiry
- Gathering evidence: Performing knowledge
- Accountability and Accounting: Two different processes

Collaboration and assessment

- Student reflections: "Could you see it? Could you feel it? What touches you? Can you relate?"
- Students as audience for their peers' work
- Assessment as part of learning—not an afterthought
- "Accountability that a junior high student understands"

Processes for Arts Assessment

- Revision: Reworking ideas, media, and perspectives
    - Song lyrics as revision
    - Video reflection as revision
    - Seeking and receiving feedback on the work
- Rubrics
    - Scoring work
    - Integrating criteria for art and content
    - Checklists for students and teachers

Performance assessment: Presenting and representing work

 Exhibition: Making the work public

    Parent and community roles in assessment

 Self-evaluation

    Reflecting to learn

    Providing feedback for future units

4

Beyond The Unit:
Assessment and
the Learning Cycle

THE #2 PENCIL: ARTS INTEGRATION AND TRADITIONAL ACHIEVEMENT MEASURES

Arts integration initiatives face a persistent and intensive challenge to address issues of accountability in an age where academic standards, time on task, and bell-to-bell learning are the norm. If external standardized measures drive policy in many schools in this country, how then can the arts validate their presence as an integral part of the educational process? How do arts integrated curricula contribute to achievement? Do they raise test scores?

Assessment, like the very substance and quality of the (arts integration) program, is an area that requires utmost attention for the sake of students and teachers, arts administrator David Flatley says. *Marketing is everything.* Arts integration markets itself in communities and schools where it has been taken seriously. Why? Because it does contribute to student learning. Orozco School Principal Rebecca de los Reyes says: *I don't care how cute the activity is, how much fun the kids have, or how much art they are doing. Show me how it's related in a meaningful way to the objectives and standards, and to the curriculum. Show me how you focus on those things to help students achieve.*

Information collected in schools where arts integration has taken hold suggests that standardized test scores are positively affected by the presence of the arts in classrooms. Schools where the arts have been a consistent presence show gains in both reading and math scores. More studies continue to mount, validating the interaction between quality arts programming and student achievement (Catterall, 1997; Parks & Rose, 1997). The National Endowment for the Arts (NEA) reports that analyses of test scores across a range of schools consistently show the following:

1. Students in arts-focused schools usually have higher than average test scores than students enrolled in other schools in their district or state.
2. Standardized test results of students in arts-focused schools compare favorably with those of students enrolled in more academically selective schools even when the arts schools do not pursue selective admission policies.

3. Some evidence suggests that some students with low to average academic preparation perform at a higher level on standardized tests when enrolled in arts-focused schools. Students with more favorable academic preparation sustain their strong academic performance.

4. Students who enter arts-focused schools with above average academic performance do sustain these levels and often improve their performance on standardized tests during their enrollment in arts-focused schools (OMG, Inc., 1991).

In Chicago, we have also found consistent anecdotal as well as statistical evidence that arts integration contributes to achievement as measured in standardized ways (Catterall, 1999). Tammy Steele, coordinator for the Bridgeport-Armour Square-Near North Partnership, reports: *Was it worth it? Student reading scores at Healy School had risen from 37.8% at grade level to 60.0% reading at grade level. The Iowa Test of Basic Skills in math rose from 49.0% at grade level to 72.7%, and science scores climbed from 52.9% to 66.3%. These scores may not prove that an arts integrated curriculum causes scores to rise, but they absolutely prove that so much time "wasted on the arts" did not cause scores to fall.*

The Whirlwind Performance Company in Chicago also conducted research on how their drama programming contributed to students' achievement in reading as measured by the Iowa Test of Basic Skills. Their study reported encouraging gains, thanks to the focused attention to the integration of specific reading skills and drama techniques. Whirlwind's research validates earlier work relating significant gains in reading comprehension with creative drama activities (Burns, Roe, & Ross, 1988; McCaslin, 1990).

Principal Dr. Ron Clayton reports that data collected by the Chicago Consortium for School Research at Walsh School show similar increases in the area of reading. He claims that the initial purpose for introducing the arts-based curriculum projects was to improve the students' understanding of reading material and enhance their test scores. Over a 5-year period, he attests to a continual growth in the children's levels of comprehension. He does not hesitate to attribute his students' success to the efforts of artists and teachers to make learning meaningful through the arts.

Catterall and Waldorf (1999) prepared the most extensive evaluation report of CAPE documented in *Champions of Change: The Impact of the Arts on Learning* (available on the Kennedy Center web page: *http://artsedge.Kennedy-Center.org*). The researchers performed a total of 52 test score analyses of CAPE and comparison schools. CAPE schools were compared to other Chicago Public Schools in a variety of ways. In none of those 52 analyses did nonCAPE schools outperform CAPE schools. Here is a sample of what Catterall and Waldorf found:

A very strong case can be made for CAPE program effects in reading and math at the sixth grade level, and a moderate case can be made for CAPE program effects in reading and math at the third grade level. The middle and high school years consistently show test score improvements since the planning years, and the high school grades tend to show larger advantages for CAPE schools in the implementation years (post–1995) than in the planning years (1993–1994) (p. 54).

They continue: *There appear to be strong and significant achievement effects of CAPE at the elementary level and especially by sixth grade. In high school there are positive gains for CAPE versus comparison schools that, while notable in size, do not achieve statistical significance because of the small number of CAPE high schools (p. 56).*

That said, what else might arts integration contribute to the conversation about assessment? Standardized test scores reveal a comparison of how one child compares to another child on his or her grade level with respect to specific, predetermined skills. Is there more we can learn about what and how children learn? Is there other information that is valuable to parents, the community, teachers, and the students?

Catterall and Waldorf also explored other benefits of arts integration offered by the CAPE approach. Teachers and artists reported growth in what may be called *personal* and *social skills*, such as responsibility, self-management, team participation, and work with diverse individuals. Teachers and principals observed greater motivation to learn, positive behavioral changes in limited English proficient students, and positive changes in teacher–student relationships.

Some researchers are justifiably concerned about the use of standardized test scores to justify arts in education. Harvard-based researcher Lois Hetland: "We don't ask history to justify itself on the basis of whether it raises English scores. It's valuable on its own" (2000).

If arts experiences are valuable to children, we need to continue to explore exactly what *is* valuable about them and how those experiences contribute to schooling.

"Assessment is not so much a test as an episode of learning," Wolf and Pistone noted (1991, p. 8). The practices described in this chapter indicate other approaches to assessment that provide relevant information to parents, educators, and the students about what they are learning. They are meant to complement traditional means of scoring and assessing, not replace them. They represent learning that has been part of the *elegant fit* of arts integration. As *episodes of learning*, they require more than a #2 pencil.

BEYOND THE #2 PENCIL: PLANNING AND DOING AS ASSESSMENT

The word *assessment* comes from the French *assidere*, which means "to sit beside" (Herman, Aschbacher, & Winters, 1992). The root suggests an approach to assessing how students experience the arts in classrooms and schools. "Sitting beside children" implies that we observe, listen, watch, and collect data to better understand what they are struggling with. Assessment is really the process of collecting information that helps students, parents, and teachers understand how the students are doing.

Jessica Hoffmann Davis, an artist and scholar, suggests that we must ask this question of an artistic product: How does this mode of presentation inform the process—developing understanding (Lawrence-Lightfoot & Davis, 1998)? This concept of *representing to learn* (Daniels & Bizar, 1998) generates a whole new battery of tools for teachers who must, on a daily basis, access what their students are doing with curriculum.

Such assessment brings the best of art and science together to paint a rich picture of students' experiences. Clifford Geertz (1983), an anthropologist, calls this process in research *thick description*—an apt name for a thorough assessment and reflection process as part of teaching and learning. Thin description is what many parents receive routinely as a single letter grade on a report card. Thick description is informative and useful; it pushes us toward new insights, toward revision and re-working, toward continuing the learning cycle.

If we view assessment in the French sense, it becomes a close cousin to re-search. Take the word apart: to *re-search* means literally to "look again." Assessment becomes a process of inquiry, questioning, and looking for something. Assess-ment requires that one look again at the history of the students, the context of the school, the community, and the other learning experiences that teacher and stu-dent have together in that classroom. In contrast to that multiple-choice stan-dardized test, authentic assessment finds history and context questions vitally important; they are the maps. Assessment does not only happen after the arts unit; it happens within the educational experience.

The point is to gather *evidence* of content and skills learned. Jim Beane (1997) calls this *performing knowledge*. That term is most certainly something that artists and stu-dents who are learning to think like artists do. Assessment in an arts integration classroom involves exhibition and performance perhaps in conjunction with tradi-tional testing. It incorporates self-evaluation, the design of rubrics, and the involve-ment of students in establishing standards of quality. It centers on thoughtful reflection—not just at the end when the product is unveiled, but at each step along the way. The process of assessment is as integrative as the arts project.

How can such a complex process of assessment answer the calls for accountabil-ity? *Accountability* seems to often be confused with *accounting*. Accounting—that is, the process of gathering, organizing, and reporting information—summarizes a child's performance in the past quarter, semester, or year. Accounting looks at what is over and done, in the past. The numbers are then posted in the newspaper, and schools and children are compared across the county. In contrast, accountability is a much more in-depth process; it presents a *system for use* for actually interpreting and acting on those numbers (Earl & LeMahieu, 1997).

Accountability need not be antithetical to arts integration. Accountability and assessment are both processes that contribute to our understanding of arts edu-cation. The arts can actually deepen teachers' awareness of children's abilities (Goldberg, 1997). Teachers continually report surprise and even shock when they see what students have learned and can do using the arts. The least likely child is often the one with the most insightful reflection. Learning and utilizing the tools of assessment—to uncover that learning in those least likely children—is one of the most validating outcomes of an arts integration assessment approach.

THE ROLE OF COLLABORATION IN ASSESSMENT

Esther Lieber's high school ESL/bilingual students read their poetry aloud for the class. She has built an atmosphere of trust and community so that they are ready to be both audience and performers. They are also prepared to give response. When they listen to a peer's writing, Esther asks them, "Could you see it? Could you feel it? What touches you? Can you relate?" They are learning the tools of reflecting on their own experiences and perceptions; they are also learning to assess deeply and collaboratively. Those four questions push students to assume the responsibility for the quality of work that is done in that classroom. They are all responsible for setting the expectations. Students complete this approach by having autograph parties of their class poetry books. She reports that students who may not otherwise do so show up first period on the last day of school to participate. Several of Lieber's students have gone on to participate in city-wide writing contests and poetry slams.

What are the students learning in Esther Lieber's ESL/bilingual English class? How can we tell? If we can identify what they are learning, what can we use for evidence? These are the assessment questions. Lieber's students have learned "what it is to work as a critical audience" (Wolf & Pistone, 1991, p. 24). Throughout the designing of projects like this, the teacher and the students ask questions of the work; they probe for understanding and clarity; they examine the works and try to articulate what they see and hear. They may take photographs and write in journals. They establish rubrics or other such criteria for quality, and they learn to critique based on those indicators. They have products and they have traced their processes. They can articulate what they have learned in terms of techniques, skills, and content. They can do so in terms of facts and concepts. They have been *doing the work of assessment* ... all without a #2 pencil.

The process is collaborative at each step, just as working **through** the curriculum was collaborative on the part of students and teachers (see chap. 3). "Since students present, demonstrate, and exhibit their work for the group, knowledge is not simply something individuals accumulate for themselves. Rather it is put to use for the **group's** further understanding of the problem or issue around which the unit is organized" (Beane, 1997, p. 61). In the prior examples, students could not do the required assignments alone. They need the consistent input, feedback, and individual talents of the group. If the process is collaborative, then shouldn't the assessment strategies also be? Group assessment is knowledge being put to use.

Dancer Kathleen Maltese structures many opportunities for her student artists to observe, notice, and name what they are doing as they make their dances. She helps students learn how to really see their work by becoming each other's audience. *One group at a time gets up and presents the dance they're working on, which is valuable because then everyone has the opportunity to give feedback and discuss what they saw; we're training to be observant, to notice things,* Kathleen explains. This is just what Jim Beane was talking about; students present their work and the group learns something from it.

Artist Kim Salerno also talks about building assessment into the integrated lesson process: *We took the specifics of what I talked about regarding portrait painting, and we introduced them to five specific criteria, then we tested them on it. They had to make a painting and decide what three aspects they were going to address and how they were going to do it ... they defended their choices in their journals. Their painting became a tool for assessing their knowledge.* In this example, the student's painting became a collaborative tool for assessing their knowledge. Assessment is occurring as an integral part of the teaching, not something separate from it. The students were learning to articulate their point of view as speakers and persuasive writers.

These examples really demonstrate how teachers and artists can construct a conversation between "producers and perceivers" about what they have been working on (Lawrence-Lightfoot & Davis, 1998). It is a negotiation. The perceiver or audience attends to some aspects of the work and the artist/student to others. Together they interpret the experience. Textile artist Eleanor Skydell says: *The process of making art is never finished until the critiquing is done. If you don't do the critique, you miss out on the response of other people to your work—the knowledge that you've touched someone else.*

Teacher John Nieciak of Mark Sheridan School describes the video project in which junior high students write mystery stories after an intensive study of the genre of mystery and the nature of the writing process. Once the stories are written, a video artist introduces the video/technology component. *Students are then placed in small groups to decide which story will be adapted to video. This decision is based on criteria provided from the video artist. In groups, students write a script and story board, and design and implement an action plan to produce a movie. Students respond to this portion of the lesson very seriously. Students know that their names and faces will be on the video to be viewed by all! This is not only built-in accountability; it is accountability that a junior high student understands* (see Table 4.1). Accountability that a junior high student understands is the goal; collaboratively, students become responsible for a building block of authentic accountability.

The assessment processes described below are compatible with assessment in arts integration projects. Teachers in areas outside arts integration use these processes. But the ways in which teachers and artists have used them **within** arts integration may stretch our view of just what assessment can be in classrooms. These processes can be applied to other areas of the curriculum, but they have real viability when the arts are integrated with other subjects in a meaningful way. They are the tools we can use to see what students know and are able to do.

PROCESSES FOR ASSESSING: "SITTING BESIDE" LEARNERS

Revision: Looking at Assessment as a Spiral

Reggio Emilia teachers develop projects that involve spiraling experiences, exploring themes and events relevant to the lives of children and the community. Through the project, discussions consisting of children's questions, answers, and responses to activities are shared among children and noted by the teachers. The children's current ideas are compared and contrasted to their initial ideas through the use of many symbolic media like words, movement, songs, drawings, block building, and shadow play. Through reflection and repetition, children are guided into deeper experiences (Keenan & Edwards, 1992).

The operative metaphor for the Reggio Emilia arts-infused preschool program is the *spiral*. This metaphor informs the Emilia philosophy: Learning is never finished. Students revisit ideas again and again in different media and from different perspectives. They spiral back to ideas that compel them, each time in a new way with new information. If we take this same concept and apply it to assessment of learning, what are the implications for how we measure growth?

A Sheridan School parent envisioned this notion of spiraling as a way to infuse the arts throughout the grades in her school. *I think it's a good idea to start some kind of art program in kindergarten, and each year, as they go to a different grade, they can develop in a deeper way in that art area. By the time they get to eighth grade, they have mastered it. We do that with everything else in the curriculum, but somehow we don't do it for the arts. And we should.*

Arts integration is a great vehicle for students to revisit concepts in different media. In fact, the revisiting and translating back and forth between different media may be at the heart of integrated studies. It is the translating between media that generates higher order thinking and deeper learning.

TABLE 4.1

Mystery Video Unit—Assessment Linked to Goals and Standards

Grades 6–8 Mark Sheridan School

Teacher: John Nieciak   **Video Artist: Deb Diehl**

Language Arts Objectives

1. Students will demonstrate understanding of characterization.

2. Students will sequence narrative events in written story and video.

3. Students will collaboratively select and adapt one of their own original mystery stories to video.

4. Students will distinguish between mystery and suspense.

Video Art Objectives

1. Students will understand creating structure as an important part of video process.

2. Students will structure a mystery storyboard.

3. Students will recognize elements that make mystery genre distinct.

4. Students will recognize audio/FX as an important sensory element and be able to demonstrate its use.

Assessment Tools

Story Checklist

1. Are there at least two typed pages?	Yes	No
2. Does exposition include setting?	Yes	No
a crime?	Yes	No
a question of "who did it"?	Yes	No
3. Does the story establish characters with motive?	Yes	No
4. Does the story name a detective?	Yes	No
5. Are there physical clues that can be videotaped?	Yes	No
6. Is a criminal revealed based on evidence provided from the clues?	Yes	No
7. Is there a resolution?	Yes	No

Process Assessment

1. Working in Groups

  a. Name three benefits to working in a group.

  b. Give three to five examples of how those benefits were evident or could have been evident in your group.

  c. Describe what you contributed to your group.

  d. Describe what you could do next time to make your group work more productive.

2. Summarizing your Learning

  a. Describe what you learned about mystery as a story genre.

  b. Describe what you learned about working in groups.

  c. Describe what you learned about video technology and special effects. (Use three to five technical words or descriptions in your summary.)

In reflection sessions, students discuss and write about their experiences with the art forms, reflect on the qualities of their work, and exhibit what they have learned. This expression of ideas is necessary to continue the learning cycle. Sometimes curricular concepts being integrated only come together through such discussion and representation.

The Whirlwind ACES Partnership initiated the use of memory boards to record and display artifacts of student learning in each arts integrated unit. They were inspired by the documentation created in the Reggio Emilia classrooms and in the traveling exhibition, *The Hundred Languages of Children.*

ACES artists and teachers took photographs of the different lessons embedded in an integrated unit, mounted the photographs in sequential order on a black display board, and often asked their students to write captions and draw pictures that described each step of the process. These memory boards, which made learning visible to students, were displayed in the classroom, in the school hallways, and at culminating exhibits and events.

The boards created a collective class memory and served as an assessment of how well the students remembered and retained new ideas and experiences. At the end of each semester, the artists and teachers in the ACES partnership came together to share their work. They used the memory boards to exhibit, explain, and reflect on their work in the classroom.

Singer/songwriter Amy Lowe comes into a classroom to help students reflect on their learning through song writing (see Fig. 4.1).

I go into a classroom after students have experienced artists for a 15-week session. I interview them as a group, and then we brainstorm together. I put on the chalkboard everything that they remembered and experienced from their work with the artist. I then talk them through the process, and we mold it into a song as a group. So their actual memories and experiences get talked about, and we finalize it all in a song.

It is really wonderful for me to go in and ask the students what they felt about the experience and what they learned. I will always talk to the teacher beforehand to find out what the intent was. The teacher will say, "This is what we wanted to do and tried to do, and this is what we did do." Then we'd all be pleased and surprised by hearing the voices of the children. The children will remember the songs, and the songs will reinforce the experience.

I've always believed that music is a great learning tool. It's a great vehicle for solidifying an idea. Sometimes it's a song that can get the essence of an emotion. Songs can capture something in a moment.

When teachers and artists realize that their students are *not* making connections, they can go back and teach minilessons or reteach ideas in a new way. There are bridges and gaps in both student learning and team teaching. Such a process is not easy, and there are no shortcuts. But students' learning is at stake, and there can be no compromise. Artists and teachers understand the need to revise and spiral back to different teaching strategies; they must exercise the same discerning care that is needed to make elegant artwork.

The use of video is a valuable tool in arts integration during a process of reflection and revision. Artists ask questions such as, *What is strong here? What really works for you and why?*, says dancer Donna Mandel. Video is also a way to bring home the notion that there is tangible learning occurring here, something that *is* happening, although the students consistently report this as "fun." Dancer Angelia Pfeifer

Audubon School, 3rd grade Teacher: Laura Goulding,
Visual Artist: Abi Gonzales, Weaver: Amy Lowe

The objective of this Integrated Curriculum Lesson (ICL) was to study Chicago's architectural structures and designs and make children aware of their surroundings. Children were taught to use clay by forming designs with different shapes and tools. Plaster and paint were poured over the designs and then put on display so that the children saw what their finished ornamental designs would look like. The class took a walk around the school to look at the different architectural designs, and each student drew his or her own interpretation of the designs. Students' final models are mounted and displayed.

Amy Lowe, singer/songwriter, then went in as the weaver and, together with the children, wrote a song that synthesized the process of the ICL.

> First we looked out the window at
> the designs on the rooftops.
> Kept the image in our minds.
> Together we went for a walk.
> We went into the hallway like
> detectives on a search.
> Looking for a design
> to begin our research.
> (REFRAIN)
> Architectural design
> Never before caught my eye—whoa
> Architectural design
> I am now aware of the
> architectural design.
> Sat down on the steps then we copied
> The design onto a piece of paper,
> that's how we learned to make
> perfect lines.
> Then we found a piece of clay, with
> a paper clip scooped out designs.
> Then we added colored plaster to
> preserve it for all time.
> (REFRAIN)

Courtesy of Lakeview Education and Arts Partnership

FIG. 4.1.   Integrating social studies with Chicago architecture.

says: *Sometimes it takes the kids looking back at the end to realize that we're actually doing something that's supposed to be learning. And then they integrate everything. I ask, "What did you like about what you did? What really made you understand?" They reflect on it and that's the way they grow.*

Ongoing assessment during arts integration is self-correcting and generative. Myrna Alvarez, community arts organizer, says it this way: *When you work with art, you can never do something wrong because whatever comes out, it's still your creation. Children are able to take their failures a little better and they're able to get right back in there and start all over again. In schoolwork, sometimes it's frustrating because once you do it wrong, they mark it down and you're wrong, and it's wrong. But with art, it's easier because if you do something wrong, you can fix it.* This is a whole new way of looking at assessment; this is a process that generates risk-taking, curiosity, and new ideas. It is also a process that a teacher could observe and learn from, noting where skills may be lacking and how intervention might be useful.

Some teachers have used this approach in their teaching beyond the arts. Tests become more like learning opportunities when students have the opportunity to revise, rethink, retake. Projects become stronger and deeper when, after response and feedback, they can be overhauled or redone. A central part of the work of arts integration is the seeking and receiving of feedback, which can then be reintroduced to the learning cycle. Orozco Principal Rebecca de los Reyes says: *Teachers need to be given the time to show that it may not work the first, the second, or even the third time. But at least in time you know that you're actively reflecting and finding ways to make it better.*

Videographer Deb Diehl says: *It's hard to launch new things. It takes a lot of thought and hard work. You polish them up by the third or fourth year. Then they're elegant—then they are polished stones.*

Using Rubrics

A rubric is a set of scoring guidelines for evaluating students' work. In medieval times, a rubric was a set of instructions or a commentary attached to a law or liturgical service and typically written in red. Thus, *rubric* came to mean something that authoritatively instructs people (Wiggins, 1998). Why do teachers use rubrics? How have they been useful in arts integration classrooms?

The arts integration approach to learning seems especially compatible to the use of rubrics as part of an authentic assessment system. If we move back in time and recall the medieval use of the word, we are reminded how today's modern rubric for assessment can also be *instructive*. **Assessment is a form of teaching**. Designing and using rubrics with children teaches them while they are also learning to critique and be critiqued on the quality of their work.

Lincoln Park High School's freshman physical education class constructed an assessment for a Rites of Passage/Seasonal Dances arts integration process (see Table 4.2). This rubric is detailed and includes both written and performance components. The scoring is in the form of points and percentages and is converted to a letter grade. But the letter grade finally attached is accompanied by a wealth of information related to the student's demonstrated knowledge of movements taught as well as historical and cultural information related to each dance.

McCosh School offers a similar blending of performance and literary objectives in the Teacher's Checklist for Drama/Playwriting (see Fig. 4.2). These examples re-

TABLE 4.2

Rites of Passage/Seasonal Dances—Lincoln Park High School and Hedwig Dances

Scoring Rubric

Variable	3 OUTSTANDING	2 MEETS	1 LITTLE EFFORT	0 NO ATTEMPT
A. Participates in dances of diverse cultures	Demonstrates leadership on more than one occasion; up and with the group at ALL times; shows willing attitude	Up with group at all times and shows willing attitude	Participates with group at least half of the time (at least 25 minutes)	Does not participate in dances
B. Uses basic steps, patterns, & positions	Performs dances with 80%–100% accuracy, and displays stylistic ability	Performs dances with 50%–79% accuracy	Performs dances with 20%–50% accuracy	Does not attempt to execute dances
C. Follows music using dance	Rhythmically adept at all times, moves on beat with music	Moves to the rhythm of the dances 75% of the time	Moves to the music 50% of the time	Does not follow the music
D. Demonstrates confidence in leading and following	Able to move with partner as a unit, able to lead and follow partner/group through spatial patterns, and steps correctly and effectively	Able to lead and follow partner/group through spatial patterns and steps with 50%–70% accuracy	Shows some attempt to dance with partner and follow the group (with less than 50% accuracy)	Does not dance with partner and/or does not follow group
E. Creates variation on learned movements	Rearranges six or more learned movements from Week 1 incorporating these movements into a repeating combination	Rearranges four to five learned movements from Week 1, incorporating these movements into a repeating combination	Rearranges two to three learned movements from Week 1 within a combination that can repeat	Does not create dance variations
F. Identifies the backgrounds of the dances; role of the dance within its culture, and similarities and differences between dances (written exam)	Answers 20–25 questions correctly	Answers 12–19 questions correctly	Answers 8–11 questions correctly	Answers seven or fewer questions correctly

Total Score   A = 15–18 (83–100%)   B = 12–14 (67–77%)   C = 9–11 (50–61%)   D = 6–8 (33–44%)   F = 0–5 (0–28%)

veal the potential for integrated assessment that is consistent with an integrated approach to teaching.

Fifth-grade students at Hawthorne and Agassiz Schools present yet another way to conceive of assessment as an integral part of learning and teaching. *Poem for 2 Voices* has a Language Arts Assessment Rubric for the writing of the poem. Then students are asked to complete a Drama Assessment using their poem (see Table 4.3).

They are receiving feedback about the tangible aspects of their writing that are considered important for the creation of a poem. But they also have the reading of their poems videotaped for review by their teacher, artist, and student reviewers. This is a powerful learning tool that taps into students' strengths on different levels and in different capacities.

French teacher Maureen Breen and Actor Ralph Covert describe a similar process for integrative assessment that happens on the high school level. Their approach showed the students that they needed to take this integration seriously (see Appendix D for Unit Plan). French teacher Maureen Breen says:

They had to show up the day of the test having thought about the most important grammar that we had learned this term. They came in, divided into groups, and were given cards with scenarios described on them. There were nine fundamental grammar categories, and the students had to use a minimum of six in the skit. They then prepared their performance in about 20 minutes and presented skits instead of taking a traditional final exam. When you get put on the spot, if you can reach back and pull something out, then you know you've actually learned it.

There were two scoring grades for the exam: One had the French goals on it and one had the Drama goals on it. Ralph filled out the assessment in his area and I did the assessment on mine. We added them together and that was the score for the final:

Drama Skills	**French Skills**
Focus, concentration, staying in character	Language easy to understand; articulation, pronunciation
Supports partners	Use of new vocabulary
Sufficient volume	Six full sentences in French per actor
Facing audience, open stage picture	Skit delivery in French, start to finish
Starting performance within 30 seconds of being called	Appropriate grammar difficulty
Fun factor	Grammar accuracy
	Title given in French
	Skit ending dramatic/clear ("La Fin!")

Testing looks very different in such a classroom. There were definite standards here, but the products were far from standardized.

Actor Ralph Covert adds an important postscript:

The A students are not always necessarily the students who flourish with this kind of active teaching. Some of the kids with discipline problems, with attention problems, really take off. The kids who are good at following the rules and spitting them back out are not necessarily the kids who are thinking.

READING RESOURCE TEACHER CHECKLIST

James McCosh School

Teacher _____   Date _____   Grade _____

CHILDREN'S NAMES

Marking Key + Regularly 0 Sometimes – Never													
Literary Objectives Recognizes Story Elements:													
Foreshadowing													
Conflict													
Climax													
Resolution													
Shows awareness of historical fact in association with literary fiction													
Performance Objectives													
Demonstrates understanding of performance elements													
Projection													
Loudly													
Clearly													
Shows appropriate expressions													

Comments _____

Artist in Residence: Mr. Charles Moore

FIG. 4.2

TABLE 4.3

Assessment Rubrics for Language Arts and Drama: Poems For 2 Voices— Fifth Grade at Hawthorne and Agassiz Schools

Language Arts Assessment Rubric			
Points	1	2	3
Fluency	Poem seemed choppy and segmented	Most of the poem is fluent, some choppy parts	Poem has smooth flow and sentences blend together easily
Rhythm	Poem has no obvious rhythm	Parts are rhythmic, but some parts have dissonance	There is a rhythmic quality to poem from beginning to end
Descriptive	Word choice does not create mental images	Some mental imagery is created by words, but some parts are nondescriptive	Mental imagery is created by word choice throughout the poem
Colorful words chosen	Word choice is mediocre	Some colorful words chosen, but most seem arbitrary	Word choice indicates specific selection
Spelling/ grammar	More than two mistakes	One to two mistakes	Spelling and grammar are correct
Format	Format not followed	Some mistakes in format	Format followed correctly

Total Points Grades
17–18   A
15–16   B
12–14   C
10–11   D
Less that 10   E

Drama Assessment Criteria—Each poem performance must have examples of the following:
➢ **Characters**: Circle two words in your poem that would make good characters. There must be a character for each person who participates in the poem. Each partner must act out a character.
➢ **Gesture**: Circle three words that would make good gestures. When performing your gestures you must have examples of gestures, that are mirrored, repeated, and transformed.
➢ **Group Structure**: Circle two words that would make a good sculpture. You must have at least two, and everybody in the group must be part of the sculpture when you perform.
➢ **Extra Credit**: To receive extra credit, you can add your own ideas to the performance or perform more than one of each of the assigned tasks.

Drama Assessment Rubric Note: Student performances were videotaped for teacher, artist, and student review.
Check Plus   Student included and demonstrated all the assigned drama tasks from final assessment instruction sheet in their final performance and performed additional tasks on their own design.
Check   Student included and demonstrated all the assigned tasks from final assignment instruction sheet in their final performance or all tasks except one and added one of their own ideas.
Check Minus Student did not include and demonstrate all the assigned drama tasks from the final assignment instruction sheet in their performance or performed all but two and added their own ideas.

There's so much anonymity in a big high school. Unless you have some unique, exotic talent, a way to get your feelings across, you're just a name on a roster, and that's a terrible feeling. When you can get up and do improvisation, it's like you're telling people, **"This is me. I have skills. I can do this."** *There were zero students out of five classes, who weren't fired up. You couldn't tell who was formerly an A student and who was a D student from the energy and attitude. Everybody there had ownership ... OF A FINAL EXAM!!!*

Performance Assessment: Representing and Presenting the Work

I hate competitions and prizes. When things are all about the final event, that's not good. But the satisfaction with a finished product makes a big difference. It's part of what we're hoping will happen, says textile artist, Eleanor Skydell.

In keeping with the trend toward more complex and more informational assessment tools, performance shows some promise of playing a major role in assessment as instruction, as information, and not as an endpoint. Performance assessments *represent a set of strategies for the application of knowledge, skills, and work habits through the performance of tasks that are meaningful and engaging to the students,* as one teacher's guide describes them (Hibbard et al., 1996). Although the idea of judging students' learning by something other than a test may be new to many teachers, it is not new to the arts and to teachers who engage in arts integration. For artists, the performance or demonstration is how what is inside of a person moves outside, so one can look at it more closely. Performance helps the participants think about what they are doing and why.

Table 4.4 shows a variety of ways for students to demonstrate what they have learned through tangible products. Arts integration, however, suggests that a product may be just one aspect of a culminating activity. In fact, these products may serve as the framework for demonstrating learning or performing knowledge. There is the *knowing*, exemplified in the creation of a *thing*; then there is the *doing*, exemplified in the creation of a performance. There is the *representing* and then there is the *presenting* of knowledge. Both dimensions, often interchangeable, work together to present a rich picture of learning.

Arts integration affords an opportunity to compile student portfolios that reflect the process of learning as well as the final products. Music students can write critiques of their performances, keep portfolios of their marked music, gather audiotapes, and write journals about their progress as individual musicians and as a group (Wolf & Pistone, 1991). They make "rehearsal a setting in which to think, choose, and reflect" (p. 26). Students write their musical histories and construct histories of others' through an interview process. Portfolios in such classrooms become avenues for discussion. They highlight "moments of understanding" and point toward "pivotal pieces" in a student's learning (p. 51).

Esther Lieber's high school ESL/Bilingual students created a book of poetry called *Voices of Our Hearts* (Figure 4.3). The book was the final product that represented their understanding of poetry as a means of expression. The students then performed their poems for their classmates. They received a public response to their poems. It is this juxtaposition of representation and presentation that makes the poetry powerful. Esther admits that her expectations were expanded as the

TABLE 4.4

**Ways for Students to Represent and Present Their Work:
Demonstration and Performance as Assessment**

Representing Student Work Demonstrating Knowledge	Presenting Student Work Performing Knowledge
Advertisement	Dance
Blueprints	Debate
Book report	Demonstration
Bulletin board	Dialogue
Cartoon	Dialogue
Collage	Discussion
Data log	Dramatization
Diagram	Experiment
Drawing	Improvisation
Essay	Interview
Fact sheet	Monologue
Flow chart	Newscast
Graph	Opera
Journal	Opinion poll
Letter	Pantomime
Magazine article	Performance
Mural	Play
Newspaper	Public service announcement
Notebook	Questions
Opinion paper	Rap
Outline	Role-play
Pamphlet	Skit
Photographs	Song
Portfolio	Speech
Puzzle	Storytelling
Questionnaire	Video-recording
Radio script	
Report	
Research paper	
Review	
Scrapbook	
Sculpture	
Timeline	
Travel log	

unit concluded: *What I was expecting was better language use. I got it. What I wasn't expecting, that I also got, were these well-captured moments that the other students acknowledged. What's more ... they are still writing poetry, months and even years after the unit was over.*

This teacher recognized that rich reflection and public assessment of student work extended the possibilities for her ESL students. The creation of the poetry book brought some closure to a unit of study. The students even had an Autograph Party the last day of school for which everyone showed up. But the conscious and careful expression that represented a new sensibility in students as performers and audience members continued.

Exhibition: Parental and Community Response

There's a difference between work in your own studio and a piece that you do to finish and exhibit. It's that issue of integrating all the parts to make a whole that never was before. I love that, taking a bunch of things that used to be something else, or that weren't much, but then making a whole new something, says textile artist Eleanor Skydell.

Is the phenomenon that Eleanor describes also true of students in schools? Do they see the process of integration and the ultimate exhibition of their work as something somehow different than the normal schoolwork that has no audience beyond the teacher? An exhibit "has an invisible ingredient – a constant, almost ruthless assessment," Wolf and Pistone (1991, p. 7) say. The very possibility of exhibition urges students to think about "a whole that never was before" and put their best efforts into their work. Skydell continues: *When the artwork is made public, it starts to assume a life separate from you, and it has the opportunity to start working on you. You enter into a dialogue with your work once it goes public; it gives the work an opportunity to enter into a dialogue with your public.*

Arts integration products are an ideal way to bring a school community together. One grade level or class has access to another's work. They serve as audiences for each other, and they also serve as analysts and critics. They can provide valuable feedback to the student artists while learning to articulate what they see and hear as audience members.

Positioning student work and performances in the community rather than just in the school building seems to draw in community members and parents. The actual **site** where the work is done becomes critical. Assessment becomes part of a larger initiative to involve people in the work of teaching and learning. Myrna Alvarez speaks about how this worked with Latino parents in her community: *They see me, and they say, "Weren't you at the park with the school children?" I say, "Yes," and then they ask me what else our community organization does. They sign up for services and assistance with learning English!*

Parents as assessors? What are the implications of bringing parents into this aspect of the learning cycle? One parent firmly attested to the quality of work done by students at her school: *These children are doing something that other people should see.* Another parent says: *The taxpayers have to say, "We want this at this school. We want you to underwrite it."* Parents who know what their children are producing begin to act as activists. They cannot advocate if they do not see and know what their children are experiencing. Parent Terry Cook says: *Schools are always, to some extent, driven by what the parents want for that school. Even if they don't want anything, the school is driven by that. If we know something works, we can fight for that.* Parents can be the most vocal advocates

FIG. 4.3. Voices of Our Hearts: Student Bilingual Poetry Book (this page and facing page)

Fear

When I walk on a street in Chicago, I don't feel
safe. I feel I'm being
                    Followed, step
                            by step
Street by
            Street...all from a horrible past in Guatemala!
            Heads cut off, fingers, ears,
            Nails pulled off. Lit cigarettes used to burn
            Eyes, backs, then forced to be swallowed.
            People tied to the back of cars and horses
            Pulled for entire blocks...
Much, Much more that I can not say.
I don't even feel safe in Chicago
            in my own home
                when I'm
                        alone.

Carlos Gonzalez

Reflection

by Juan Mendez

A teenager is imagining in his brain a picture of his feelings.
Even if he is not talking, there are emotions that someone can
feel without any voice; so I tried to expand his heart, and in his
heart there is a pride for his culture, and for where he is from
and where he is now. Therefore, I made two triangles together.
It means for the geographers a graphic of the Americas.

I see two hearts, one on each side. One is a happy human heart
and one is a sad heart. There are strong emotions: worries,
confusions, questions, healed wounds, hopes and expectations.

A drop from his heart is revealing his feelings and it's joining
with more drops of hearts from the rest of us, so we make a sea.

These feelings we have inside spread and ripple throughout our
lives and this movement touches the lives of others.

once they understand the power of the arts for their children. I *think we've all been in school and we've all crammed for tests and the day after the test, the information is gone ... But when kids learn through the arts, they remember, they retain it*, one parent announced.

Parents notice the power of the arts to give their children voice: *Sometimes, the student is there to absorb the material that has been presented on the blackboard from the teacher's notes and then transform it into student notes. That's the job of the students. But in the arts, students' perceptions are valid, maybe just as valid as the teacher's!*

At Ray School, the students collaborated with artists and teachers to solve a problem at their school. The noise level in their school cafeteria was an ongoing issue for children and parents. The school community decided to apply their arts expertise to address the problem. After some consultation, they made a series of banners reflecting areas of the curriculum and hung them in the cafeteria. Exhibition of the artwork offered an aesthetic solution to a school community problem and made the arts in the curriculum visible and concrete. The students at Lakeview High School, working with the art department, transformed the look of the building with hallway murals and mosaic and ceramic installations (see Color Insert D.b).

Making the arts processes visible for parents helps them look at their own children and begin to understand how they learn. A high school parent recognized that the arts integration helped his son learn to be disciplined: *It's the discipline of not only learning his lines for a play, but in realizing that he has deadlines to meet. The discipline that they learn through the arts transfers into other academic areas. They finish that science project on time because they have learned that, in order to perform, they have to finish the work*. How does one assess such learning? Does it appear on the standardized test? Many parents identify time management, personal responsibility, and self-discipline as essential learnings, and yet they are not often measured by a paper- and pencil-test. Broadly based assessment, which is collaborative and inclusive, has the potential to teach all involved about these extra growth areas. Parent Beverly Urschel from Agassiz School describes an authentic kind of assessment, which she does unwittingly, in a letter to the editors of this book. Her letter outlines criteria for learning that could easily be organized as a rubric:

My seventh-grade child has always learned more from doing things rather than just reading about them. He enjoys working creatively with his hands and takes great pride in his finished work. A lesson that he learns from acting it out or thinking creatively to produce a finished product, will stick with him much longer than one that he merely reads about or on which he is lectured.

Most of the time, Marc does not talk about his experiences or lessons in school. However, this was not the case with arts integration units. The artists approached their theme from a variety of ways. In so doing, Marc began to look at a topic from many different perspectives. He has begun to think things through more globally and from many different angles. His self-esteem has been given a big boost when he has produced a creative piece or when he has solved a problem using a different approach.

How does this mother know when her son in learning? She notes that he learns when he (a) works with his hands, (b) acts it out, and (c) produces something. What is the evidence she cites that he has learned? He (a) looks at things more globally, (b) looks at a topic from different perspectives, (c) looks at a topic from different angles, (d) produces a creative piece, and (e) solves a problem using a different approach.

Among the seven key developmental needs for early adolescents is the need for "creative expression" (Scales, 1991). In other words, young people need to be able to express who they are and what they think to the outside world. Thinking differently about audiences for student work is one way to adapt the school curriculum to address this need for creative expression. Local libraries, amphitheaters, parks, and gallery spaces are excellent venues for exhibiting student work (see photos, p. 108). When this kind of event occurs with more than one school participating, students see their own work in a much larger context. They learn to revisit their own understandings of quality. They see new possibilities. Arts coordinator Tammy Steele says: *When students perform in public, they understand the connection between hard work and looking good. They become willing to work hard.*

There is another aspect to this idea of exhibiting and taking students' work out into the community: Teachers begin to see the community through a different lens. Many teachers do not teach in the community in which they live. They may not have the incentive or opportunity to know more about their teaching community than the front of the school or the parking lot. Field trips are often beyond the budgetary limits or they become massive administrative headaches for individual teachers to orchestrate. Arts integration may be the impetus for teachers to visit a museum, attend a concert, and experience what their students might experience. One principal noted that teachers in his school have started to look to community agencies and park districts to determine what resources they have that could be used on a regular basis by the classes. Some of those resources simply aren't duplicated within the school building, such as a dark room for photography or a kiln for firing pottery.

When we look at what students have produced and are exhibiting, we can ask how this mode of presentation informs or clarifies the process. How does exhibition develop understanding—for students, parents, and community?

The presentation, the actual performance, is really another piece of the work. It is part of the work, and gathering the response of others to that work is part of the learning process, says artist Eleanor Skydell. What students and teachers hope to have achieved may not in fact be what observers have seen. Eleanor Skydell says further: … *maybe you could have done a little bit better, maybe the audience member could have looked more closely, but that relationship among the artwork, the artist, and the audience member is what is important. This three-way dialogue informs the artist.*

We once again return to the issue of dialogue and collaboration. A three-way dialogue—between student–artist, the product or performance, and the receiver–audience—informs assessment. Teachers no longer own the process. We have not yet begun to tap the potential for looking at assessment in this way.

Self-Evaluation

We must constantly remind ourselves that the ultimate purpose of evaluation is to enable students to evaluate themselves. Educators may have been practicing this skill to the exclusion of learners; we need to shift part of that responsibility to students. Fostering students' ability to direct and redirect themselves must be a major goal—or what is education for? (Costa & Lowery, 1989)

The Smart Museum of Art hosts an exhibit of student work and a concert, to conclude their MusArts program, where students explore the expressive qualities of music through the visual arts. Students and their parents from ten participating schools have the opportunity to see a wide range of responses to the same project across many schools.
The Smart Museum is a partner with Murray and Ray School in the South Side Partnership.
Photo: courtesy of Mary Ellen Ziegler and Smart Museum of Art.

A culminating exhibit of student art work from the LEAP Partnership is an annual event at the Beacon Street Gallery in Chicago. The exhibition provides a sense of closure and celebration for the students, teachers, and artists.
Photo; courtesy Beacon Street Gallery and LEAP.

Beacon Street Gallery artist, Conor McGrady, sets up a mini-exhibition inside the first-grade classroom of Margo Brown at Audubon School.
Photo; courtesy Beacon Street Gallery and LEAP.

Costa's comment is an apt reminder of our purpose in assessing student learning through arts integration. We want our students to be good judges of their own work; we want them to set goals and realistically understand how to achieve them. Self-evaluation is being used more and more in classrooms to help *shift the responsibility* to students for their own learning. Self-evaluation can be simply described as a response to three basic questions: What did you do? What are the strengths you've discovered? What are the gaps in knowledge and practice you've discovered? Although the particulars may vary and the level of detail required might be different for different age levels and degrees of expertise, if a student can respond to these three issues, he or she is beginning the journey of self-evaluation. Seventh grader Eve Ewing notes, A *good teacher/artist has to be more focused on what the students **think**, not just what they do.* Accessing how students think about their work and what value they put on it may be one of the most important outcomes of authentic assessment.

"The primary reason for assessment is to teach students how to be rigorous critics of their own work" (Wolf & Pistone, 1991, p. 8). Teacher Marie Schilling used self-evaluations during her fourth-grade Animal Arts Project. Students were asked to write an essay that responded to these four questions:

What animal did you select for your project and why?

How did working with the arts (writing, mask making, music, and movement) help you think about or learn about your animal?

What did you learn about yourself while you were studying the animal or using the arts to explore the animal?

What part of the Animal Arts Project did you like the most? Why?

The questions Marie posed to her students reveal the depth of meaningful self-evaluation. She asked them for specifics of their knowledge, not just about the animal that was the focus of their research, but also about their own processes. She asked them for their opinions and preferences. This is a most important aspect of self-evaluation; we know that students learn from what they enjoy doing. If we can understand more about *what* they actually become engaged with, we can design learning experiences that address those areas. It's not just a question of what we need to teach, but also how we could be more successful in teaching it. Reflective assessment questions can get to the heart of that and help teachers teach.

One student wrote: I *selected the puma because it is beautiful and graceful. I think that it is the most graceful animal on earth. I like its talents too. The arts helped in a way that is hard to explain, but I'll try. I got to experience how the puma moves and sounds. Making the mask gave me an idea of what it felt like to be a puma. At home, I jumped off the top bunk onto my prey, which was a stuffed raccoon. I would like to have the puma's talents. I'd like to jump as high, run as fast, and be as strong. However, I don't want to live in the wild.*

Kyle Westbrook uses student evaluations in his American History/Jazz Poetry Project. His high school students are asked to evaluate their own learning, the unit, and the substance of the arts integration. Feedback from students helps strengthen future work in arts integration, as Kyle's experience suggests (see Appendix D for Unit Plan).

Self-evaluation instruments can be specific to a particular art form or unit; they can also be general enough to use across units, classrooms, and experiences. The Mexican Fine Arts Center Museum in Chicago designed a self-evaluation, written in both Spanish and English, in which students are invited to reflect on their work with artists and consider how their learning might be connected to learning in other subject areas. They are also invited to draw a picture of what they did with a visiting artist! (See Fig. 4.4).

Wendy Anderson designed self-evaluation instruments for specific projects and for the whole quarter's work in her middle-school science classroom (see Fig. 4.5). Using such instruments allows her to examine students' needs and interests as well as to determine what they believe they have learned in science during the term.

Assessment is part of the learning cycle, not separate from it. Meaningful assessment extends the definition of learning to include representation and presentation. It involves performing knowledge and offers the opportunity to expand the community of assessors beyond the classroom. It affords teachers the means to connect classroom units, topics, and themes by helping students recognize applicable skills and concepts to use and reuse. Students and teachers who experience assessment as episodes of learning begin to understand that assessment is "a matter of offering informed judgments, not simply a matter of marking the number correct" (Wolf & Pistone, 1991, p. 24).

One high school parent describes the arts integration process as a matrix: *The matrix helps the brain organize information and access different aspects of the content area and the art form. The matrix is a grid inside our heads in which behavior, feelings, perception, and knowledge all interact.* Assessment belongs in that matrix and can help move the analysis of what and how students are learning from "particular exercises toward large projects" (Wolf & Pistone, 1991, p. 53).

We return to the *elegant fit* metaphor for arts integration (see chap. 2). If concepts are integrated elegantly, so too should assessment be part of the fit. The matrix becomes rich and evolving; one cell informs another; one way of knowing informs another. All work together to further learning and growth.

WEB SITES RELATED TO ASSESSMENT

http://www.cse.ucla.edu—National Center for Research on Evaluation, Standards, and Student Testing (CRESST)—New Directions in Student Assessment

http://www.nap.edu—National Academy Press

http://www.carfax.co.uk—Assessment in Education

http://www.fairtest.org—Transforming Student Assessment

School:

   escuela: _____

Name of Artist:

   nombre del artista: _____

Grade:

   grado: _____

Date:

   fecha: _____

☺ I enjoyed the art activities the artist had us do.   YES SOMETIMES NO

   Me gustarón las actividades que el artista hace con nosotros. Sí A VECES NO

☺ I found the art activities interesting. YES SOMETIMES NO

   Yo encontre ques las actividades fuerón interesantes. Sí A VECES NO

☺ The artist let us work on the activities in our own way. YES SOMETIMES NO

   El artista nos dejo hacer las actividades en nuestra manera. Sí A VECES NO

☺ I can do things I could not do before the artist came. YES SOMETIMES NO

   Yo puedo hacer cosas que no podia hacer antes. Sí A VECES NO

☺ The artist showed us what we were to do. YES SOMETIMES NO

   El artista nos demostró lo que deberemos hacer. Sí A VECES NO

☺ Name one thing now that you did not know before the artist worked with your class.

   Escribe algo nuevo que no sabías antes de que el artista trabajara en tu clase.

☺ I learned some things from the artist that I can use in the following school subjects.

   Aprendí algunas cosas que puedo usar en las siguientes materias:

Language Arts	YES	A LITTLE	NO	Math	YES	A LITTLE	NO
Arte de Lenguaje	Sí	UN POCO	NO	Matemáticas	Sí	UN POCO	NO
Science	YES	A LITTLE	NO	Social Studies	YES	A LITTLE	NO
Ciencia	Sí	UN POCO	NO	Estudios Sociales	Sí	UN POCO	NO
Gym	YES	A LITTLE	NO	Art	YES	A LITTLE	NO
Gimnasio	Sí	UN POCO	NO	Arte	Sí	UN POCO	NO

☺ If a friend asked you about this program, what would you tell your friend?

   Si un amigo te preguntara sobre este programa, qué le dirias?

☺ Draw a picture on the back of this page of what you did with the artist.

   Dibuja también que hiciste con el artista en el otro lade de esta pagina.

FIG. 4.4. Mexican Fine Arts Center Museum Student Self-Evaluation Instrument
Courtesy of the Illinois Arts Council Art in Education Program and the Mexican Fine Arts Center Museum.

Self-Evaluation—Science

Directions:

I.   Think back over Quarter 3 in science. (You have worked on the periodic table or the body of elements project. In addition, you studied and created the solar system or space exploration.)

II.   Answer questions, on a separate piece of paper, accurately, clearly, and neatly.

III. Remember to include your name, the date, and your homeroom number.

   A. Thoughtfully answer each of the following questions:

      1. What was your favorite activity this quarter?

      2. What are the five most important things you have learned this quarter?

      3. What did this quarter make you think about?

      4. What are two of your strengths in science?

      5. What is the best thing about having you as a group member?

      6. To what extent did you contribute to your group's assignment?

      7. How often do you complete your homework (0%–100%)

      8. What do you still wonder about?

   B. Grade yourself (A, B, C, D, or F) in the following areas:
      (Copy the word in bold onto your paper and write your grade)

      9. How could you improve your learning next quarter?

      Responsibility for Learning   _____
      Your Attitude   _____
      Cooperation/Encouragement   _____
      Amount of Read/Research   _____
      Understanding of Vocabulary   _____
      Amount of Effort/Focus   _____
      Your Contribution   _____
      Consistent Homework   _____
      Neatness/Clean up   _____
      Creativity of Project   _____
      Final Quarter Grade   _____

      10. Final Question: What do you know about simple machines?

FIG. 4.5.   Self-EvaluationScience
Courtesy of Science Teacher, Wendy Anderson, Audubon School

Self-Evaluation—Science   (continued)

Written Project Self-Assessment

Assignment 1:	Describe the process and product of your project.

Think about:

What was your assignment? How did your group decide to approach your task? As a group member, how did you contribute? What did you read about? What did you do? What did you think about? How did your cooperate, encourage, lead, assist, ...? How did you like your final product? What did you learn? What do you still wonder about? If you were to do it over, what changes might you make? Who were productive, creative members of your group? How do you know?

Organize your paper following the Hamburger Method:

(Top Bun)

Paragraph 1:	Introduce yourself and project. Explain purpose for writing. Give reader a preview of paragraphs to follow.

(Meat, Lettuce, Tomato ...)

Paragraphs 2, 3, 4:	Explain what you did, how you did it, who helped, how you contributed, what you made, why you made it, etc. (For more ideas, see questions to think about.)

(Bottom Bun)

Paragraph 5:	End your paper. Conclude. Tie everything together. Restate main ideas from your introduction. Remind reader of your purpose and most important thoughts and ideas.

Project Assessment Rubric

Assignment 2:	Grade your work and project using the following rubric.

Name: _____

I.   Process

Cooperation and Encouraging	0	1	2	3	4
Responsibility	0	1	2	3	4
Effort/Initiative	0	1	2	3	4
Reading and Research	0	1	2	3	4
Contribution	0	1	2	3	4

Comments: Process Total: _____

Process Grade: _____

II.   Product

Aesthetics	0	1	2	3	4
Accuracy	0	1	2	3	4
Neatness	0	1	2	3	4
Evidence of knowledge gained	0	1	2	3	4
Presentation	0	1	2	3	4

Comments: Process Total: _____

Process Grade: _____

FIG. 4.5.   Self-EvaluationScience   (continued)
Courtesy of Science Teacher, Wendy Anderson, Audubon School

REFERENCES

Beane, J. (1997). *Curriculum integration: Designing the core of democratic education.* New York: Teachers College Press.

Boston Globe. (2000). *Harvard study casts doubt on 'Mozart Effect',* Sept. 21.

Burns, P.C., Roe, B.D., & Ross, E.P. (1988). *Teaching reading in today's elementary schools.* Boston: Houghton Mifflin.

Catterall, J. (1997). *Involvement in the arts and success in secondary school.* Los Angeles: The UCLA Imagination Project.

Catterall, J. (1999). *Achievement Data for CAPE schools.* Unpublished preliminary report, Chicago Consortium for School Research.

Catterall, J. S., & Waldorf, L. (1999). Chicago Arts Partnerships in Education Summary Evaluation. In E. B. Fiske (Ed.), *Champions of change: The impact of the arts on learning.* The Arts Education Partnerships, The Presidents's Committee on the Arts and Humanities, GE Fund, John D. and Catherine T. MacArthur Foundation.

Cost, A. L., & Lowery, L. F. (1989). Techniques for teaching thinking: The practitioners' guide to teaching thinking series. Eric Document 404837.

Daniels, H., & Bizar, M.. (1998). *Methods that matter: Six structures for best practice classrooms.* York, ME: Stenhouse.

Earl, L. M., & LeMahieu, P. G. (1997). Rethinking assessment and accountability. In 1997 ASCD *yearbook: Rethinking educational change with heart and mind* (pp. 149–168). Alexandria, VA: Association for Supervision and Curriculum Development.

Geertz, C. (1983). *Local knowledge: Further essays in interpretative anthropology.* New York: Basic Books.

Goldberg, M. (1997). *Arts and learning: An integrated approach to teaching and learning in multicultural and multilingual settings.* New York: Longman.

Herman, J. L., Aschbacher, P. R., & Winters, L. (1992). A *practical guide to alternative assessment.* Alexandria, VA: Association for Supervision and Curriculum Development.

Hibbard, K. M., and others. (1996). A *teacher's guide to performance-based learning and \ assessment.* Alexandria, VA: Association for Supervision and Curriculum Development.

Keenan, D. L., & Edwards, C. (1992). Using the project approach with toddlers. *Young Children,* 47(4), 31–35.

Lawrence-Lightfoot, S., & Davis, J. H. (1998). *The art and science of portraiture.* San Francisco: Jossey-Bass.

McCaslin, N. (1990). *Creative dramatics in the classroom* (5th ed.). New York: Longman.

OMG, Inc. (1991). *Understanding how the arts contribute to excellent education: Study prepared for the National Endowment for the Arts.* Philadelphia, PA: Author.

Parks, M., & Rose, D. (1997). *The impact of Whirlwind's reading comprehension through drama program on fourth-grade reading scores.* Chicago: Whirlwind Performance Company.

Scales, P. C. (1991). A *portrait of young adolescents in the 1990s: Implications for promoting healthy growth and development.* Carrboro, NC: Center for Early Adolescence.

Wiggins, G. (1998). *Educative assessment: Designing assessments to inform and improve student performance.* San Francisco: Jossey-Bass.

Wolf, D. P., & Pistone, N. (1991). *Taking full measure: Rethinking assessment through the arts.* New York: The College Board.

Bridgeport-Armor Square-Near North Arts Partnership

A.a. Students from Mark Sheridan School work with teacher John Nieciak, and Street-Level Youth Media video artist Theresa Jones, to make their mystery videos. The students create the scripts and story-boards, act, direct, shoot, and critique their video work.
Photo: Theresa Jones

A.c. A Healy School student painting inspired by the photography of Robert Capa uses the compositional elements of foreground, middle-ground, and background. The painting project was directed by art teacher JoEllen Kerwin in collaboration with the Terra Museum of American

A.b. Sixth-grade students in Paulette Ryan's class at Healy School create a dragon banner for an all-School China Fair celebrating Chinese history and culture.

A.d. Healy School eighth graders rehearse a segment of their dance performance, "Who We Are" directed by dancer, Rosemary Doolas. The students take accusing robotlike postures that express a theme of being Undernourished.

Photos:
Courtesy of Tammy Steele

ETA / Muntu Arts in Education Consortium

B.b. Musician Ernest Dawkins assists parents in their own artistic development during a parent arts workshop.
Photo: Arnold Aprill

B.a. Classroom teacher Mary Hoover, from McCosh School works with playwright Charles Michael Moore, to assist a student in the dramatic interpretation of literature.
Photo: Arnold Aprill

B.c. The Muntu Dance Theater of Chicago brings dance and cultural awareness to Chicago public schools.
Photo: Kwabena Shabu

Hawthorne / Agassiz Elementary Schools Arts Partnership

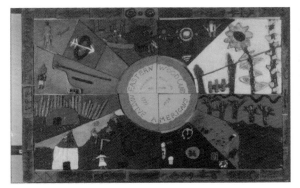

C.a. Fourth-grade students from Agassiz School create a ceramic-relief mural showing symbols of Native American life of the Eastern Woodland Tribes. The mural project was lead by art teacher Donna Pekin, classroom teacher Anne Casey, and Lill Street Studios artist Lisa Harris Mason.
Photos: Scott Shigley

C.b. (left) & **C.c.** (right)   Seventh-grade students from Hawthorne School create ceramic-relief artwork showing images of Illinois Ecosystems and Habitats. Under the direction of science teacher Sonja Oliveri, and Lill Street Studios artist Lisa Harris Mason's students research the animals and plants in each habitat, make sketches at different natural sites, learn about texture and composition in clay design, and create each piece in small groups.

C.d. Eighth-grade students from Hawthorne School worked with Lookingglass Theater director David Kersnar, and teachers Monica Sullivan, Eleanor Nangle, and Carlton Oquendo to produce a multi-media performance, *Journey to Freedom*, on the civil rights movement. The collaboration with Lookingglass is an annual tradition that includes the participation of the entire eighth-grade class.
Photo: Karen Maude, Lookingglass Theater

Lakeview Education and Arts Partnership (LEAP)

D.a. Lakeview High School students in Elena Robles' biology class, with art teacher Susana Erling, create a diorama of a coral reef that shows their understanding of diversity and interdependence within an ecosystem. Photo: Elena Robles

D.b. Lake View High School art student recreates a part of Michelangelo's Sistine Chapel in the hallways of the school. Photo: Miriam Socoloff

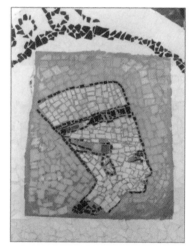

D.c. Mosaic detail of an ancient Egyptian head. Ravenswood School. Photo: Scott Shigley

D.d. Middle school students at Ravenswood School create a mosaic time-line wall that highlights art and culture throughout the centuries with art teacher Kitty Conde and artist Eduardo Angulo Salas. Photo: Scott Shigley

Lincoln Park High School Partnership

Students from Lincoln Park High School work with textile artist Eleanor Skydell and chemistry teacher Pat Riley, on the many phases of an integrated unit, The Chemistry of Color—Acids and Bases Meet Color and Hue.

E.a. Teams of students dye fabrics in silk baths.

E.b. Students measure boards to make a grid and produce a larger pattern block.

E.c. Students manipulate color patterns by assigning hues and values to each piece.

E.d. Students place the final design on a board.

Photos: Pat Riley

Pilsen Arts Partnership

F.a. Life-size cut-outs are painted by neighborhood children in an after-school workshop offered by Pilsen Arts Partnership artists. The finished artwork was created for the annual Dia del Niño, Children's Day Celebration.

F.b. Second-grade students in Elizabeth Casper's classroom at Walsh School perform their version of "Strega Nona" by Tomie dePaola, under the direction of artist, Jean Parisi.

F.c. A bilingual class from Walsh School works in the Clay Studio at the Casa Aztlan community center. The students study the pottery of the Southwest and use the methods and designs of indigenous potter Maria Martinez. The students work under the direction of Pros Arts artist, Tatiana Rodriguez Giles, and teacher, Irene Mendoza.

Photos courtesy of Pros Art Studio and The Pilsen Arts Partnership.

South Side Arts Partnership

G.a. Third-grade students from Ray School work with Najwa Dance Corps artist Andrea Vinson, on a dance performance about Chicago History. The children collaborated in small groups to create the movements for the dance. Third-grade teachers Sharlean Brooks, Ellen Crabill, Bill Salvato, and Rochel Walton partnered with Andrea to create a culminating performance that included dance, set design, dramatic readings, and song.
Photo: Scott Shigley

G.b. A student from Murray Language Academy models a self-portrait mask made in Mary Ellen Ziegler's art class. Middle-school students explored the themes of self-image and urban culture through mask-making and writing.
Photo: Mary Ellen Ziegler

G.c. Seventh-grade students at Ray School in Shenethe Williams' classroom, show off their Constitution Quilt. Every student researched a concept or an amendment from the United States Constitution and designed a corresponding visual symbol for the quilt.
Photo: Scott Shigley

Tlahui Mexican Fine Arts Center Museum Partnership

H.b. Orozco School students wear masks and costumes created for their annual "Dia de los Muertos", Day of the Dead, neighborhood parade. (With art teachers Jennifer Jensen and Ed Pino, and the seventh-grade Humanities team, including Victoria Turbov, Aandraya DaSilva, Gerado Vivas, Maria Economou, and visiting artists.)
Photo: Courtesy of Ed Pino

H.a. Orozco School students display their drawings of Olmec heads representing Mexico's earliest civilization for a parent conference night.
Photo: Victoria Turbov

H.c. A first-grade student at Telpochcalli School works on a mural on underwater life, directed by artist Guillermo Delgado and teacher Liz Chase Vivas.
Photo: Guillermo Delgado

(Also see book cover for more Telpochcalli School student work)

H.d. Orozco School students build a Day of the Dead Altar for the Mexican Fine Arts Center Museum's annual exhibition. The altar celebrates the traditional Mexican holiday and honors the memories of loved ones who have died.
Photo: Ed Pino

5

Chapter

Science and Art: Lessons From Leonardo da Vinci?

Connections Between Science and Art

- Making fundamental science concepts concrete
- Teaching for understanding
- Visualizing scientific processes
- Relating arts processes with scientific principles

Moving Arts into the Science Curriculum

- Motivating students
- Building community
- Showing others what happens in the science

Working Through the Curriculum

- Teacher-selected topic
- Artist initiative for project
- Learning from each other
- Making time in the schedule
- Supporting difficult concepts
- Working with diverse learners

Arts and scientific problem solving

- Uncertainties, constraints, and conflicts

Going Beyond the Unit

- Assessment through performance: The project as assessment
- Assessment through reflection
- Long-term impact
- Challenges and incentives for doing it again

5

Chapter

Science and Art:
Lessons From
Leonardo da Vinci?

by Diane Deckert

*This chapter illustrates the **into, through, and beyond components of arts integration outlined in this book**. Thanks to Wendy Anderson, Ed Metzl, and Elena Robles, science teachers in Chicago Public Schools, for their rich contributions.*

DANCING WITH LEONARDO

What could art have to do with science? This question reflects the conflict between these two ways of looking at the world that exists in the minds of many people today. Yet that conflict hasn't always existed. When science in Europe was starting to take shape as a discipline during the Renaissance, it was considered a close relative of art. One person who exemplified the connection between art and science was Leonardo da Vinci, who combined his exploration of the natural world with his artistic expression through drawing, painting, and sculpture. Since Leonardo's time, science and art have been divorced, with science usually seen as rational and analytical and art often considered subjective and emotional. So what could art possibly have to do with science?

That question is easy to answer when you visit Ed Metzl's classroom at Lincoln Park High School. Students in his physics class are bending and stretching to warm up for their day's work with dancer Peter Sciscioli from Hedwig Dances. In one recent session, the students explored the concepts of average velocity and acceleration as they performed a series of going-across-the-floor exercises. They measured the distance and the time it took to either walk, run, or perform their movement phrase from one point to another in the room.

Today they examine Newton's Laws of Motion. As they stand motionless, Peter explains that they are experiencing how an object with no net force acting on it remains at rest. Next, they push a partner across the room, experiencing what level of force is required when the partner is first walking and then running. Again, Peter makes the connection to the concept—he describes how the pushing represents the force in Newton's second law, which states that the acceleration of a body is directly proportional to the net force acting on it and inversely proportional to its mass. He asks the students who were pushing a hefty partner to switch with someone pushing a partner with less mass. Besides the smiles on the students' faces, there are also flashes of insight as they literally feel the meaning of Newton's laws.

Ed Metzl, a teaching veteran who left the classroom to run a business and then decided to return to what he really loved, wishes he could find an art experience this meaningful for every topic in his curriculum. He says, *I want the kids to understand. You walk out of physics and you know everything, but a month later, you remember that F=ma and that's about it. You had memorized all these formulas, and to me that's not physics. Dancing is helping them to understand. It's real life physics as opposed to textbook physics.*

SCIENCE + ART = UNDERSTANDING

Ed isn't talking simply about his students remembering what they've learned. He's interested in them understanding Newton's Laws of Motion kinesthetically—through their own bodies. Dancing provides the students with a sensory experience for the abstract notions of inertia and acceleration, thus building a bridge between the rational knowledge involved in physics with the subjective knowledge felt in their physiques. This connection, which Leonardo would find entirely natural, is powerful. The physics concepts are made concrete through dance for those students who might struggle with them in a purely abstract form. Because the students also know what the concepts mean in actual experience, they can reason about them and apply them to problems more meaningfully.

Understanding is a major goal for the art projects that Elena Robles does with her students at Lakeview High School. In her high school biology classes, her students use drawing, movement, and sculpture alongside their textbooks. Sometimes Elena starts with an art project so that the students will be able to make sense of the more difficult concepts they'll read about later in their textbooks. For example, the students create a storybook about genetics by pasting cut-outs representing the amino acids in DNA into the correct double helix shape. When they start, the students may not have any previous knowledge about DNA, but Elena plunges in, explaining that the construction paper pieces represent four different amino acids—the building blocks of DNA. On another page, the students color, cut, paste, and label the parts of a cell involved in protein synthesis while she describes their functions. All of this serves a specific purpose: to create a visual image of the microscopic structures of a cell and to develop the vocabulary needed for the rest of the study. Elena observes, *If I had the students read a chapter, it would go in one ear and out the other. It doesn't mean anything to them. However, once they start to make their storybooks, they have a visual picture, and then we can go to the textbook.*

At another point in their study, the students construct an inflatable walk-in cell. One group of students assembles large sheets of plastic into a 6-foot-tall balloon, ironing the seams to create a weld. A box fan pointed toward the interior inflates the balloon into a gigantic, oversized cell membrane held up by a foam-core armature hanging from the ceiling light fixture. Using recycled materials such as plastic soda bottles and styrofoam peanuts, other students fashion mitochondria, endoplasm, and a nucleus with chromosomes and then suspend them inside the inflated membrane. Along the way, they are discussing which materials will best represent the cell structures—conversations that Elena notes for her informal assessment of their learning. When the cell is finished, the students walk inside and imagine that they are molecules, perhaps of glucose, for example. Elena's goal is for her students to understand the microscopic structures of the cell and their functions: *We were able to do some visualizations where you are the molecule and you're passing through cellular structures, and then we go over the functions, and they know exactly what's going on in the cell. I think that just helps to clarify what's so abstract for students.*

Students select yarn or peanuts on a plastic hose to represent the ribosomes on the endoplasmic reticulum. Students then glue these items onto the nucleus of the walk-in cell to represent chromosomes. She trusts the artistic representation of her students' knowledge. This doesn't mean that she relies solely on the art projects for assessment, but they broaden the range of ways that students can both learn and show their learning.

Elena reports, *Many times I have been challenged by colleagues with the question, "Do you think you're doing your program justice by using art?" I'm a high school teacher, so that's an issue for me.* Using art projects as an integrated part of the curriculum is common in elementary classrooms, yet Elena and Ed choose to integrate art into their high school science curricula despite the pressure to cover content and prepare students for high-stakes assessments like SATs—pressures that can crowd out any activities.

Educators must ask whether the arts and the science curriculum are truly in conflict. When designed carefully, arts integration projects can involve fundamental science concepts. Dancing to understand Newton's laws of motion and creating the DNA storybook illustrate how the concepts in the science textbook were embedded in the art project.

For another example of art and science integration developing student understanding, walk through the hallway of space created by Wendy Anderson's seventh- and eighth-grade students at Audubon Elementary School. Black paper covers the walls to suggest the vastness of space. One side of the hallway displays a timeline of space exploration vehicles, whereas the other side presents the planets in the solar system. A label provides background information about each item, such as the mission dates and construction costs, or about each planet, such as the length of the planetary year and the composition of its atmosphere. Inside Wendy's classroom are books that the students wrote and illustrated to go along with their display.

The project began with a day introducing visual artist Eduardo Angulo Salas. Wendy, who recently started teaching seventh- and eighth-grade science after teaching fifth grade for 6 years, thinks it's important for her students to get to know the artist as a person, what he or she does, and how the project is going to meld science and art. Wendy and Eduardo described the project as an *installation*, and Eduardo showed examples of installations created by a variety of contemporary artists. He also showed slides of his own paintings and discussed how growing up in Venezuela affected his development as an artist.

Getting to know the artist helps the students understand the art processes involved. The students see that art may take on a form different from their stereotyped notion of painting or sculpture. They start to understand that art means exploring an idea and making choices about how to express that idea. They recognize that art involves observation and solving problems just like science does.

Once Wendy's students knew what an installation was, the seventh graders selected an object in the solar system and the eighth graders picked a spaceship or satellite to learn about. From then on, research and art went hand in hand. When the students learned about the size and structure of a spaceship, for example, they had to decide how to engineer a replica using cardboard, tape, construction paper, and paper maché. For the planets, they blew up balloons and beach balls and covered them with paper maché. Partially finished projects hung on wires from the ceiling, the only place to store them until they were done, making everyone duck and dodge Explorer One and Sputnik, Pluto and Mars as they had made their way around the classroom. As they were working, they used trade books, magazines, and newspaper articles to help them decide how to create the structural features of their space vehicles or which colors to paint the planet's surface. Wendy remembers, *They were looking at books at the same time as they were plastering things on and getting the details and checking to see if they had it right.*

MOVING ARTS INTO THE CURRICULUM

Motivating Students

In addition to promoting understanding, arts projects include a benefit often not found in textbooks: They motivate students. Whatever their age, we know that meaningful learning occurs best when students are actively engaged. The hallway of space project incorporates several elements to motivate students: an artist's expertise and enthusiasm, active learning directed by the students' choice of which object to research and represent, and the challenge of creating an art project for a real audience. How could students *not* feel motivated? Wendy reports,

When those kids walk down that hallway of space, not only do they feel very proud of it, but they feel that much more attached to space science. They were coming in with, "Ms. Anderson, did you see on the news about this, about that?" It also affected the other students, because they walked through the hallway of space and said, "Oh, cool! I want to be in your classroom next year," and "I want to do this." A lot of them thought they didn't know how to do Sputnik, and at the end they felt they could do anything. And that's a really good positive attitude they'll bring with them wherever they go.

As science teachers, Elena, Ed, and Wendy want their students to learn the science content of their curriculum, and they know that their students need to be motivated and actively participating to learn best. They value arts integration because it builds a deep understanding of the science concepts and lures their students into taking a personal interest in learning.

Building Community

Arts integration projects build a sense of community among students. One of Wendy's students wrote, *Walking and looking through the hallway of space makes me feel good because I was actually a part of this.* Wendy points out, *There's kind of a group unity that* they're getting, as opposed to "I did well in this test" or "I did this." There's that real group feeling of, "We were able to do this." The arts integration projects encourage teachers, artists, and students to think big, and their big ideas require teamwork to realize. There's nothing like a real assignment that's too big for one person alone to encourage students to work as a team. Even students who are reluctant to pay attention or contribute to group activities become active. Because the projects often require other skills besides the ones traditionally valued in schools, students who may struggle with typical school assignments may suddenly find that they are flourishing. For one of her bilingual students in particular, Wendy explained, *I think the art really helps to show what the kids are thinking. Take Omar, for example. The other kids see what he can do in art, and then they have more respect for him, and it just kind of boosts him up all the way around, and so he really contributes more and becomes a valuable member of the group.* With a different avenue to display their talents, these students may also find that their social standing has moved up several notches in the eyes of their peers.

Communication Made Easy

With the benefits of greater understanding, student motivation, and community building that arts integration brings to these science classrooms, there's another payoff in terms of communication with the rest of the school, with parents, and with the wider community. Although not every arts integration experience leads to some sort of product, many of them do, and they're usually very attractive and appealing.

When parents came to pick up their middle-school child's report card, Wendy found that the hallway of space made her students' learning readily apparent: *I had parents saying things like they wished they had brought their camera, and some even went home and got their cameras. I think the kids were really proud to show it. It was suddenly easy to tell parents what we did this quarter.*

One art project from Elena Robles' biology class, a diorama of a coral reef measuring 8 feet high and 10 feet wide, found its way to several venues (see Color Insert D.a). It started as a learning project about the diversity and interdependence within an ecosystem. Her students crumpled old wrapping paper and other recyclable materials to form a life-size slice of a coral reef that they covered with a self-hardening plaster compound and then painted. They each researched and modeled a plant or animal and mounted them in the appropriate environmental niche of the reef. Elena describes how the project engaged her students: *The kids got so interested that they wanted everything to be exactly the right way. They were using books to look up the colors of the fish and gather other specific information. They put certain fish in certain places; for example, they put the sea urchins close to the bottom. So there was a lot of meaning behind where they attached their creatures.*

When it was time for a teacher appreciation luncheon and later a parent meeting at the school, the students added low evocative lighting, shells, sand, and a length of slinky blue fabric pooling on the floor beneath. It was so impressive that it went on display for a time in a local art gallery. Elena and her students were understandably proud of their work; through their diorama, the school, parents, and community all had a chance to appreciate their learning, which wouldn't have happened if the students had only read a textbook, answered questions, and taken a test.

WORKING THROUGH THE CURRICULUM

Integrating Science and Art

Given the pressures in many schools for students to do well on high-stakes assessments, classroom teachers tend to become territorial about their curriculum; they often see any time spent on art as decreasing the time they have for their *real* curriculum. Ed, Elena, and Wendy are not immune to these pressures, yet they choose to integrate art into their science programs because, as Wendy says, *You're teaching your science curriculum. The arts are just another way of showing it.* In addition, these teachers appreciate how arts integration leads to an increase in their students' understanding of the science content, greater student interest, and a broader range of opportunities and styles for students to demonstrate their knowledge and to communicate their learning to their peers, parents, and the school's community. Although their primary allegiance is to their science curriculum, they value the arts in their classroom.

So how do these science teachers manage the tension of balancing their science curriculum with the art process? What does it take for an artist and a science teacher to work together this closely?

A Dynamic Collaboration

Teaching always involves making choices about what to do and for how long. With expectations to *cover* a curriculum and develop the students' skills, one of the issues that immediately crops up in integrating art and science involves choosing the topic and the related project. The decision about how much classroom time to spend on it follows closely behind. There are a variety of routes to making these decisions for a successful arts integration experience.

Sometimes the science teacher initiates the collaboration based on a chosen topic. In creating the coral reef, Elena led the way:

I had gone scuba diving to a coral reef on a vacation, and I was in heaven—it was beautiful. I really wanted students to feel what I felt when I was there. Plus, there was so much biology in the coral reef. So I had a vision of what I wanted to do, but I knew that I couldn't do it myself. I went and found the art teacher (Susanna Erling) in my school and asked, "Can you help me? How can we get this kind of texture to create the kind of look that I want?" (See Color Insert D.a.)

Another arts integration project started when Elena was interested in working with a particular artist and his art form—photography. They jointly chose the topic of tree identification and then designed a project where the students would photograph trees and make bark prints and leaf prints.

Although Elena took the initiative in approaching the photographer to support her science curriculum, she also listened to his concern about some fundamental art skills that the students needed:

We talked about what he would do, and he said, "Well, I think I need to teach them composition." So we dedicated the first day to composition. We had the kids draw a flower on a piece of paper, and some of them would draw a little, bitty flower, and then we'd talk about all that extra *space. But I wasn't doing the talking—Bob was. And by talking about framing the flower a little better, by the time we got outside to actually do the photography, the students had that understanding of that form of art.*

Although in some cases the teacher may solicit the artist's participation, in other cases the artist takes the initiative in suggesting a project. For example, Ann Boyd, the first dancer from Hedwig Dances with whom Ed worked, had been a biology major during her undergraduate work and had also taken some physics and kinesiology classes. Using Ann's knowledge of the science of movement, they designed a curriculum unit that they called the Physics in Motion. Ed's role was to make the links to the physics vocabulary and concepts (see Appendix D for Unit Plan).

Integrating art and science is not a simplistic choice between the teacher taking the lead while the artist supports the teacher's initiative or the reverse. Usually it's a balancing act involving the artist's expertise, the art process, the science teacher's experience, the science content, the time frame, the prescribed curriculum, and the amount of flexibility that the teacher can exercise regarding the curriculum. Thus, each arts integration experience takes on its own identity through a dynamic collaboration.

Learning From Each Other

One of the strengths of integrating art with science comes from combining these two disciplines that usually don't mix, with resulting experiences that are more powerful than either one alone. For this to happen, both the artist and teacher need to let the other bring their expertise to the table and avoid trying to make the artist into a science teacher or vice versa. Elena comments, *Because if I say to the artists, "Well, you have to do it this way," then their creativity is stunted.*

Communication between teacher and artist is essential. This is true for any collaboration, but especially for one that encompasses art and science. Each discipline uses its own language and makes its own assumptions about how what's real and what counts as important. Integrating art and science requires the artist and science teacher to cross these boundaries into each other's world. It takes time together to chat, ask questions, and explain so that artist and teacher get to know each other and respect each other as experts in their fields.

It's important for the artist to understand the science content of the arts integration project. The science teachers appreciate the artist's willingness to learn the science fundamentals if needed. They lend science books to their collaborating artists and spend time together in person and on the phone so that the artists are familiar with the goals of the science curriculum. In a mutual exchange, the artists inform the science teachers about the nature of the art process.

In some cases, however, arts integration can work without either the teacher or artist having much knowledge of the other's area. Then an arts collaboration becomes a two-way street in terms of growth. Each collaborator—artist and science teacher—needs to learn the other's language: The vocabulary of the art forms along with the science content. When the artist and teacher both broaden their knowledge base of the other's field, the possibility for deeper integration of art and science is strengthened.

A dynamic collaboration requires that the artist and teacher to have a clear understanding of each other's roles and the emotional security to be able to turn to the other person and admit ignorance. It's tempting for a teacher or artist to avoid participating in a project that they do not completely understand and that makes them feel vulnerable in front of another adult, not to mention a room full of students. However, admitting ignorance and demonstrating a willingness to learn provides a wonderful role model for students. As the artist or teacher partially explains things during a class session and then turns to the other to fill in the blanks, students can see the power of teamwork in action.

Making Time in the Schedule

Coordinating class schedules with the artist's availability presents a challenge for arts integration. The three teachers in this chapter met this challenge in several ways. One solution is to rework the schedule of the curriculum. For Ed, the Physics in Motion project is so powerful that he rearranges the sequence of his curriculum topics for the semester to allow for the window of time when the artist and science teacher are able to work together.

If the curriculum topics can't be rearranged, then the teacher and artist must think creatively to find a way to utilize the artist's particular expertise within the given topic during that block of time. For example, Wendy had wanted to work on the topic of trees with her artist collaborator, but because his schedule made him available when she was going to be teaching astronomy and space, those were the topics that they used.

Supporting Difficult Concepts

Selecting a topic for an arts integration project can grow out of a teacher's concern about teaching a particularly difficult concept. Elena noticed how projects such as the DNA storybook and the walk-in cell helped her students understand topics that are often hard to grasp. She considers the topics where her students will need additional support: *What I do is I try to look at my curriculum and ask, "What is a tough unit? What do the kids have a hard time understanding?" What I try to do is get a project together with an artist so that the students can walk out of there saying, "I really got it."* Far from impinging on science territory, there is little tension between the science content and the art process when arts integration illuminates the dark corners of the curriculum.

Students who feel overwhelmed by a difficult topic sometimes resort to inappropriate behaviors to avoid the challenge. They may also interpret the presence of an artist as a signal that it's time for fun and games and no real learning. However, even challenging topics become accessible when the artist and teacher are very clear in communicating their vision of how the project will integrate art and science. For the Physics in Motion project, Ed says, *The way it's presented, it's a lesson so that they understand more about motion, more about forces, more about energy. It's not, "We're going to have fun and dance around." If it were not as well structured, the students probably wouldn't take it seriously.* The lesson plans that Ed and Peter prepared demonstrate the thoughtful structure undergirding the integrated activity that contributed to its success (see Appendix D: Physics in Motion).

Diverse Students, Diverse Resources

In a classroom of students with diverse interests and learning needs, teachers face the need to differentiate their instruction. Compared to activities where verbal intelligence rules through the spoken word (usually of the teacher) and the written word (usually from the textbook), one of the main benefits of integrating the arts into science is that it provides visual, kinesthetic, and tactile avenues for students to both learn and demonstrate their knowledge. However, arts integration should not be construed to preclude language-based learning. Indeed, some art forms such as poetry and drama rely on language. Providing books and videos can support the students who are *word smart*. Elena talks about the role of books in her arts integration projects: *I think I'm using them a little bit more because there are different kinds of learners. We're tuned into the visual learner because this is an art project. What about the nonvisual learners? The real important thing is to find a balance in the kinds of activities we do.* In this sense, the arts integration project resembles other student-directed research activities where the teacher—with or without an artist—functions as a facilitator instead of the exclusive source of knowledge.

It's important for the science teacher, who knows the students well, to share that knowledge with the artist. Elena and her collaborating artist do a run-through of the process, taking turns to talk through the activity and then each offering advice to the other to smooth out the rough spots. Elena explains her role:

> *I get to be the student and I get to see what's going to happen, so I can intercept and say, "Now wait a minute, at this point the students might get a little lost, or maybe could you be more visual? Put it on the overhead so it's very clear to the kids." Because to the artist, it's their specialty, so they're very clear on it, but it's a new subject for the kids.*

Problem Solving at the Core

The core of the science and art integration projects often involves problem solving. The goal of integrating art and science is not simply to tack on an artistic expression of what the students have learned once they've done the *real* science. Instead, the artist and teacher guide the students through a problem-solving process where art and science function hand in hand.

For an idea of how problem solving is at the heart of arts integration with science, consider the codex project in Elena's classroom. First the artist introduced the idea of a codex as a book made of long folded strips of paper and showed slides of some spectacular examples of Maya and Aztec codexes made of bark paper. The project involved making paper and trying to replicate the colored sheets of the codexes so that the students could document the highlights of their biology studies for the semester in their codexes. There were some paper-making materials that the artist had experimented with and some that he had not. As the students started trying different fibers, some problems came up. Elena remembers, *We tried carrot fibers, and it would turn brown. We tried all kinds of stuff—we put flowers in there, and we blended it up, and some of it kept color. To me, the best one was wheat grass—no discoloration at all.*

Meeting the Challenges

The problem-solving nature of projects like this brings challenges for the artist and teacher. For one, it may be difficult to trust the process when the outcome of the problem or the final result of the project is uncertain, but grappling with the *muckiness*—to use Wendy's term—of a real problem is what makes it both art and science. Often the artist and teacher will find themselves cheering each other on through the ups and downs of starting a project. As the project gets underway and the trickle of student interest and energy grows into a torrent, the project takes on a life of its own. *All of the projects that I've done have really developed as we went along,* comments Wendy. *We come up with more ideas as we go, refine them, and change and make the project better.* To successfully guide such projects as they evolve, flexibility and communication are key characteristics.

Another challenge stems from the time constraints of a class period. Many teachers find it difficult to work within a limited time frame of 40 to 50 minutes, and it's often even more difficult for artists. With the project usually spanning multiple class periods, it's helpful to establish routines of getting supplies, cleaning up, and storing unfinished projects so that as much time as possible can be devoted to actual work.

There's also the issue of different working styles. For example, one person may be organized with materials and the other not; one person may want to plan the structure of the class period beforehand, whereas the other may want to *wing it.* Sometimes a similar style between the two can be detrimental as well, as when both the teacher and artist feel most comfortable processing the experience verbally: The teacher and artist can end up doing all the talking! Although these stylistic issues might seem trivial on the surface, they reflect the need to share control. It takes commitment from both the teacher and artist to communicate and trust their collaboration to result in a greater sum than either of their two parts.

BEYOND THE UNIT

Assessment Through Performance and Reflection

The day finally arrives when the project is finished … or is it? The beautifully illustrated codexes, the photographs mounted on the wall, or the installation of the hallway of space can deceive everyone involved into thinking that they're done, but they're not. Some of the most powerful connections are made when the students, teacher, and artist take the time to reflect on their experience. Asking why and how prompts responses that make the learning more conscious and cement the meaning of the experience in everyone's minds. Sometimes that reflection can take place informally, perhaps in casual debriefing, such as "Why did you choose to put the angel fish at the bottom of the reef?" or "How did the color of your replica of the planet Mars show what Mars is like?"

Formal reflection is also valuable and can be embedded in various forms of assessment that include not only the traditional paper-and-pencil tests but also alternative assessments. Wendy explains the multifaceted assessment that she used for the hallway of space project: *I gave the students a grade on their process and their product. I had them do a self-evaluation. They wrote and illustrated a book about their individual planet or spaceship, and they did a book evaluation. They even had to read each other's books and give each other a grade.* For the students' individual project and their books, Wendy generated lists of characteristics with a scale of 1 to 5 for her to assign grades and for the students to grade themselves as well. She also prepared questions for student self-evaluations (see Fig. 4.5).

The project can be an assessment. When Elena had groups of her students draw diagrams of different kinds of cells and present them to the class, she could see whether they represented all the different structures of the cells and could explain their functions. The poems that her students wrote about the endangered animals that they had sculpted and attached to a mural also functioned as a performance assessment: Elena looked for factual information about the animals' habitats, adaptations, and threats to their survival.

When the students' learning occurs through the arts, performance assessment is a natural choice. Wendy speaks of this in terms of application: *I mean, your goal is for them to be able to to apply this knowledge in some fashion … to be able to use the knowledge that they've learned. So you're seeing that in their projects.* It challenges teachers and students to think of different ways to document their learning, for example, with photos and video in addition to traditional written evaluations. Above all, assessing arts integration work challenges teachers and students to develop the ability to see the meaning in the artistic expression. They must both encode and decode the message in the medium of art. They must function as artists.

The Long-Term Impact

We've seen that integrating art into science through the collaborative teaching of an artist and a science teacher can be powerful, but is it an isolated experience? Wendy, Ed, and Elena all emphatically disagree. Like the variety of ways that artists and teachers make their decisions about the topic and project for their collaboration, the long-term impact takes various shapes as well—from a close replication to adaptation to inspiration for future projects that integrate art and science.

Some of the projects become embedded in the formal curriculum, as in the case of Physics in Motion project, which Ed, as one of the writers for the Chicago Board of Education's day-to-day lesson plans, has inserted as the culmination of the mechanics unit. To work with an dancer, however, usually requires funding. Unless a teacher is able to participate in a program such as CAPE, Ed acknowledges that not every teacher may have the expertise and time to write a grant to fund such an artist. To repeat the Physics in Motion project, Ed states, *I want an artist there because he is far, far superior in leading the activity than what I could do.* Elena feels that she has learned enough through working with the artist in certain projects that she can implement the same experience on her own:

I don't believe that it's necessary to always have the artist in the classroom [in subsequent years], but the teacher can learn to do what the artist does without the artist. When the artists and I were working together, they would come to one class. But many times, I would do the same activity three or four other times during the day with my other classes, so I become pretty good at being the artist and the teacher at the same time. This was, I thought, an important thing, because then you're training the teacher.

Elena's experience points out the importance of a true collaboration between the artist and teacher. Because Elena participated in the art project, first as a learner and then as a teacher, she integrated it not only into her curriculum but also into her repertoire as a professional. The long-term impact on the teacher is greater when the teacher doesn't sit back and observe while the artist and students engage in the process. Just as active participation is a key factor for the students, teachers make the connections and understand how to facilitate the experience independently when they personally engage in the process.

However, the scope of the arts integration project is a factor in the teacher's ability to replicate it without the artist. Sometimes it takes an artist to help manage the complexity and length of the process; simply having two adults to facilitate can also make the difference when the process involves intense amounts of energy.

Whatever the size of the project, when teachers decide to strike out on their own and replicate a project, they will likely find that the first time is demanding; if they survive that experience, the next time will be easier. Wendy remembers, *The second year that I did the "elements in me" project [creating a life-size illustration of the chemical composition of the human body], I thought I was going to kill myself, but the third year, it was easy* (see photo).

Even if teachers decide to replicate the arts integration experience, Wendy counsels them to expect things to turn out differently. She notes: *That's what makes it exciting—you're not stale. You can't plan everything that will happen. The whole point is coming up with something creative, not just to manufacture the same project again.* If a teacher tries to exactly replicate the experience, the students might get the message that the goal is for them to produce the same result as the previous year's students, and then the focus is on the product and not the processes of learning and artistic creating. In addition, the students will be different; because arts integration asks students to take an active role in making connections and expressing their understanding, the experience may take a different route, leading to another version of a final product.

Thus, adaptation is one way that these science teachers continued to integrate art into their classrooms without an artist. They didn't change the activities, but they adapted the scope of the project to fit their resources of time and energy. Elena explains, *Once you have all that information, you say, "Well, I can maybe do it on a smaller scale," and you learn to do it by yourself.*

Once these science teachers took the plunge and tried integrating art into their science curriculum, they noticed that they started looking at their teaching differently: They began looking for other ways to integrate art to reap the same powerful benefits in other units. They realized that there were many more possible activities that could nurture their students' understanding. It opens doors in their thinking so that they can then lead their students into more meaningful learning.

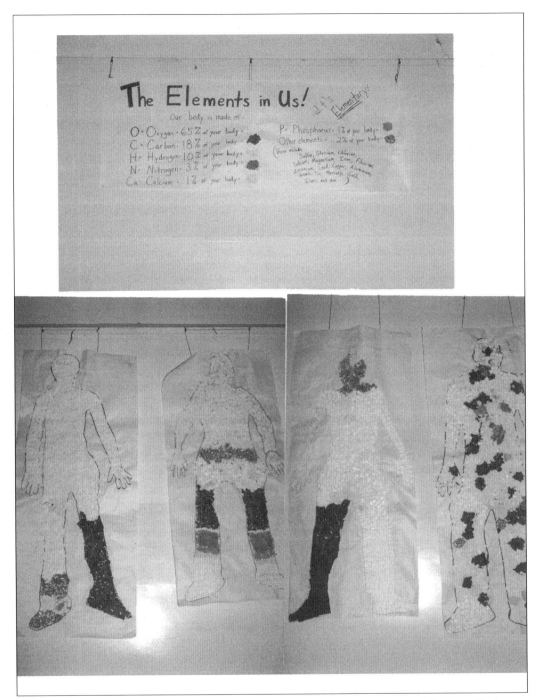

The Elements in Us: Students make life-size illustrations of the chemical composition of the human body in Wendy Anderson's science class at Audubon School.

BACK TO LEONARDO: ERASING THE LINE BETWEEN ART AND SCIENCE

Integrating art and science has been successful for these teachers even though none of them is an artist. They have been able to bridge the gap that has opened in the popular imagination since the days of Leonardo da Vinci, which suggests that the gap may not be as great or even as real as it is perceived to be. By rethinking the relationship between art and science, we may be better able to understand how arts integration in science can work.

For many people, art takes on certain forms usually associated with museums and galleries. A broader conception of art recognizes that process is a fundamental characteristic of art—a process that involves finding ways to express a message, hopefully in a new and fresh way. When engaged in this process communication, artists may not know ahead of time what the product will look like, but instead are guided by the desire to express what they want to communicate. Their choices of subject matter, materials/media, size, style, and so forth depend on what will convey their ideas best.

The process of art also involves examining ideas and making connections between ideas and the physical perception of the world (i.e., through the five senses). Visual art is not simply a visual (or auditory, tactile, or kinesthetic) experience; music is not simply a collection of sounds. Instead, art is concerned with the ideas represented in the painting, sculpture, movement, or other art form.

Thinking of art as a process of exploring ideas and communicating them brings the similarities with science into focus. As Leonardo demonstrated, early scientists were often working out of an artist's sensibility—that is, an interest in the *why* of the observed appearance. Like art, science seeks to uncover the patterns and relationships in our world. Although the scientific process, with its emphasis on empirical, quantifiable evidence, is the conventional image, much of science is also found in breakthroughs of insight. Deciding what to study, which data to gather, and what sense to make of the data often involves scientific insights that are just as intuitive as analytical. Many scientists consider the aspect of their work involved in coming up with original ideas to be like that of art; the *eureka*! effect functions in both.

Science and art, then, require a similar approach to making sense of the world that involves observing, exploring relationships and patterns, and communicating ideas. For students who are immersed in an arts–science experience, the question is not "Is this art or science?", but "What does this mean?"

A SATISFYING EXPERIENCE

For Ed, Elena, and Wendy, there's another reason for them to integrate art into their science curriculum: As teachers, they find it inherently motivating and satisfying. Ed reflects, *It's different [for the teacher and the students], so it's something that will catch the kids' interest. Also, it might be fun, and that's the whole thing—for me to enjoy what I'm doing.* That enjoyment stems from the satisfaction of teaching well—of effectively reaching the students and seeing their progress. Wendy declares, *It has been very rewarding all the way around. One of the things I just really like is that it helps me teach the way I'd like to teach. I'm not the sole giver—I'm just the guide. I'm helping them with ideas, but really a lot of it is coming from each other.* The satisfaction of their students' learning is the incentive that these teachers have discovered in arts integration.

A motivation for teachers also comes from the collaborative aspect of the integration. When two people work together, each person's energy fuels the other. The presence of an artist also signifies that there is tangible support for what matters most to a teacher: teaching well. Elena recounts, *I needed the resources and the support. For me, that's what the artist stands for. It really is motivation for me, not only for the students. The artist motivates me as a teacher to pursue these extra activities.* For teachers who have little contact with other adults during the day, there's the pleasure of sharing the excitement over the students' achievement with the artist. When teachers are enthusiastic about taking risks and expanding their teaching repertoire, they pass their excitement onto their students.

Despite initial appearances, art and science are not such strange bedfellows after all. When a science teacher and an artist collaborate to integrate their two disciplines, each of them is encouraged to expand their way of looking at the world. As a result, they can guide their students in a process that makes meaning of the world through the power of both science and art.

Arts Integration Snapshot

Telpochcalli School:
Mexican Culture at the Heart of Curriculum

Arts integration can affect the philosophy and curriculum of a whole school. The following stories illustrate how two Latino schools have embraced the arts in very different ways but with very specific goals and powerful results. Thanks to Angelica Ahlman, Guillermo Delgado, Gabriela Chong-Hinojosa, Lydia Huante, Rita Arias Jirasek, Patricia Martinez, Mari Carmen Moreno, Alfredo Nambo, Erin Roche, Vicki Trinder, and Tamara Witzl for their contributions to this snapshot.

Telpochcalli Elementary School is a small school with a large and passionate vision. Telpochcalli (Nahuatl for *the house of youth*) is located in the Mexican-American community of Little Village; most of the students are of Mexican descent. The school is dedicated to making connections between the students' lives outside the school—including their language, heritage, family and community—and the teaching and learning inside the school. Mexican art and culture, integrated throughout the curriculum, provide a bridge to that end.

A first-grade student at Telpochcalli School enjoys posing for the camera while he works on an underwater habitat mural.

On a warm May afternoon, theatre artist Angelica Rocio Alhman works with the sixth- and seventh-grade classroom of Telpochcalli teacher Alfredo Nambo. Their students are practicing monologues, organized around the theme of *tolerance*, for a public reading to take place after school at Casa Azul, a local coffeehouse.

Angelica asks the class to recall a performance they have seen by a professional storyteller. She wants them to draw lessons from his presentation to heighten their own performance skills. She directs their attention to the comic timing that the storyteller used—or, as she puts it, *la pausa grande*—the grand pause.

One student remembers that the actor asked a witch in his performance, "Are you *crazy*?", and the witch paused for a really, really, long time before answering, "Yes, ... as a matter of fact, ... I am!"

The other students laugh as they recall the hilarious effect of such an exaggerated silence. Angelica encourages them to add dramatic tension to their own readings by inserting pauses in their speech. Students read their work, and the class makes suggestions on how to improve the rhythm of each reading. They revise and critique their work based on a nuanced response to a professional performance.

Alfredo reminds the class that there will be an audience at Casa Azul, so it's important that *le hechamos ganas* (we give it all we've got). There is an easy, affectionate exchange between Spanish and English conversation, between Angelica, Alfredo and their students, and between tying formal elements of drama to the students' own autobiographical writing.

Telpochcalli students and teachers cross boundaries among disciplines, languages, and modes of expression as a matter of course and by thoughtful design. The school faculty integrates instruction across subject areas and creates thematic curriculum with Mexican fine arts and culture at the center. The school is committed to developing bilingual/biliterate students. All the faculty is bilingual; many of the teachers are Mexican-American. Instruction from kindergarten through eighth grade stresses both English and Spanish competency.

The Telpochcalli school brochure states that *the arts are woven throughout the curriculum both as a subject of study as well as a tool for teaching and learning*. Co-planning and co-teaching between the artists and teachers occur on a regular basis. Three clusters of primary, intermediate, and upper grade teachers meet for 2 hours *every* Friday to plan together. A full-time art teacher and librarian work with all the teachers. The artists, who work in the disciplines of Mexican dance, music, visual arts, and drama, are integral parts of these teams. Each cluster works with four different artists and art forms in the course of a school year.

The teams have created units of study around big ideas or organizing themes including: Immigration, Tolerance, Transformative Experiences, Patterns, and Time Lines in history, math, and the arts, and an Our Place geography unit that focuses on the reading of maps, music, and art. Concepts in the arts are used to reinforce concepts in languages arts, social studies, math, and science. Ideas from literature and history are represented in vivid murals, dramatic readings, and choreographed dances. After many years of creating arts integrated units, teachers and artists are now looking to explicitly teach the parallel processes between art forms and provide opportunities for multiple ways of knowing the curriculum.

How did a school with so many rich, curricular cross-currents come to be? Other arts partnerships have worked from a model that starts with a handful of committed teachers who spread arts integration slowly throughout their school, but Telpochcalli began with a whole school mission from the start. The idea for the school began in 1993 when the Mexican Fine Arts Center Museum invited teachers from the John Spry Elementary School to partner with them as part of a CAPE proposal.

Tamara Witzl, now principal of Telpochcalli, explains: *It occurred to me and a fellow teacher at Spry School that this would be a great opportunity to create a school within in a school. We told the Museum that we had a group of teachers interested in integrating Mexican art and culture, and they wrote us into the proposal. When the Museum received the CAPE grant, we separated ourselves into a small school. We restructured our school and created common planning time for teachers and artists because we knew that we didn't want the arts to be add-on extras.*

Telpochcalli teachers worked as a school within a school for 2 years and then applied for and received autonomous status from the Chicago Board of Education. The Mexican Fine Arts Center Museum assisted with professional development for the teachers and hired and trained the artists in residence. The Small Schools Workshop, affiliated with the University of Illinois at Chicago, was instrumental in providing technical support in restructuring the school.

Rita Arias Jirasek, educator and curriculum consultant working with the Museum, led teacher training sessions for a full year. Rita says: *We were very lucky that the teachers were willing to look at the curriculum and take it apart. One of our benchmarks was that anywhere that we could integrate the culture of Mexico, in an art form or in history, we were going to try to do it. There were very interesting projects that came out of that openness to experiment with curriculum. Many teachers had never had the opportunity to look at year long plans ahead of time before. It was very exciting.*

Sixth-grade teacher Vicki Trinder agrees: *Rita was enormously helpful. She taught us how to create unit webs. We would start with a theme, pull in all the content areas, add the assessments, and then try to integrate the assessments into a larger holistic unit plan. We make curriculum planning the heart and soul of everything we do, and at the center of that, is the arts—so we don't have to try and swim in two oceans.*

When the initial Telpochcalli faculty moved into a new building in August 1996, they worked as teachers, administrators, and janitors all at once. They had to scramble to find desks and chairs, paint the walls, and organize materials in preparation for their students. Parents who chose to enroll their children in the new school supported the school's educational philosophy and forged a strong bond with the teachers in their new venture. There is a sense of family and camaraderie at the school, where teachers are invited to student's confirmation parties and students have danced at a teacher's wedding.

Teacher Alfredo Nambo says: *The idea at our school is not only to tell our parents and our community that we respect this culture, but to actually integrate it—to bring it into the classroom and talk about it. To open it up not only to ourselves , but to other teachers, to artists, and return it back to the community.*

The border crossings at Telpochcalli are both philosophical and literal. Most of the families have immigrated from Mexico. For some, this is their first school experience in the United States; others have lived in Chicago for many years. But there is a constant state of movement between Mexico and Chicago. Many families, pulled by economic necessity, have immediate relatives living on both sides of the border.

The middle cluster teachers addressed the very personal theme of immigration with their third- and fourth-grade students. They read immigration stories from around the world to understand that displacement and adjustment to a new life is a universal issue among all cultures. They interviewed their own parents, wrote down their stories, and revised and reworked their writing in peer groups. They then selected the most vivid stories to dramatize. Jessie, a student working on this unit, wrote:

My family is my mother, my two sisters and me. We came to Chicago because my father was here. Before we came, my mother told me that we were moving, and I started to cry. At first I was very sad, but later I began to feel content because my family was going to become complete. When I got off the plane and saw my father, I cried with joy. He held me and told me not to cry....

At the culminating presentation, parents heard their own stories in the voices of their children. Parents and teachers were deeply moved. Teacher Alfredo Nambo spoke for many when he recalled, *The show spoke directly to me. That was my story on stage.*

Angelica introduced the show to the audience and explained that one student, Ramon, would not be in the show because he had just moved to a new school. She was emotional as she realized that Ramon's gift to the school would be his story, and that stories are often all we have to hold onto in times of change. To everyone's delight, Ramon was in the audience and had returned to hear his work performed by the rest of his class.

At Telpochcalli, there is a constant interpreting and reflecting on the experience of being Mexican-American. The teachers and students create rituals that mirror rituals in the larger community. Each year students build altars to celebrate the Day of the Dead—a holiday with both religious and cultural significance.

Students are accustomed to creating the altars with a different theme each year, but one year the altar took on profound, personal meaning. Two sisters, students at the school, tragically died in a house fire. Their brothers survived and returned to school. The entire school community was in mourning. Art teacher Patricia Martinez worked with the students to build a Day of the Dead altar to honor and remember the girls. Everyone participated, including the brothers. The altar was also rebuilt at the Mexican Fine Arts Center Museum's professional Day of the Dead show. The show drew a tremendous following of people from around the city. The students came to the opening night and told stories about the girls to large crowds of people.

Rita Arias Jirasek says: *The kids worked out their grief when they built an altar to these children. They had seen the altars built over and over again with a different focus each year, but this time they were able to use the ritual to express something so important to them. They transformed the experience from one thing to another and turned to it as a time for solace. It was an incredible gift.*

The results of the school's vision and commitment to developing an integrative program of learning through the cultural arts are impressive. Student attendance is incredibly high at 97%. Test scores are steadily improving. Students have a sense of themselves as artists and are becoming more sophisticated in their art making and thinking. Students who were not willing to perform publicly 2 years ago now come forward to star in a play or dance, as they begin to trust their own process. Girls are encouraged, as empathically as boys, to speak out and take on leadership roles.

Gabriella Chong-Hinojosa, third- and fourth-grade teacher says: *We are such a small community that we can provide one another with different perspectives on how to help each student really shine. We know that if one student doesn't like dancing but likes to draw, she can make a contribution there. We are open to each others' ideas and suggestions.*

The school is committed to professional development. The teachers work to renew themselves as educators, attending summer institutes, workshops, and classes. Telpochcalli and Orozco School teachers recently traveled to Mexico on Fulbright scholarships for a 5-week intensive study of Mexican history and culture. Lydia Huante, Director of Museum Education, says: *The teachers were able to experience first-hand the country, culture, and people of Mexico. They came away with a more profound understanding of themselves, their students, and what they were trying to teach.*

The walls at Telpochcalli are filled with murals, including a primary school mural on the Gift of Corn, and murals in the bathrooms that record different kinds of journeys—from immigration to the journey from girlhood to adulthood (see Color Insert, H.c). The students' thinking is made visible through their bilingual writings hung on the walls, their discussions in the classroom, their research projects, and their exhibitions and performances.

Student artwork hangs on the gallery walls of the Mexican Fine Art Center Museum. The exhibit, *Cuentos y Re-encuentros* (Stories and Encounters), features work from this Tlahui-CAPE partnership of the Museum, Telpochcalli, and Orozco School.

Startling and beautiful self-portraits and collages made from pieces of painted tissue paper and found print material hang on the turquoise and magenta walls. Rodolfo's blue-green face with wistful soccer-ball eyes suggests a map of the world. Argenis' background includes an Old Navy logo and a Mexican *amate* (bark painting); a hybrid of cultures is layered within the colored tissue paper. These children, led by Telpochcalli visual artist Guillermo Delgado, have reinvented images of themselves (see cover).

Arts integration is working at Telpochcalli School. It permeates the curriculum and it draws parents and community members into the process of teaching and learning. It engages the culture of the children and it provides a way to bring the school community together on many different levels. Within this supportive environment, Telpochcalli students are piecing together the best of many worlds to develop as sophisticated and successful learners, artists, and young adults.

Arts Integration Snapshot

Recognizing Culture as Curriculum:
Orozco School Presents Student Artwork in a Digital Age

by Connie Amon

It's 2:35 p.m. and eight students sit around a table in the Learning Center. Amid munching on cookies, they fight over the sign-in sheet and exchange comments about the day's events with each other, the adults who are there to teach them, and those who stop by for a cookie of their own. Although the cookies may seem insignificant to an outsider, they are very important to us. The eight students are committed to staying after school for an extra hour and a half 2 days a week. Besides the fact that many of them haven't eaten all day, by 2:30 in the afternoon we all could use some extra nourishment.

The students have been chosen to be at the table by the technology coordinator and their classroom teachers. These are students who, although not necessarily the best in their class, have demonstrated a commitment to learning, a willingness to try new things (especially in the area of technology), and a dedication to their work. They have agreed to become a part of the Web Team, and they know the requirements of the job. Although at times they may whine and complain, they are conscientious workers, and they understand that they are responsible for documenting and presenting the work that they and their peers have created in their arts-based humanities program to the world.

The Jose Clemente Orozco (JCO) Academy Humanities Web Site became a reality in the fall of 1996 when we received a grant from the Illinois State Board of Education to fund the equipment, training, and personnel that would make the web site possible (*www.orozco.cps.k12.il.us*). JCO had been working with the Mexican Fine Arts Center Museum and neighborhood artists for 2 years prior to this time. Teachers in the seventh grade had also been working collaboratively to integrate the arts into the curriculum—not as a separate subject, but as a means to learn content. One of the art teachers involved in the program expressed interest in publishing student work over the Internet, and the idea for the humanities web site was born.

As an extension of Orozco Academy's humanities program, an interdisciplinary program that emphasizes language arts, social studies, and the fine arts, we proposed to design and maintain an Internet web site that would include student research, student artwork, and lesson plans and activities that Orozco faculty had developed for the humanities program. We worked in conjunction with members of the Mexican Fine Arts Center Museum (through the Chicago Arts Partnership in Education/CAPE), which is located in our school neighborhood, local and visiting artists, the UIC (University of Illinois at Chicago) Neighborhoods Initiative, and onsite technology-multimedia specialists.

The web site provided motivation toward an end result that was global and somewhat revolutionary in scope, encompassing the learning of many graphics, publishing, and critical thinking skills. The project necessitated team teaching and cooperative learning as teachers and students involved in the humanities program collaborated on and incorporated the key decisions involved in researching, designing, and building the site into their existing curriculum. We spent the first 3 months of the project brainstorming and developing ideas and have continued to reflect and alter our ideas and the site as projects and people evolve and change.

The integration of multimedia and online resources with the curriculum helped meet the diverse learning needs of students and teachers. Although some students excel artistically, others excel as writers or editors. Some students have excelled as managers of information and at pulling things together. As global publishers, both students and teachers have been motivated in all aspects of creating the site. Pictures drawn or designed for the site must be perfect, fonts chosen must fit exactly, and text needs to be edited again and again.

The focus of the humanities program is on the art and culture of Mexico and Mexican-American communities in the United States. Ninety-nine percent of the Orozco student population is Mexican or Mexican-American. We believe that our students have much to offer the world about the history and future of Mexican and Mexican-American cultures and art (see Table 1). The creation of an Internet site that emphasizes these cultures and art has been a strong message to the community, students, staff, and the broader society that their work is valued and significant in a global context. Through the site, students, guided by their teachers, have contributed to a global knowledge base by designing and displaying their own work (see Appendix G for Scope and Sequence).

The primary goals for the project have been as follows: to integrate technology and the arts into the curriculum so that they become tools for learning content area subject matter, not as isolated skills or subjects; and to provide faculty and staff with the relevant, student-centered, ongoing professional development necessary to ensure the successful integration of technology and telecommunications.

To meet these goals, we designed the following objectives:

1. Create and maintain a Web site which incorporates student and teacher work in a multimedia, global format;
2. Establish and enhance communications globally and locally with other schools, artists, professionals, students, and communities of Pilsen and the world;
3. Provide increased access to and availability of resources, both online and in person; and

TABLE 1
J.C. Orozco Humanities Program
Grade 7—Integrating Social Studies, Art, and Language Arts
Themes: Storytelling and Art

Europe and the Middle East	Mexico and the Americas (art based)
Quarter One: Foundations of Today's World • The Roman Empire • The Origins of Judaism • Early Christianity • Islam	**Quarter One: Celebrations/Rituals of Mexico** • Mexican Independence Day—story based on interview • The Olmecs—large-scale chalk heads with presentation • Day of the Dead—costumes, parade, and illustrated essay • (see Color Insert H.b)
Quarter Two: the Making of Europe • Europe in the Middle Ages • The Renaissance • The Reformation	**Quarter Two: Folk Art and Classic Murals** • Holiday Mercado—Milagros, Christmas cards • Teotihuacan—nature motif murals
Quarter Three: the Clash of Empires • Early Civilizations in the Americas • Spain: The First Modern Empire • Great Britain's Sea Empire	**Quarter Three: Architecture and Myth** • The Maya—building a Mayan city • The Aztecs—write and illustrate Codex • Sor Juana—introduction of poetry
Quarter Four: New Nations/ past Traditions • The Forming of Mexico • Life in the English Colonies • The United States: From One Nation, Many	**Quarter Four: Nation and Self in Mexican Art** • 20th Century Mexican artists—mural painting, retablos, portraits, guest artists • The music and dance of Mexico—guest artists • Performance for variety show

4. Provide training for teachers and students in the use of multimedia, tele-communications, and the use and integration of technology with the curriculum.

Back to the cookies. After reviewing what has been completed and receiving their assignments for the afternoon, students break off into small groups or work individually. Some students may be scanning artwork that students have created, such as parts of their codexes or illustrations drawn for their Olmec stories. Some may be scanning portions of a map or original artwork they have created (e.g., graphics for button icons).

Other artwork is not so easily placed on a flat surface or sized to fit in a small space. Some students might be in classrooms, taking digital pictures of student-size Olmec heads (see Color Insert H.a), Day of the Dead masks (see Color Insert H.b), or two- or three-dimensional replicas of Mayan cities. Other students might be capturing images on videotape.

As resources and materials are gathered, students work on designing and creating pages for the web site. Images that are downloaded from digital or video cameras, or pictures or drawings that have been scanned, must be cropped, resized, and *giffed out*, or saved in the proper file format for viewing on the web. Buttons must be created that link pages together, text must be added and then edited, and backgrounds must be chosen from available programs or created as original artwork. Students work in sophisticated programs such as PageMill and PhotoShop to prepare pages and images. They also learn to utilize the "Draw" features of more simplistic programs such as ClarisWorks to create headers, graphics for buttons, and backgrounds. Pages begin to take shape and then come together. Although visitors to the site might take these pages for granted, the students understand just how much work has gone into a completed page (see Fig. 1).

After 2 years, our web site has grown to a formidable size. The site now incorporates work from all of the major art projects included in the humanities program: Day of the Dead ofrendas (altars; see Color Insert H.d), frescoes Teotihuacan style, Olmec heads, Mayan cities, Aztec codices, pop-up Virgin of Guadalupe stories, retablos (thanksgiving installations), and scratchboard representations of student poetry, along with student writing, information about each of the Meso-American civilizations that are studied, as well as our own neighborhood of Pilsen in Chicago. Through their work on this project, our students have expanded their learning and some have become webmasters extraordinaire. Here are some of their comments about working on the web site (Fig. 1 shows Olmec stories and art):

It's really fun, and we get to do research. We get to take pictures, draw, scan pictures, and we mostly get to work on the computer. I learn to do other things that I never knew before on the computer. Like I never knew how to scan, or draw pictures in a computer. **Carlo**

Doing the Teotihuacan page was hard to do ... very complicated. I learned how to get onto the Internet and research what I'm looking for. **Maria**

What I like about the Web Team is that I have been learning new things about all the civilizations and it's fun. I also like to work with everybody because everybody helps. **Karina**

Working on the Web site has been exciting and fun. These past months have been great and I have learned a lot about PageMill, Ofoto, PhotoShop, TextureScape and many more programs. I usually work on facts with my teacher. I know that I have learned more about the early civilizations in Mesoamerica, and that has helped me a lot in my studies. **Ruben**

In addition to mastering the technological skills necessary to develop the site, such as scanning, cropping pictures, and *giffing out* images, the students have used their writing, editing, and artistic talents to plan and design the site, making sure that everything fits logically and creatively. We have watched and listened as students have struggled with pictures and text, exclaimed when animation has worked, and sat silently glowing over a finished page. Our students have presented the site to public audiences at two different technology conferences. In the spring of 1997, we presented at the Tech2000 Conference in Springfield; in the spring of 1998, we presented at the Inaugural Illinois Student Technology Conference in Oak Brook. Not only have people been impressed with the site and our students' artwork, but they have also commented on how much they have learned about the content our site covers.

We have found, through our work with the humanities program and with the students involved in this program, that the combination of art and technology is a very powerful one. Technological tools—computers, cameras, scanners—are also creative tools—a medium that students can use to create, develop, or alter artwork they have created using more traditional methods. Technological tools can also be used to display student work to a global audience of critics and supporters.

Sometimes it's difficult to imagine our lives without technology. At times it seems as if we wouldn't be able to communicate without telephones, fax machines, and e-mail. As technology becomes increasingly important in every facet of our lives, it is necessary for schools to become places of technological literacy and innovation. Teachers and students need to be given the chance not only to learn about new technologies, but to use them and incorporate them into daily classroom life. Students do not contemplate how things have changed in the digital age; they just live it (Table 2).

Olmec Stories

Defender of the Olmec people

In 1100 B.C. in the rain forests of Mexico, there was a man named Flying Eagle. He was a carver of sculptures for the Olmec people. One day he was traveling to a village because his mother was ill.

He always prayed to the Sun and the Moon for protection. As he was praying, a jaguar jumped out and attacked him because he had a weapon in his hand.

The Sun and the Moon were listening to Flying Eagle pray when he was attacked by the jaguar. The Sun and the Moon sent down their son, Eclipse, to save Flying Eagle from the jaguar. Eclipse started to fight with the jaguar. The jaguar gave Eclipse scars on each side of his face. Eclipse hit the jaguar so hard that the jaguar ran away.

Flying Eagle carved the Olmec sculpture of Eclipse because he was so grateful to him and his parents, the Sun and the Moon. The people used the Olmec head as the Defender of the Olmec People.

Omeccal Head

This Olmec head is named Omeccal. He was a warrior. He was the leader and the most intelligent of the whole army. He killed 25 warriors in 30 minutes.

Omeccal lived in the rain forest. He was killed by a traitor from his army. In his house the traitor killed him. He had two sons. Omeccal liked the jaguars.

He was important because he was very rich and he was very famous. He beat the powerful man called Tiotimecca, but Omeccal killed him with great strength and power.

The army of Omeccal was the most powerful. They didn't kill with weapons, they killed with their own strength.

When he was little he started to study karate and he beat all the kids. He was the best in karate and in his house he collected all the trophies and all the belts.

One son of Omeccal was Taimecc. He was a warrior like his father and he also studied karate. The other one was Amecc and he was an artist. He made masks of jaguars.

After Omeccal died, people in his town started to make statues of Omeccal and tell stories about him. His sons became famous like Omeccal.

FIG. 1. Olmec stories and art: Orozco School web site - this page and facing page   (see also Color Insert H.a).

Our Olmec is the lord of the jaguar. A long time ago a man built this Olmec head because the legend said that a little boy's face was in an Olmec's head that was the lord of the jaguar. He was a little boy and his name was Zuaiky-Zuaiky.

One day he was in the forest and he came eye to eye with a jaguar. Zuaiky and the jaguar were fighting and Zuaiky won. The people decided to make an Olmec with the boy's face.

The young boy lived in the forest by himself because he liked to live alone. When Zuaiky was older, he was out hunting one day when a strong storm came and lightning struck him. Nothing happened to Zuaiky because he had armor on that protected him. After this happened, whenever Zuaiky wanted it to rain, it would rain.

Zuaiky was important to the people because he commanded the rain and the jaguar. When the people needed rain they went to him. Nobody ever messed with him because he was too powerful.

The Olmec Head of Tiotimeca

This Olmec head was important to the town. He was a man and his name was Tiotimeca. He lived in Titioguacan. Tiotimeca was an important man because he was a good man and a good hunter.

He had a pet named Mecazi that was a jaquar. They used to go to the forest together and when they had hunted too much he gave some meat to the poor people. But one day Mecazi died and Tiotimeca was really sad.

Tiotimeca decided to make a hat with the head of his best friend, Mecazi. He said that it was going to be his lucky hat.

Five years later Tiotimeca died because he was a warrior and somebody killed him.

All the town was saddened by his death.

Then the people decided to make an Olmec head in honor of Tiotimeca. On his head they made his lucky hat, with the head of his pet, Mecazi.

TABLE 2

**The 3 Rs of New Technology in Integrated Curriculum:
Research, Relationships, and Representation**

INTO: As teachers and learners move INTO the curriculum, new technology
    allows them to access a wider range of original sources for RESEARCH:

    Web searches to research prior knowledge
    Digital "cut-and-paste" skills to store documents from original sources

THROUGH: As they work THROUGH the curriculum, they draw on an expanded set of
RELATIONSHIPS with co-learners and co-teachers:

    E-mail relationships
    Listserv relationships
    Video conferencing relationships
    Electronic discussion groups and bulletin boards

BEYOND: As they move BEYOND the curriculum, technology provides new tools of
REPRESENTATION for documenting, reflecting on, and presenting work:

    Digital cameras, graphics, and scanning software
    Electronic spreadsheets for charting and graphing
    Video and sound editing
    Software for presentations (such as Powerpoint)
    Creating CD-ROMS, desk-top publishing
    Web sites, cybergalleries, on-line magazines

Note. Courtesy of Arnold Aprill.

Chapter 6

You Don't Have to Do It Alone: Initiating and Sustaining Collaboration

Unexpected Allies

- The kids
- Your peers
- Arts teachers on the faculty
- School administrators
- Partnership coordinators
- Parents, community members, and arts organizations
- Colleges and universities

Building an Arts Program in Your School

- Learning from past efforts
- Starting with what is
- Evidence of arts integration in a school
- Documentation as key element

Scope and Sequence: Looking at the Bigger Picture

- Showing breadth and depth of arts integration
- Demonstrating what students are learning
- Illustrating connections with goals and standards
- Planning with teachers and artists
- Defining questions to form partnerships
    - Example: Discussion of a partnership

Commonly Asked Questions—and Possible Responses

- Doesn't it take time?
- Isn't it sometimes artificial?

- Shouldn't the arts be separate disciplines?
- Shouldn't reading, writing, and mathematics come first?
- What if teacher or artist is not engaged?
- Aren't we too busy to reinvent the wheel?
- How will we pay for it?

Meaningful Partnerships and Meaning Learning

- Collaboration
- Simple transactions and joint ventures
- Long-term conversations
- Listening to each other across boundaries and separations
- Being producers and consumers
- Creating the renaissance

6
You Don't Have To Do It Alone: Initiating and Sustaining Collaboration

So, say you are intrigued by this notion of arts integrated teaching. You think it's important for kids; you think it's valuable for your development as an educator, but you are concerned that you can't do it alone with all the other demands on your time, attention, and energy. You don't have access to an artist at the moment, and you aren't confident of your ability to read music, dance, act, or paint. This chapter's title, "You Don't Have to Do It Alone," is intended to give you some suggestions for where to turn for support, ideas, and inspiration.

This chapter helps us take a moment to see arts integration as part of a bigger picture beyond the individual classroom. First, we introduce you to some unexpected allies. Then we describe what arts integration planning might mean for a whole school community. We do this by examining how a scope and sequence of arts integration is a useful talking tool among teachers and artists, as well as parents and administrators. Then we discuss the design and evolution of partnerships, providing a look at one partnership—the ETA/Muntu Arts in Education Consortium—through the eyes of its participants.

You have unexpected allies waiting for you at every level of the education and arts communities, hoping for your help as much as you are hoping for theirs. In fact, we almost named this book *Unexpected Allies* because we believe so much in the power of collaboration to do this important work.

UNEXPECTED ALLIES

The Kids

Begin with the students. Young people, when given access to materials and a little guidance on structuring time and space, are often more than ready to become your artist partners. We have seen a group of middle-school students transform a regu-

lar classroom of cooperative learning groups into a dance studio, a composers' fo-
rum, a playwrights' workshop, a painters' gallery, and a poets' gathering without
anyone losing focus or productivity! It was as if invisible walls protected each ener-
getic cluster, and in each little cell arts activities were being led by students.

Having a compelling focus for the non-arts content, so that the arts activity
serves a real purpose, assists students in becoming leaders. For example, in that
middle-school classroom, students *needed* those arts forms to represent a novel
they were reading in literature circles and took initiative in applying those art
forms. Greater student leadership opens up time for teachers to conference with
individual students. Teachers can work with small groups who are focused on a
specific means of representing their learning through an art form. When students
become leaders and artist partners, teachers can become fellow explorers,
ethnographers, and curators. Expanded roles for students expand the roles of
teachers.

Vivian Gussin Paley has built an entire kindergarten curriculum around student-directed storytelling and dramatic play, as documented in her 1990 book, *The boy who
would be a helicopter*. Karen Gallas has created an indelible portrait of first- and second-grade students as lead artists in her 1994 book, *The Languages of Learning: How
Children Talk, Write, Dance, Draw, and Sing Their Understanding of the World*. In *You Gotta BE the
Book*, Jeffrey D. Wilhelm (1997) recorded how a class of reluctant eighth-grade readers
were transformed through their emergence as dramatic artists. James Herndon's
well-known books *How to Survive in Your Native Land* (1971) and *The Way It Spozed to Be*
(1965) are crammed with examples of student-initiated learning through the arts.
(Both Herndon's texts are now out of print.) In *Drama for Learning*, Dorothy Heathcote
and Gavin Bolton (1995) explored how students of all ages assume the "mantle of the
expert" to deepen their learning in all areas of the curriculum.

We have found that the students have much to say about how to make arts integration work. A Lincoln Park High School student group conversation about this
collaboration revealed that these young people know what will make this venture
successful. Here is some advice they had for artists:

Artists need to have patience and tolerate kids if they come here to work.

*They are coming into our environment, so they need to know how to adapt like how we act and
like how our class schedule works. Just like how like maybe the teacher acts and like giving up the
classroom.*

It's not like every kid in every class is going to be open to learning something that has to do with art.

You have to be crafty because kids are more open to learn if they don't think they're learning.

*Trick us. Trick us into being happy. Trick us into thinking we're having fun. It'll work. I don't
think you have to trick us necessarily, but just let us know this is something new and different.*

Just try it. You don't have to be good at it. Just try it once. That's what you tell them.

*But a good artist teacher has to be more focused toward what the students think than on how
the students do the art … at least at first.*

These high school students also had some suggestions for their teachers who
were trying this work for the first time:

I think teachers need to prepare themselves and not think that the artist is coming in trying to unravel everything the teacher has already taught. Or that kids are going to automatically want to do this all of the time. It's just a new experience. Teachers have to understand that what they're teaching is important, but this person is just coming in and trying to make it more interesting for kids.

The teacher should allow the artist to do what he came to do.

Yeah, just give them the stage.

No, I think the teacher should participate with the students, because a lot of teachers haven't been introduced to this sort of thing in college.

When in doubt, ask the kids.

Your Peers

In CAPE partnerships, after 5 years of having some form of arts integration present in their schools, 54% of teachers reported having developed one integrated unit and 24% reported having created four or five units (Catterall & Waldorf, 1999). 71% of teachers surveyed in CAPE schools reported teaching their units more than one time. If more than half the teachers in CAPE schools participate at some level, there is real potential for the arts in all schools. It's clear that once teachers experience the arts in their classrooms, they see the value and they support the initiative.

All you need is one other person who shares your vision. Find out who else at your school or in your arts organization is interested in arts integrated teaching. Assess who has skills in the arts and in education. Poll your peers. And don't just look in the obvious places. Who'd have thought that the chemistry teacher was a blues guitarist? Who'd have thought that the cellist in your community orchestra has a degree in teaching mathematics? Chicago's Pulaski Elementary School has an extraordinary Latin rhythm band that was organized by a member of the school's support staff.

Arts Teachers on the Faculty

The arts teachers on the school faculty are wonderful allies and resources in arts integration work. The arts teacher, with a commitment to teaching sequential art curriculum, is a crucial advocate for the arts in schools. Working together, the art teacher, classroom teacher, and artist can develop students' skills and aesthetic sensibilities in the art room *and* the classroom, both as discrete subjects of study and as vehicles to represent ideas in other content areas.

JoEllen Kerwin, art teacher at Healy School, says: *The school looks to me for support as someone who will be enthusiastic from the start on a creative venture. The artists, teachers, and coordinator know that I will be there to listen, brainstorm, and contribute because I want the artists here. This [arts integration] project has really enriched Healy School.*

The specialists should be invited onto the team to work and plan alongside the teachers and artist. Within a well-structured work context, every side has a lot to offer. The in-school art teacher knows the students, has a body of valuable curricular knowledge, and can help facilitate good working relationships. The classroom teacher knows the curriculum and the needs of her students. The visiting artist brings in a special area of expertise that can expand the existing curriculum and shares her or his studio practices and processes with the students.

JoEllen has worked closely with CAPE dancer/choreographer Rosemary Doolas for many years. They collaborate to create an annual eighth-grade interdisciplinary performance, supported by the Illinois Arts Council, a state agency. (Local Arts Councils can be a great source for additional revenue to bring professional artists into the schools. See Appendix L for state contact information or find your local arts council on the Americans for the Arts web site: *http://www.artsusa.org.*)

JoEllen says: *Rosemary and I brainstormed together on our first collaboration. I had taken a teacher class at the Art Institute. As my final project I proposed an art lesson where there would be a visual Underground Railroad throughout the school, with different stations in front of each classroom. All I had to do was tell Rosemary this idea and she went off! I was the seed and then it exploded. She turned it into a really amazing performance!*

Since that first successful venture, they have each brought ideas to the table to design this eagerly anticipated, ritual eighth-grade event. The most recent performance, initiated by Rosemary Doolas, involved the Terra Museum of American Art, the photographs of Robert Capa, video, music, and student dances that expressed "Who We Are" (see p. 47 and Color Insert A.c).

The art specialists need to participate in arts-integrated work as part of their regular duties, not as add-on extras. JoEllen has structured her involvement in the Healy School performances in ways that are congruent with her teaching goals.

JoEllen says: *I'm not only going to do the scenery for a play. For me to end up with good work to support a project, I have to have complete lessons and units. I always have many segments to my lessons that lead up to a final work. Whatever I do, I always start with individual student work that can be pulled together for a collaborative finished piece.*

Other art teachers in CAPE schools have also chosen to work across art disciplines with the visiting artists. Lakeview High School art teacher Susana Erling was thrilled to bring Redmoon Theatre puppeteer, Frank Maugeri, into her sculpture class. Together they created a shadow puppet play based on a short story by Latin American author, Gabriel Garcia Marquez. Frank taught Susanna and her students how to build puppets, create a puppet stage, adapt myths for the show, and expressively manipulate the puppets. She loved watching Frank encourage different talents in her students as they responded to his teaching style.

Miriam Socoloff, head of the art department at Lakeview High School, invited playwright Jackie Murphy into her self-portrait classes. Miriam wanted her students to expand their definitions of self-portraits to include the written word. She felt a writer would have a better feel for generating autobiographical writing and would add another dimension to her teaching. Both Miriam and Susana gained a partner, colleague, and friend with whom to exchange ideas and grow professionally.

New arts integration ventures will find themselves without the added luxury of professional artists on their curricular team. These schools should look to the "acres of diamonds in their own back yards"—the resources of their own faculty.

Kitty Conde is the instaff art teacher at Ravenswood Elementary School. She works closely with the classroom teachers to jointly develop arts integrated curriculum. She has forged a special relationship with the third-grade team, often finding *elegant fits* between their science curriculum and her art objectives. She is implementing a book-making and illustration unit that supports the seventh- and eighth-grade classrooms' Young Authors project. Kitty is well loved and respected throughout the school; she is also recognized as a strong ally to turn to when teachers are looking to create meaningful curriculum.

As in all successful integration work, there need to be clearly defined roles for each member of the team. No one will be happy to feel that their work is *only* at the service of the other teacher's goals. Not all visiting artists, classroom teachers, and art teachers will see things eye to eye, share the same instructional philosophy, or agree on how to divide up their work. But it is worth the effort to bring the art specialist into the mix. When it works, it really works, and everyone is enriched by the experience.

These collaborations are only possible when they are supported by creative scheduling that leave time for the specialist, teachers, and artists to meet together. Art specialists, especially in the elementary schools, often work with students during the classroom teacher's prep periods. Their participation in co-teaching with classroom teachers and visiting artists, or attending planning meetings during the school day, may not be possible. Instead, building leaders need to look for ways to designate time, such as staff development days, for the art specialists to sit with other members of the team. That way, the art teacher's expertise and ideas can be accessed by everyone. For example, Telpochcalli School has set aside Friday afternoons, with an early dismissal for students, to allow the whole school faculty, including the specialists, to be present at team meetings (see Arts Integration Snapshot: Mexican Culture at the Heart of Curriculum).

The art specialist who works as a respected team member often becomes a leader in the school community. Culminating art exhibits and performances galvanize parents' and the school district's support for the school, the art program, and for the role of the arts in increasing student capacity. CAPE art and classroom teachers have also become leaders in their professional communities. They have directed workshops, served as consultants, and traveled nationally and internationally to meet with artists, art specialists, and educators also working in arts partnerships.

Opening up the classroom to the art room and the outside world corresponds with contemporary art-making and education practice. Public artists are drawn to projects that are interdisciplinary, that connect the arts with cultural, historical, and identity studies; and that engage communities in the art process. This interest dovetails with the interests of educators who also create interdisciplinary work and who reach outside the classroom to access the community as part of their students' education.

Although some art teachers, classroom teachers, and artists in the partnerships were initially reluctant to give up the boundaries of their own disciplines, after years of successful work they have come to agree with the sentiments of collaborator and art teacher JoEllen Kerwin:

Healy School is an interesting enough place that people with big ideas come from the outside, and that has always been good for me. You can get very isolated as an art teacher; these projects pull me out and open me up. They broaden me. I am pulled into something bigger, and I don't know what's at the end of it. And the end is very exciting.

School Administrators

School leaders can become great advocates for the arts especially if they are approached for help instead of for permission. Approach your administrators as collaborators; indeed they can be. A teacher at Brownell Elementary School in Chicago, in love with opera, approached her principal about developing an opera program. The principal, who was looking for innovative ways to deepen the school's language arts program, responded warmly and approached the ETA Creative Arts Foundation theater to help with artistic resources. Under ETA's guidance, the school hired a playwright in residence who trained students and teachers. Classroom teachers and the music specialist at Brownell collaborated; the school began producing an original opera annually, written and performed by the students, and presented at a local college and on a local cable TV station. One teacher and one principal got things going.

Principals can also encourage a wider scope for arts integration in a school. Cydney Field, principal at Ray School, says: *It was, at first, a matter of getting everybody to buy into it, so I said, "OK, let's take baby steps. Let's try one unit, one project per classroom." We started one grade level the first year and then I think it was three the second year. We branched out on each end; now the entire school including the preschool is involved. And what I found was that it really created a lot of energy among everyone. That's been very, very positive.*

Partnership Coordinators

Every group needs leadership and management. A leader listens, pulls together a vision, excites the group, and inspires the discipline that it takes to reach the goal and to persevere when quitting seems better. Managers shepherd the resources and direct them toward the vision. Both qualities need not be in the same person. In an effective team, different people can take on different roles. Good management is invisible. It is only when things go wrong that the group cries out for a manager to fix it! (Tammy Steele, Coordinator of the Bridgeport/Armour Square/Near North Arts Partnership)

The individuals who coordinate the arts collaboration work in a school play a key role in the project's success. The larger and more complex the team, the greater the need for a strong coordinator. The coordinator may help with creating and maintaining schedules, structuring time for planning among teachers and artists, facilitating meetings, planning training sessions, and keeping the group on track.

The coordinators provide the glue that holds the team together and helps the group to discover its own capacities. Jean Parisi, director of Pros Arts Studio in the Pilsen Arts Partnership, works to access the resources and talents of the team members, the school, and the community. Jean says: *The reason that I can do this work is that I live in the neighborhood. I know all the partners, and I try to stay open to what resources are out there. Discovering and unearthing treasures is a part of this job. When we first began, I met with Myrna Alvarez at Casa Aztlan (a community organization). She heard our plans and said, "Wow! You work in clay; I think we have a big old oven upstairs." And sure enough, they had a kiln that we restored and now use in our after-school program. The coordinator learns what everyone has to offer and makes sure that everyone gets credit for what they do* (see Color Insert F.c).

A new venture is not as complex as these long-term partnerships. However, for the work to proceed and develop, it is important to appoint someone to be in charge of nurturing the effort. A shared and sustained community vision makes this work successful.

Parents, Community Members, and Arts Organizations

Some arts organizations are beginning to provide their artists with the professional development they need in education methods. The East Bay Center for the Performing Arts in Richmond, California, and the Community Music School in London require their artists to go through extensive educational training before they work with schools. At the same time, states and districts throughout the nation are rethinking their policies and approaches to teacher preservice, inservice, and professional development. Arts organizations and arts education partnerships have an important contribution to make to this discussion.

In the Chicago Arts Partnerships in Education Summary Evaluation, Catterall and Waldorf (1999) asked participants about the relationship between CAPE and the wider community. They reported that community support seems to be coming mainly from the localized schools. That is, the immediate community is most likely to know and care about the arts in their neighborhood school.

In some CAPE schools, parents are very active. Catterall and Waldorf (1999) stated: " ... in one partnership a group of parents simply took the CAPE project on from the beginning and helped with planning, grantwriting, and scheduling" (pp. 61–62). Although that may not always be the case, parents can be very strong advocates.

Parents can be artists too. The Hawthorne–Agassiz Partnership includes in-school visual arts specialists, parents, and community members who are professional artists. Poll parents in your school. Who gives private music lessons? Who has performed in community theater productions? Who has a degree in art? Find out.

Community members who may also be gospel singers, quilters, or jazz percussionists are likely allies. The local Chamber of Commerce may have a directory of artists who may welcome the opportunity to get involved in your school. Give it a try.

Parents we interviewed were some of the arts partnership's strongest allies. They had ideas, volunteered time, raised money, and sometimes inspired their children. *The children here have a great opportunity,* one Hawthorne School parent noted. *We didn't have this when we were in school. They should grab everything they can and learn from it. Later on, they can say, "I did this" or "I know that."*

Most arts organizations and many park districts and community organizations have arts education programs that work with schools. Coordinator Jean Parisi sees the value in cultivating these resources: *I think that the arts do make a difference, but what makes the most difference here is that we've built a community—a community of caring adults, of teachers, artists, students, and parents. One of the key things about our partnership is that we recognize that the schools can't do everything. You can't just integrate the arts in the classroom because the students leave at 2:30. So this partnership has always extended into the neighborhood* (see Color Insert F.a).

Many cities have several local organizations devoted entirely to providing arts education services. Your state or local arts council (see Appendix L) may have a roster of artists that specialize in working with schools. In any case, be ready to talk to any provider about what *you* want out of the program. Arts integration requires more than just receiving delivered services (see web site *www.arts4learning.com* for a national directory of artist partners).

Colleges and Universities

Universities are not only joining arts education partnerships as a useful strategy for connecting to their communities, but they are starting to provide professional development for artists and arts teachers. Columbia College and the Erikson Institute in Chicago are developing teacher training and child development programs for practicing professional artists. The School of the Art Institute of Chicago, the University of Illinois at Chicago, and the New England Conservatory have each created programs that consciously connect art and music teachers to contemporary professional arts practice.

Parents we interviewed at Sheridan School suggested that schools look for practicing teachers to help with the arts: *The way to do it would be to get more participation from college students. It seems like if you bring someone in who is in the second or third year of college in a particular field, it would be good for everybody. Students have to do internships. Why can't it be in the public schools?*

In an innovative program at the University of California, teachers are receiving part of their preservice training at the Armory Center for the Arts, a community-based arts education center in Pasadena. University arts education program leaders and studio art organizers are just beginning to understand their potential for making emerging artists available to schools.

In CAPE's West Town Partnership, a whole crop of young artists just recently graduated from Northwestern University developed arts integrated curriculum at Peabody Elementary, Otis Elementary, and Wells High School through Northwestern University Settlement Association and an Americorps grant. Universities seeking to create positive relationships with communities and public school systems provide professional development, conferences, support networks, fiscal agency, and even fundraising and evaluation for arts integration initiatives.

CAPE's Lakeview Education Arts Partnership is facilitated by the Chicago Teachers' Center of Northeastern Illinois University. Universities often create arts in education initiatives, such as Project Zero and Project Pace at Harvard University. California State University San Marcos collaborates in a cultural partnership program called SUAVE (Socios Unidos para Artes Via Educación) or United Community for Arts in Education. Arts integration will be deepened as programs like these mature and spread.

FROM CLASSROOM TO SCHOOL: BUILDING AN ARTS PROGRAM

Effective and meaningful arts programming continues over the long term. It consistently builds on past efforts; it is not a temporary phenomenon that disappears when a particular teacher or particular principal leaves the building to take another position or when a grant ends. The challenge of building and sustaining such an arts integration program in a school is an art in itself. To begin with, you might take a serious look at what is happening **now** with respect to the arts. Where is there an arts presence in the curriculum? To what degree is art included in yearly goals or school improvement plans? If a stranger walked into your school, would she or he know that the arts were important?

The arts partnership work at Hawthorne Elementary School began in the primary grades. (See a description of Hawthorne teacher Wendee DeSent's kindergarten curriculum, *Making Shape of Our Environment*, in chap. 3). Over the course of 5 years, the program has spread to the entire grade levels from kindergarten through eighth grade. Year by the year, the program has grown with support from a group of committed teachers and artists, parent leader and project director, Mary Lou Schmidt, the in-school coordinator, Wendee DeSent, artist coordinator, Angie Pfeiffer, and the school principal, Sandra Mawrence. Many pieces contributed to the whole school buy-in of the program. The primary teachers shared their successes with their colleagues, the school's already high test scores rose in the course of the 5 years, and the students moved up grade levels. With them came the momentum and desire to expand the program to the upper grades.

David Kersnar, artistic director of the acclaimed Lookingglass Theatre Company, has worked as a coordinator in the arts partnership and a performing artist in the upper grade classrooms. For the past 3 years, he has teamed with teachers to direct an eighth-grade performance that brings together history, language arts, and drama. This integrated arts performance has become an eagerly anticipated, annual ritual for the graduating class. David says: *There is a real flexibility at Hawthorne on how teachers can use the arts partnership program offered at each grade level. We want teachers to decide what excites them, and let them grab that. The eighth grade teachers wanted to make their assembly performance more pertinent and meaningful for their students.... So we made* performance *the* Big Idea *of our work.*

David worked with teachers Carlton Oquendo, Monica Sullivan, and Eleanor Nagle to develop this year's show, *Journey to Freedom*, based on the history of the civil rights movement. Carlton Oquendo adapted speeches and historical narratives for the script; David developed the performance with the input from the students (see Color Insert C.d).

The students researched and studied the history of the civil rights movement in the 1960s in class. A core group of students worked with David using the process that Lookingggglass Theatre members use to create their professional work. They came together as an ensemble, working from photographs and text, to create images for the performance. All the 65 eighth-grade students participated, some in the core group, and others performing music from the period, or working behind the scenes as stage managers and set designers. Everyone added his or her voices to the choir.

Sydney Sidwell, parent of an eighth grader, says: *We were all incredibly proud and moved. You could really see the students working as an ensemble. They supported each other and made sure everyone got credit for their work. The performance really illustrated to us what arts integration looks like.*

David Kersnar was particularly pleased that teachers recognized the importance of choosing students for the core group who might not otherwise be thought of as high achievers. There is now the understanding that participation in the arts can reach students in new ways and give students with different talents the opportunity to excel.

The ensemble metaphor applies to the current school-wide support for the arts integration at Hawthorne. The Local School Council voted to increase financial support for the arts partnership, teachers acknowledge the contribution that a professional artist can make in the life of their classroom, and the principal stands behind the process. Teachers, parents, artists, and students agree with Kersnar that arts integration has become *part of the cultural fabric of the school.*

Virginia Vaske, Principal at Murray School in Chicago, explains what happened in her school: *What I did not think would happen is the vast amount of art, visual art, music, dance, theater, whatever, that would be done in kindergarten through eighth grade. You walk into this school now and you can tell that art is something that is valued. That wasn't true before. We're pretty close to institutionalizing what's done.* Figure 6.1 is a tool for examining your school as it is now with respect to the arts. It is also a useful vehicle for communication with staff members, community, and parents.

We have learned that there are other things to look for over the long term when the arts play a viable role in a school:

1. School attendance—Students are more likely to come to school if they know there are arts activities happening regularly.
2. Homework patterns—Students are more likely to complete homework with understanding when they are actively involved in the arts in their classroom.
3. Mobility rates—Families are more likely to remain in a school if they are actively participating in arts-related projects.
4. General parent involvement—Parents are more likely to attend and participate in more facets of their children's education if they have had some interaction through the arts. A parent in a CAPE school commented on yet another benefit: *Yes, it's very, very wonderful to have something like this ... to be able to have something like this in your school and grow up and say, "I went to that school, I graduated from that school, I became someone in that school."*

All of these elements of an arts integrated school climate point to the consistent need for *documentation* of arts events, arts curriculum, and the impact of the arts on school environment and learning. *Documentation*, the recording of what you, the students, and all arts participants do, think, and feel, is critical for success. Well-documented work serves as a tool to advocate for future programming. It is a way to highlight strengths and describe informed goals for the future. David Flatley (1998), an arts coordinator for the Lakeview Education Arts Partnership, says: *Partnerships that succeed in facilitating systemic change are those that have an eye toward the ongoing development of authentic documentation, a portfolio or collection of materials that demonstrates the consensus in the network. It should not be a process of backtracking or creating a blitz of materials only when needed. How this material is presented to the community is part of the equation, not only because educators should determine how well a subject has been taught or how well a methodology works, but because the evidence and articulation of authentic learning breeds support for the creative initiative.*

How then can teachers, artists, and administrators document their work in ways that they can actively use and display to the larger community? We have found that there is one particular kind of documentation for those working with arts integration that can be a real vehicle for conversation and learning in a school: the **Scope and Sequence**. A **Scope and Sequence** can be a powerful reflective piece for refining your teaching that is both enlightening and user-friendly.

Evidence of Arts Integration in a School

The arts are a meaningful presence in your school if there is evidence of the following indicators. Which ones apply to your school? Which ones would be important as goals? How would you work toward the ones that are not evident right now?

- art in the hallways
- when kids are asked what's important in their school, they mention the arts
- arts specialists (music, drama, art, dance teachers) are included in whole staff planning
- artists are/have been present during the year
- teachers involved in arts projects are communicating often with others who are not
- school staff and students are connected to art in the community
- there is a real relationship between the artists working with your school and the teachers, not to mention the students
- there is evidence of the arts in formal and informal teacher lesson plans
- the school calendar reflects the arts as it relates to other areas of the curriculum (e.g., when the sixth graders are studying Egypt, they are also involved in making Egyptian hieroglyphic drawings and displaying them for the whole school)
- there is sharing of the arts with parents and community
- there is a connection between inschool and after-school programming in the arts
- there is evidence of the arts in reading and writing assignments
- the arts are a regular part of teacher-made tests and other assessments
- the arts play a role in inservices during a school year
- there is a pattern of the spreading of impact over several years; more teachers and students become involved and more grade levels are included
- there is planning time provided for teachers to integrate the arts collaboratively, and there has been useful staff development for teachers to know how to use that planning time well

FIG. 6.1. Evidence of arts integration in a school.

SCOPE AND SEQUENCE:
LOOKING AT THE BIGGER PICTURE

What is a Scope and Sequence? Typically it is a graph, table, or chart that illustrates how often and in what depth specific topics, skills, and strategies are taught and learned. Useful Scope and Sequences show not just **what** was learned, but also *how* it was taught. Useful Scope and Sequences *also help participants ask and answer questions* and *provide information that is useful for the future*. Meaningful Scope and Sequence charts are shared with students, are exhibited for community members and parents, and are fluid and easily changed. They may even have moveable parts and places for response and feedback (see Appendix G).

A Scope and Sequence that shows arts integration is most helpful if it does the following:

1. Shows breadth/depth/ and order of events, usually at a glance;
2. Refers to **student learning**, not just what teachers and artists have done or what themes/topics have been addressed;
3. Shows grade levels, topics/themes, length of time spent on units, goals addressed, and arts goals addressed;
4. Shows progress over time; and
5. Shows an order of events/units based on a rationale or philosophy.

Some of the CAPE partnerships have been using Scope and Sequences to help plan for the future and discuss their work with partners. Table 6.1 presents some questions to consider during three planning/assessing meetings as you, your partners, and even your students look at some graphic representation of what you have accomplished—or hope to accomplish as you plan for arts integration.

Scope and Sequences are helpful as dialogue for what the students experience and how they are being well served in and through the curriculum using an arts integration approach to learning. Scope and Sequences focus on student learning and what the students really receive as a function of the arts programming across the curriculum. Dialogue about what students are learning and what art forms are being addressed is central to any initiative that intends to be more than a brief opportunity for some students.

It is also important to look at the adults in the partnership and assess how the collaboration has worked—for the benefit of all those invested in its success. There are three possible ways to look at this "big picture" that we have noted for you in the Appendix H (Stringer, 1996). One approach involves the asking of interpretive questions—the Who, What, How, Where, When, and Why questions that help partners assess progress and success. A second approach is essentially a Partnership Review, in which the mission, goals, structure, operation, and general issues of concern are articulated and discussed by the partners. The third approach to partnership evaluation is a form of concept mapping. In this approach, artists and arts organizations, teachers, administrators, and parents participate in drawing or diagramming the partnership, perhaps in the form of a timeline or a series of concentric circles that indicate what has been happening with arts integration and who has been involved. Although these three approaches are not the only ones available, they do point to different styles of program evaluation—one of which will probably be useful to you as you go forward in a partnership.

TABLE 6.1

Questions for Discussion about Scope and Sequence: Three Planning Meetings for Arts Integration

Meeting 1
A. Before even looking at your materials, what do you hope students have gained or accomplished in this partnership over the last year? List those things being as specific as you can.
B. Do you/your partnership have different aims for older students than for younger students in the school? Explain.
C. Are there some things you hope were gained or accomplished for each given grade level? Explain.
D. What do you hope to learn by looking at a scope and sequence for arts integration at your school/in your partnership? What do you hope to learn that you don't already know? THIS IS IMPORTANT.
Meeting 2
A. How do the integrated arts projects fit into the rest of the school year?
B. Do you see any transfer or connection between what students did during an integrated arts unit and what they did at other times of the year?
C. Which arts forms received most serious teaching and attention? Why?
D. Which art forms would you hope to focus on in the next 3 years? Why?
E. How does the teaching and engagement of an art form increase in sophistication as the grade level increases? (For example, how do the drama skills build or increase in complexity as students move up through the grades?)
F. What, if anything, do you notice is missing that you believe should be incorporated in a viable arts integration approach at the school/in your classroom?
Meeting 3
A. What standards were addressed in and through arts integration projects at each grade level or for each unit?
B. What standards did not receive attention directly and purposefully through arts integration projects?
C. How would you draw—or describe in writing—the relationship between the textbook and the art form in an arts integration unit that you are familiar with?
D. How does assessment systematically appear in your Scope and Sequence ... at each grade level and with each arts integrated unit?
E. Is there a common assessment across grade levels used in the partnership? Explain.
F. Is an assessment tailored for each unit? Explain.
G. Are art skills systematically assessed? (Where/When in the Scope and Sequence?)

Dreeszen, Aprill, and Deasy (1999) suggested three sets of Key Questions that partners should be asking themselves: (a) when they begin thinking about a new partnership, (b) when they have decided to collaborate, and (c) as the partnership matures (see Appendix I). These questions are wonderful springboards for action; it's powerful to ask yourselves questions as you proceed.

DISCUSSION OF A PARTNERSHIP: THE ETA/MUNTU ARTS IN EDUCATION CONSORTIUM

The concept of collective responsibility is central to traditional African culture. The ETA/Muntu Arts in Education Consortium was organized around the understanding that "it takes a village to raise a child," meaning that all members and entities in the community must assume the mission of educating and socializing the children. Therefore, the Partnership sought, through the arts, to strategically plan for the cognitive and social development of children within the context of the whole community. The creative process was seen as consistent with the educational process (see Color Inserts B.a, b, c).

For over 30 years, ETA Creative Arts Foundation and Muntu Dance Theater, as arts organizations that speak directly to and for African Americans, have played a major role in the cultural life of Chicago. They serve as the co-anchors (coordinating organizations) of the ETA/Muntu Arts in Education Consortium Partnership. ETA's mission is the perpetuation, preservation, and promulgation of the African-American aesthetic, telling the African-American story in "the first voice." Muntu Dance Theatre perpetuates the spirit of African cultures through professional presentations of dance, music, and folklore. Both have demonstrated a long-standing commitment to young people and education.

The Partnership includes five schools (Brownell, O'Keefe, McCosh, Parkside, and the Metro Program at Crane High School) and three arts organizations (ETA, Muntu, and Community Film Workshop). From the first organizational meeting, it was understood by all the schools, arts organizations, and community resource groups in the Consortium that different schools would be at different stages of development. This was viewed not as a detriment but as an opportunity because everyone brought "something to the table" from which others could learn, and real strength would emerge from collective effort. It was agreed that developing a *process*, rather than developing one *program*, would be the guiding principle in successful planning and implementation. The Consortium also held as a value that each school would develop its own unique program, distinctive to its school environment and improvement plan.

Voices From a Shared Table

The teachers, artists, administrators, and coordinators of the ETA/Muntu Arts in Education Consortium have become a true community of colleagues. Some of the partners gathered to reflect on 7 years of working together. Here are some of their comments.

Ms. Brown [ETA Creative Arts Foundation]:

In November 1992, Joan Gray [Muntu Dance Theater] and I had talked about a consortium; we thought it would be a good opportunity particularly because they were talking about the establishment of an endowment so that the work that organizations were doing in schools could be funded long term. So that was one of the things that intrigued us. So after having come to some agreement ourselves in terms of anchoring the Consortium, we put out a call to the schools. We set forth some goals that were basically within the context of understanding that it was our obligation, as African-American people, to take control over what our children were learning and in some ways to be responsible for that. Believing very deeply in the role that the arts play in advancing the social skills of our children, we asked these various schools to join us. That way, we could share the resources and begin to understand more clearly and in a comprehensive way how the arts make a difference.

Ms. Hoover (Teacher):

I remember, just reflecting back on some of that early work we did. We had different committees that would work and were involved in different kinds of research, looking at how we would extend to other schools. We had a research and development committee that was looking at test scores and at what kind of information we might need. We had the teacher liaison committee that was talking directly to the teachers to figure out how we wanted to go about setting up the programs that we wanted to do.

Ms. Sanders (Teacher):

I had taught drama a little bit to our school prior to that and also with the after-school program, but Mr. Moore [playwright] brought in something special to us. I felt that he helped the children a lot in their speaking, their writing, and just being very interested in them, and not just having them talk with each other, but in making other people realize their talents. He comes and reinforces the characteristics of reading, the plots, and the settings so when the children are reading, they can respond. They usually write their own plays, and he goes through everything so we can see it.

One of his challenges with us was novels; we only use novels. He takes the novels that we use and he works with the students and they create their own plays. We look forward to it. That is something that we were trying to find—another way to show them that reading can be fun as well as fundamental. It has really worked; we have seen an increase in our scores. I think that is because it was reinforced. They were able to do their own writing, their own critiquing, which is really great.

Ms. Brown:

When these programs first went into the schools, what was the response of the school personnel?

Ms. Hoover:

Well, at our school, we really didn't have a problem with it. We had a program similar to it that we had started, writing our own unit using novels. But one of the things that we have to keep in mind is that when we have the performing arts teachers, that doesn't give you a free period. You have to prepare beforehand. If you are not ready, then that is going to be reflected. The children have to have some motivation beforehand. The material that he gives them before he leaves there, I am going to make sure that they have it when he comes back. Even if they have not completed it, I want to know that they have started it. Then Mr. Moore knows what he is doing is going to work.

Ms. Brown:

Is there something that people have to do in terms of the success of the program or the program even happening?

Ms. Sanders:

I think that the teacher has to be interested.

Ms. Capers (Program Coordinator):

One of the things I noticed when I visited schools is that it is very important for the administration to help implement a program like this.

Ms. Gray [Muntu Dance Theatre]:

I think that the key is the principal committing to it.

Ms. Sanders:

Dr. Watkins [principal of McCosh School] is very encouraging. Anything that she thinks is going to help a student, she will do. She is visible. She will meet with Mr. Moore and she will meet with us. Whatever is going to enhance my students' progress, I am for it. If it means that I am going to have to change some of the things that I am doing, I will do it.

Working with an artist does mean changes in our schedule—to accommodate the artist as well as the students. As long as it is something that is going to benefit the children, then I have no problem with it. We will change our lunch schedule and so forth.

The principal is committed. We were looking into getting in the arts even before CAPE. So that makes a big difference. It's up to us; the principal doesn't force feed us. If we tell her that we really didn't want the arts program, it wouldn't be here. She wants us to be happy as well. Now if it doesn't work, we can forget it. But if we see benefits, it will be here.

Ms. Capers:

We have been talking about the teachers' response and the principals' response. What about the kids? I know that one of the observations that comes back a lot is the comment from the teacher, "How did you get that child to do X, Y, and Z? We can't get that child to do anything!"

I know that some schools have challenges to contend with. I know that the test scores are an indicator, but in terms of the child's behavior and response in the classroom, even beyond the time that the child is actively participating in the arts program, have you seen changes in their personality, their willingness to listen or be involved, even if it is anecdotal?

Ms. Robinson:

I keep thinking about the students in the Metro program at Crane High School who are involved in the media literacy programs of the Community Film Workshop. They view and critique television and advertising. They are exposed to classical movies and are given an understanding of what goes on in the process. You can see a difference in their ability to stay focused and concentrate on something. This is so very important starting with kindergarten on up. I think that that is really good, and it is important that the story be told.

So many times in school and in the classroom there is nothing hands-on that directly involves the students. It's sometimes just the teacher standing in front of the class talking. The kids are not paying attention. You can see a difference with the same group of children in a class when they are writing a play or they have come up with ideas for an opera. It is like some of them just come alive. I remember one boy in a film workshop class making some very insightful remarks about characters. Before that time, he just never participated.

Ms. Robinson (Teacher):

There is no doubt that it is quite a help to their character and their academic skills.

Ms. Gray:

Yes. We see real differences. I have seen that many, many times.

Ms. Capers:

It has really given me a deeper understanding about the role that the arts play in the educational process. I didn't really understand the extent to which the arts were impacting the curriculum. I knew the kids were having a great time, and I knew they were being changed because of their involvement. I really hadn't connected it as much as I do now to how they are better equipped to deal with their academic studies in other ways beyond even the arts program. That has been a big help, and it has inspired me to do a lot more reading and research about different techniques and studies that have come out over the years about the benefit of the arts to the educational process. It has changed my thinking.

I am always impressed with the primary children. I have experience as a primary teacher, and I know pretty much what these youngsters normally do. Yet in the storywriting classes, I think they go far beyond what is usually the norm for primary kids. Their writing is excellent, as well as their grammar.

Ms. Hoover:

We do a lot of writing at our school. The students know that in their first writing, when they are writing with the playwright, he is not worried about whether it is grammatically correct at first. He wants to know whether the children are really understanding the process. He asks, "Are you understanding the definitions of the writing material that I am giving you?"

I have one little boy in my class who is a sweet child, but he doesn't do any work. He's a comedian. So the other day when they had to write about what would they be like in the year 2020, it was amazing what he wrote. Grammatically, it was all wrong. Then Mr. Moore took it and they began to fine tune it and that little boy was just so excited. I told him that when he finished it, he was to make sure that I got the first copy. I could see the difference in him because he knew that he could do whatever he wanted to do with this paper. We never grade papers in my classroom with a red pen. I always put marks on another sheet and give it to them because I don't like their papers to be marked up. He said, "Guess what? You won't get to mark this one up."

Mr. Moore (the playwright) is a role model for young males. Young boys can see that they really can write and be male. But I think that they enjoy the freedom they have to be themselves.

Ms. Gray:

What did that little boy want to be doing in 2020?

Ms. Hoover:

He wanted to be a detective. That was his whole thing—about being a detective and how he would follow the case and all. It was great for him. I told him that I was so proud of him. He has completed it and he will be the first one to read it. So he is excited now. Some of the things that those kids wrote about what they wanted to be were really great.

Ms. Sanders:

Do they see a future for themselves?

Ms. Hoover:

They see a future for themselves, and they are also learning how to proofread. With the finished project, they will come and say, "Oh, this was really messy, wasn't it?"

Ms. Brown:

How has our coming together as adults helped the process?

Ms.Washington [music teacher]:

The Partnership has given me a network of support. I don't feel all alone, and I have gotten a lot of good ideas.

Ms. Hoover:

I think that it has helped all of us because we wouldn't know what is going on at another school. It is not a competition thing. It is more cohesive, and it is working together to make sure that the program works in every school, not just one school. Because, after all, children come first. That is what we are here for.

Ms. Capers:

Our children are improving. So often they are not expected to.

Ms. Brown:

We have got to change these geopolitical-economic decisions that are being made about the ability of our children to learn. That is the root of a lot of this, singling out our children as being unable to learn.

Ms. Capers:

Sometimes a second or third grader will say, "I'm bored." In many instances, teachers need to wake up and find some way of really getting their kids involved. They need something different. It is just so short-sighted to think, "We have got to get these reading scores up, and here is this book, so sit down and read this book." We have schools that are solving these problems successfully. Their stories need to be told, and other educators need an opportunity to hear it.

Ms. Brown:

I think that what we are saying is that if we can ever break through a mind set, and people have an experience where things are demonstrable, then it can flow into all other areas. Everything takes time. The idea of arts being in the curriculum in this particular way is different from when we were in school. It gives us different ideas. I do see some progress being made as slow as it may be. We just have to stick to it and create these models. Hopefully others will become inspired.

Postscript to ETA/Muntu Case Study: The Importance of Parents

The program as designed and implemented in our partnership schools has continued and in many respects has deepened in terms of the objective of enabling the teachers to better use the arts as a teaching methodology. Based on a number of successful hands-on workshops for parents over the years, it became clear to the Consortium that parents also wanted to have an arts experience for themselves. To further our objective to bridge the gap between school and home, familiarize parents with the unique characteristics of the arts, encourage parent input about how they can assist students in the arts programs, and demonstrate to parents ways in which the arts impact learning and the educational curriculum, a series of focus groups were held along with the administration of surveys. The results indicate that, in our extension program plans, work with parents would be most effective. A series of arts workshops, including dance, mask making, theater arts, story telling, jewelry making, and media literacy, has been held with parents at each participating school. The response has been exceptional. (Postscript by Abena Joan Brown and Joan Gray)

COMMONLY ASKED QUESTIONS ABOUT ARTS INTEGRATION—AND POSSIBLE RESPONSES

Doesn't Arts Integration Take Time? Yes, it does. Planning and implementing any effective integrated curriculum takes time. Teaching arts content, including pragmatic considerations like preparing materials, setting up, and cleaning up, also takes time. Our experience has been that this is time well spent. As the information age accelerates and teachers are required to cover more and more content with students, we need new strategies for assisting students in driving their own learning in a responsible and rigorous manner.

Arts integration is one of those strategies. It requires a rethinking of the deployment of resources in the classroom—of time, materials, and the students' intellectual assets. This redeployment of resources in the classroom is central to the redeployment of community, cultural, and educational resources in the Partnerships. This rethinking process is exhilarating, nerve-wracking, and ultimately necessary to keep up with the escalating demands on teaching. The focused, self-directed learning possible in arts integrated classrooms eventually frees teachers up to give more personal attention to individual students. This process tends to be most labor intensive at the beginning, with a lot of *front loading* during the setup of projects. In time, the students become increasingly self-monitoring and self-directed. They look forward to arts in the classroom and tend to want to show how they can learn responsibly in an arts integrated environment.

Don't Arts Integration Projects Sometimes Turn out to Be Superficial? Yes, they sometimes do. Unless there is serious attention given to planning, treating the arts content *and* the other academic content with integrity, meaningful frameworks for integration, imbedding the arts learning in the larger arc of the year's instruction, and developmentally appropriate teaching, then arts infused activities become a passing entertainment that interrupts the flow of curriculum and presents a disjointed image of arts instruction. If teachers (or artists) are forced to participate, if there is a lack of support for teachers to continue their own learning in their content as well as the arts, or if student learning is not always in the forefront, arts integration can be time out from meaningful learning, rather than time toward growth and development. Arts integration is not a gimmick to be dabbled with, but rather a coherent approach to teaching and learning that can be extremely valuable when engaged in seriously.

Shouldn't the Arts Be Taught as Their Own Separate Discipline-Specific Curricular Area? Of course they should. Arts integration works best when there is discipline-specific instruction and integrated instruction, when there are in-school arts specialists *and* external arts partners, and when after-school programs are connected to and extend in-school curricular work. Some arts teachers are concerned that arts integration might encourage schools to hire fewer art, music, and drama teachers. Our experience is the exact opposite.

As Valuable as the Arts Are, Shouldn't Students Learn Reading, Writing, and Mathematics First? It is critically important that our students become come confident and competent in reading, writing, and applying mathematics. Arts integration is built on the understanding that, from the child's earliest years, arts experiences are essential to the successful development in learners of *all* symbol systems. Waiting to give access to the arts until the students are *done* with their *real* learning not only cripples students' development in the arts, but also seriously damages the capacity of the arts to deepen learning in all areas. Learners are not best served by treating the arts as a patina to be lacquered on after the real teaching is finished. One first grader told us quite clearly, "I think that without art, I would be quitting myself!"

What if the Teacher Starts Grading Papers or Leaves the Room During Arts Integrated Work? What if the Artist Launches into a Program That Has No Connection to the Classroom Curriculum? You've got to talk. Arts inte-integration is not a program delivered to classrooms for the relief of teachers or the advertisement of artists. Arts integration is a social contract between teachers and artists grounded in mutual respect for each other's knowledge and time.

This May All Be Well and Good for Highly Creative Teachers and Highly Structured Artists Who Like Redesigning Everything From Scratch. But What About Most of Us, who Are Highly Skilled at What We Do, But Are Already too Busy to Stop and Reinvent the Wheel on Top of All Our Other Responsibilities? Change is inherently difficult. It is hard to change our practice while we are immersed in it (a process often compared to redesigning an airplane while flying it), but change is inevitable. As the Red Queen in Lewis Carroll's *Through The Lookingglass* says, " ... it takes all the running you can do to keep in the same place." We need to reinvent the wheel because our students need new wheels to travel onto new highways (including the information superhighway). Children of today may live in a future world full of opportunities and challenges we cannot even imagine. To properly prepare them, we need to find ways of changing teaching practice that are inviting to all teachers, not just to the change enthusiasts. The standards and accountability movements are part of this attempt to raise the bar for teaching and learning for all teachers and all students. High expectations are absolutely necessary for school improvement, but they are also absolutely insufficient if they are not accompanied by real, effective, highly generative strategies for improving what actually happens in classrooms. Any initiative to improve schools needs to be linked to good teaching; that is what we continue to explore in this work. What is good teaching? How do we learn to do it?

One of the strengths of an arts integration approach is that it brings into the classroom an actual knowledge and skills base—a new set of expertise—that resonates with and expands the teachers' and students' existing knowledge and skills and helps them develop new repertoires of effectiveness. Educator Karen Fuson of Northwestern University calls this teaching that is simultaneously instruction for students and professional development for teachers. The presence of another competent adult in the classroom with a different skill set and with expertise in another knowledge base allows the teacher to model for the students "the teacher as exemplary learner." Virginia Vaske, principal of Murray Language Academy, comments: *It's not about learning to work harder; many of us are working as hard as we can. It's about learning to work smarter.*

How will we pay for it? Arts integration can be implemented through existing resources (such as a classroom teacher working with the school's music teacher), or with additional resources supported by external public and private funders (such as partnerships of schools and community resources). Ultimately, however, individual schools and districts must prioritize the use of their own resources if arts integration is going to be supported in any sort of meaningful, ongoing manner. Schools need clear, explicit policies articulating the importance of the arts; they also need regular access to artists and arts specialists, to high-quality professional development in the arts, to materials, and to regular, well-structured planning time. Only then can arts integration reach its full, unexplored potential for providing long-term benefits to young people. Having a few pioneering teachers and principals fighting a constant up-hill battle to include the arts is an inefficient way of improving our schools. There is a growing national interest, accelerated by access to the Internet, in school districts forming learning partnerships using community resources. If arts integration works for you and your students, tell colleagues and friends about your successes. Advocate for the arts in your school and in your community.

MEANINGFUL PARTNERSHIPS, MEANINGFUL LEARNING

David Flatley, Arts Administrator, says: *Vision needs to include living examples. Vision is found in the halls, heard in the lunchroom, and seen on the faces of children learning. The projects are living documents, full of rich detail and stories.*

Collaboration for better teaching and learning is a process; it doesn't happen overnight. Artist and arts education consultant Karen Erickson has worked with a variety of arts partnerships for years. She compares the process to dream weaving (i.e., helping others dream and creating a plan to achieve that dream). Erickson affirms the notion that a partnership is based on trust and community. That process takes time and planning, as well as leadership. She describes the procedure for "designing down the curriculum." Just as you would conceive of a finished garment and then plan the patterns and processes to get to that garment, so a partnership must work backward. What will the work look like in 5 or 10 years? What will the students be doing? What will they be seeing? What are they doing and seeing now? The dream weavers take the time to dream collaboratively with partners (Erickson, 1998).

Jane Remer, author and editor of *Beyond Enrichment: Building Effective Arts Partnerships in Schools and Your Community* (1996), described two types of partnership that occur in a cycle. The first is a *simple transaction*, in which a school engages with an arts group or an artist who essentially are vendors selling their expertise and time in a specific way for a short period of time. As you look at your resources and your support for arts programming in your school, you may see that this simple transaction may be the most feasible way to get started.

Remer's second type of partnership is far more complex and interesting. When the school and an arts organization or artist decide to work together to define students' needs and create a viable arts program, the partnership is no longer a one-time event, but can now be thought of as a *joint venture*. Only when partnerships are joint ventures over time can the arts programming be really integrative. Only when people communicate and learn from each other, sharing in teaching and planning, can a true partnership succeed. Then participants become dream weavers.

If the arts are going to become a real part of improving our schools, there has to be an honest, serious conversation among educators, artists, and community members. What's needed is a long-term conversation, along with some redeployment of resources. The arts are there, the schools are there, the communities are there, the families are there, and the resources are all there. Bridges have to be built among these interdependent but isolated communities. One of the reasons that it has been fairly easy for the CAPE model to spread (CAPE has been replicated in nine cities across the United States, the United Kingdom, and Canada) is that the model, in which existing resources commit to long-term co-planning of coherent curriculum, can be explained to someone in a fairly short time. Listeners can then decide whether to do it. It's really about spreading an idea of some trust and collaboration between people who care about our children and have not had enough opportunities to plan together how that caring can take place collaboratively in schools.

≺   ≺   ≺   ≻   ≻   ≻

So getting started isn't that hard, but there are some keys to a productive dialogue between teachers and artists. First, arts integration requires people to listen to each other, and that's often hard to do. There are separations between regions, between classes, between cultures, between languages, and between religions, as well as among urban, suburban, and rural populations. With the advent of television, we have changed from a language-based communication system to an image-based communication system. We are split between populations who communicate through text and those who communicate through pictures. There is a *digital divide* between those who are immersed in new technology and those who do not have adequate access. It seems clear that the more time we spend at our computers, the more we will need to find new ways of communicating—listening and speaking—with each other in an authentic way. The role of the arts in our society is also shifting as artists also engage in the new technology and participate in new modes of communication. Still, in the classroom, regardless of the medium, children, teachers, and artists need to continue to listen to each other.

There has been a drift in the arts away from being something one participated in to a domain split between producers of art and consumers of art. When Americans attended community dances at the turn of the century or listened to concerts at the local bandshell, they were there as a part of a community. Community choirs, folk art, street corner singers, neighborhood bands, and wedding dances are all emblems of participatory art that is also communal. That is the spirit of arts integration and it is essential for arts programming in schools for all children. Young people's experience of museums and professional art institutions need to recapture that spirit of community access and participation.

Artists, teachers, and parents have the opportunity to develop exciting, creative curriculum for children that returns them to that community, engages the skills they will need in the 21st century, and expands their world. If artists are going to reengage their citizenship, and their responsibility to share the issues of improving our schools, they're going to have to rise to the challenge of articulating who they are and why they belong in schools. There are few images of the artists' commitment to creativity and expressiveness that are compatible with the routines of class periods, bells, and external standards that we associate with schooling. There's a nagging notion in the myths of schooling that all creativity and artistic expression is some sort of irresponsible, anarchistic messing around. If you're serious, you have to be joyless and rigid! Arts partnerships reveal that nothing could be further from the truth. To learn this, however, teachers, artists, and administrators in schools and in arts organizations must listen and learn. When asked what teachers learn from working with artists, one parent responded with just three words: "To let go."

School people, policymakers, and community members can, in a meaningful partnership, realize the rigor that's involved in creativity. As Harvey Daniels of the Illinois Writing Project puts it, "Rigor doesn't have to be rigor mortis." Freedom and rigor are not opposites. When students take increasing responsibility for their own learning, as they do in arts integration initiatives, they provide practical demonstrations that we can have freedom, expressiveness, creativity, seriousness, rigor, and discipline—all at the same time—when the curriculum is rich and complex. Arts integrated teaching is the perfect arena for this demonstration.

Effective partnerships take time to develop. Productive new ideas require people to look at their old assumptions differently. Many artists remember schooling as a structure that they must resist. On entering the school archway, the dancer remembers how often she was told to stop fidgeting; the first time a visual artist revisits an elementary classroom, he recalls how he was told to stop drawing outside the lines. For many artists, their primary experience of school was one of constraint.

However, many teachers and parents remember the arts they experienced in school as a string of negative conclusions—"I can't dance," "I can't sing," "I can't draw." So the mere presence of the artist makes the teacher want to run screaming from the building! These old terrors haunt the room when the teacher and artist start politely planning together, and it may distort the negotiation between them. The only way that these demons can be dispelled is through the authentic contact that comes from shared work that is genuinely integrated. Karen Erickson calls this *viewing from both sides of the mountain.*

One of the primary functions of arts partnerships, such as the ones we've described in this book, is to encourage a discussion between people who have a shared agenda—the development of children—but who work from different frameworks. Initially, teachers may see the arts in their classroom strictly as a way to service other content fields. Artists see their work and their art forms as inherently valuable for children. Each learns what the other has to offer. It is this bumping together of different points of view that makes the work rich. We hope this book has given you permission ... permission to explore, to let kids explore, to form alliances, and to seek resources to deepen the curriculum. This is what it's really about: enriching the lives of young people in our schools. Arts integration truly creates a renaissance of meaningful learning in the classroom.

REFERENCES

Catterall, J. S., & Waldorf, L. (1999). Chicago Arts Partnerships in Education summary evaluation. In E. B. Fiske (Ed.), *Champions of change: The impact of the arts on learning.* The Arts Education Partnerships, The Presidents's Committee on the Arts and Humanities, GE Fund, John D. and Catherine T. MacArthur Foundation, 47–62.

Dreeszen, C., Aprill, A., & Deasy, R. (1999). *Learning partnerships: Improving learning in schools with arts partners in the community.* Washington, DC: Arts Education Partnership, Council of Chief State School Officers.

Erickson, K. (1998). *Dream weaving.* Unpublished manuscript.

Flatley, D. (1998). *Beyond the vision and the dollars: Succeeding with a community-based partnership.* Unpublished manuscript.

Gallas, K. (1994). *The languages of learning: How children talk, write, dance, draw, and sing their understanding of the world.* New York: Teachers College Press.

Heathcote, D., & Bolton, G. (1995). *Drama for learning.* Portsmouth, NH: Heinemann.

Herndon, J. (1965). *The way it spozed to be.* New York: Simon & Schuster.

Herndon, J. (1971). *How to survive in your native land.* New York: Simon & Schuster.

Paley, V.G. (1990). *The boy who would be a helicopter: The uses of storytelling in the classroom.* Cambridge, MA: Harvard University Press.

Remer, J. (1996). *Beyond enrichment: Building effective arts partnerships with schools and your community.* New York: American Council for the Arts.

Stringer, E. T. (1996). *Action research: A handbook for practitioners.* Thousand Oaks, CA: Sage.

Wilhelm, J. D. (1997). *"You gotta BE the book": Teaching engaged and reflective reading with adolescents.* New York: Teachers College Press.

Thanks to these participants in the ETA/Muntu Partnership for sharing their conversation:

Ms. *Abena Joan Brown—ETA Creative Arts Foundation*

Ms. *Ethel Capers—Partnership Coordinator*

Ms. *Joan Gray—Muntu Dance Theatre*

Ms. *Mary Hoover—Teacher, McCosh Elementary School*

Ms. *Nina Robinson—Teacher, Metro Program, Crane High School*

Ms. *Dorothy Sanders—Teacher, Brownell Elementary School*

Ms. *Carolyn Washington—Music Teacher, Parkside Academy*

Appendix A: Chicago Arts Partnerships In Education Funders

The Chicago Arts Partnerships in Education (CAPE) was catalyzed by Marshall Field's and has been supported by a collaboration of foundations and corporations:

Ameritech

Bank of America (formerly Continental Bank Foundation)

Chicago Community Trust

Chicago Tribune Foundation

Arie and Ida Crown Memorial

Gaylord & Dorothy Donnelley 1983 Gift Trust

Richard H. Driehaus Foundation

Fel-Pro Mecklenburger Foundation

Lloyd A. Fry Foundation

GE Fund

Harris Foundation

Joyce Foundation

Alexander Julian Foundation for Aesthetic Understanding and Appreciation

Mayer and Morris Kaplan Family Foundation

Kraft Foods, an operating company of Philip Morris Companies, Inc.

Reva and David Logan Foundation

Louis R. Lurie Foundation

John D. and Catherine T. MacArthur Foundation

Marshall Field's

McDougal Family Foundation

Northern Trust Company

Polk Bros. Foundation

Prince Charitable Trusts

Sara Lee Foundation

Wallace—Reader's Digest Fund

360° Communications

Woods Fund of Chicago

WPWR-TV Channel 50 Foundation

The CAPE is also partially supported by a grant from the **Illinois Arts Council**, a state agency.

The goal of CAPE is to improve schools by making quality arts education a central part of the daily learning experience of students in Chicago Public Schools. It seeks to fully integrate the arts with the overall educational program of schools, recognizing the cultural diversity of the city and creating for every child sequential and comprehensive arts experiences that are connected to the entire curriculum and to learning in the broader school community.

Appendix B: Chicago Arts Partnerships In Education Overviews

Bridgeport-Armour Square-Near North Arts Partnership

Anchor Organization:

- Robert Healy Elementary School

Schools:

- Robert Healy Elementary
- William B. Ogden School
- Mark Sheridan Math and Science Academy

Arts Organizations:

- Terra Museum of American Art
- Community TV Network
- Jackie Samuel
- Donna Mandel
- The Suzuki-Orff School for Young Musicians
- Hyde Park Art Center
- The Chicago Moving Company
- Pros Arts Studio
- Art Resources in Teaching
- Chicago Dance Medium
- Department of Art and Design, Chicago State University
- Creative Directions

Community Organizations:

- Chinese American Service League
- Erikson Institute
- McGuane Park

Philosophy:

The Partnership seeks to:

1. develop an arts integrated curriculum that increases students' enthusiasm for learning, stimulates creative thinking, and encourages risk taking;
2. Offer children the opportunity to engage in all art forms as independent disciplines and pursue art forms in which they have a special interest;
3. develop teachers' capacity to create and deliver integrated art lessons;
4. develop a system of writing and sharing arts units integrated with math/science at Mark Sheridan, language arts/social studies at Ogden, and multiculturalism at Healy;
5. Develop and implement its own academic and performance-based authentic assessments; and
6. increase neighborhood arts programs for after school, weekends, and summers.

Demographics:

The three participating schools are located in the Bridgeport, Armour Square, and Near North neighborhoods. The schools reflect Chinese, Latin-American, European, and African-American heritages and include bilingual programs in Cantonese, Mandarin, and Spanish.

Methodology and Timeline:

Teachers and artists revise and organize past Partnership curricula, creating 10-session units integrating fine arts and/or technology with the teaching of another subject. Participating teachers take courses in technology and fine arts and work with an artist or computer mentor in the classroom. The newly developed curricula is housed in each school's library and is presented at grade-level meetings.

Artists are working with classes at every grade level in drama, dance, clay, and video. Special attention is given to sequencing activities and sharing curricula with all teachers in a grade level. This participation has given special attention to the role that in-school arts specialists can play in developing integrated instruction in collaboration with external arts partners and other classroom teachers. Students and teachers from all three schools are given opportunities to participate in culminating events at the other schools. The partnerships offer teacher training courses in arts integration to the entire Chicago Public School system.

ETA/Muntu Arts in Education Consortium

Co-Anchors:
- ETA Creative Arts Foundation
- Muntu Dance Theatre

Schools:
- Brownell Elementary School
- O'Keefe Elementary School
- McCosh Elementary School
- Parkside Academy
- Metro Crane High School

Arts Organizations:
- ETA Creative Arts Foundation
- Muntu Dance Theatre
- Community Film Workshop

Philosophy:

The concept of collective responsibility for the education of children is endemic to traditional African culture. The ETA/Muntu Arts in Education Consortium values this concept and seeks to involve the whole community in the cognitive and social development of children through the arts. This creative education process, involving arts and community organizations, creates effective collaborative partnerships. The Consortium respects the autonomy and integrity of each school and encourages each school to develop a program that is unique and distinctive to the school and its environment and improvement plan.

Demographics:

ETA/MUNTU serves schools with African-American student populations in several neighborhoods on Chicago's South Side, including Woodlawn, Garfield, and South Shore.

Methodology and Timeline:

ETA/Muntu Arts in Education Consortium will continue the following successful aspects of the program:

- student art experiences with opportunities to demonstrate what has been learned via performances, presentations, and so on;
- parent workshops allowing hands-on opportunities in various genres;
- professional development workshops for teachers and artists; and
- LSC support and involvement.

With the implementation of the CAPE program, various partners in the Consortium who developed working relationships were able to encourage true collaboration and strengthen processes of working together. As a result, partners, students, and the community have been empowered to implement a conscious and coherent approach to the integration of arts into the educational curriculum. The Consortium is committed to continuing the arts integrated education programs in the future and to finding the requisite resources. Recognizing that the long-term objective is to enable teachers to use the arts as a learning methodology, sustainability planning will investigate the potential for and application of distance learning. Although distance learning will never supplant live interaction with professional artists, it may effectively augment the program particularly in the areas of teacher training and parent assistance appreciating the arts in the family environment.

Hawthorne / Agassiz Elementary Schools Arts Partnership

Anchor Organization:

- Hawthorne Scholastic Academy

Schools:

- Hawthorne Scholastic Academy
- Louis J. Agassiz Elementary School

Arts Organizations:

- Lookingglass Theatre Company
- Professional visual artists and dancers

Community Organizations:

- The Junior League of Chicago

Philosophy:

The Hawthorne/Agassiz Neighborhood Arts Partnership was formed to accomplish four principal educational goals:

1. Develop and implement a comprehensive fine arts curriculum for dance, drama, music, and visual art from preschool through eighth grade;
2. Develop a curriculum integrating the fine arts with other curricular areas;

3. Celebrate and explore cultural diversity through the implementation of this integrated fine arts program; and
4. Engage parents in their children's education through participation in the Partnership.

Both schools are rethinking curriculum, giving up reliance on textbook information, and focusing on integrated curriculum and participatory learning. The program includes significant involvement of parents and the Junior League. The Partnership has made friends out of neighbors. The schools had not collaborated significantly before this project.

Demographics:

Both schools are located in Lakeview, a neighborhood typified by economic extremes from luxury high rises on Lake Shore Drive to homeless shelters on Belmont Avenue. The student population of 1,000 is 40% Latino, 30% African American, and 30% White. The Agassiz student population includes 50 autistic children. Members of Lookingglass Theatre have experience in developing arts curriculum for autistic populations. The professional artists engaged in the Partnership come from diverse ethnic backgrounds, including African-American, Hispanic, Moroccan, and Ecuadorian. The cadre of professional visual artists includes several parents.

Methodology and Timeline:

The Hawthorne/Agassiz Arts Partnership anticipates three significant changes:

1. The Partnership exceeded its goal of developing and implementing arts integrated units for all grade levels at both schools. Implementing 28 units, as opposed to the last year's high of 34, provides more time and concentrates the focus of participating teachers, artists, students, and administrators. This time allows them to refine and delve more deeply into arts integrated unit activities.
2. Plans proceed to create a systematic method for sustaining the Partnership's work. In 1998, the Hawthorne/Agassiz Arts Partnership's Steering Committee, consisting of teachers, artists, parents, technical consultants, and arts administrators, participated in four intensive workshops to develop and implement a long-term strategic plan for the program. Planning continues through the Curriculum Committee and at the in-school coordinators' monthly meetings.
3. The newly created T-I-E-S/Annenberg Project is a consortium of three CAPE schools—Hawthorne, Mark Sheridan, and Healy—plus Lincoln Elementary School. The Project aims to provide teachers with professional development resources as they develop arts integrated units.

Lakeview Education and Arts Partnership (LEAP)

Anchor Organization:

- Chicago Teachers' Center/Northeastern Illinois University

Schools:

- Lakeview High School
- Audubon Elementary School
- Blaine Elementary School
- Ravenswood Elementary School

Arts Organization:

- Beacon Street Gallery

Community Organizations:

- Lakeview Chamber of Commerce
- Sulzer Regional Library

Philosophy:

LEAP encourages teachers to reassess traditional teaching methods as they restructure the curriculum to fully integrate the arts into the classroom. Teachers are also encouraged to keep current on relevant research and best practice. Administrators support the teachers' efforts by encouraging professional development, adopting clear evaluation methods, and designating financial resources. The Partnership encourages parents to accept the changes taking place in the traditional classroom and to get involved in the learning processes. Artists must be able to communicate the processes of their media to teachers and students, remembering that the goal of art integrated education is student improvement.

Demographics:

LEAP schools are located in the Lakeview neighborhood on Chicago's North Side. Student populations are primarily Latino, with significant percentages of African-American, Native-American, and Asian/Pacific Islander students. A high percentage of students receive free or reduced lunch, and a significant number have limited English proficiency.

Methodology and Timeline:

Now that LEAP has blossomed and matured to serve students in every grade level, K to 12, the focus for the current year is on planning and professional development activities that will sustain the program for the long term. Ongoing community meetings, family nights, exhibitions, advisory council meetings, and one-on-one interaction with parents and community leaders will continue, driven by the vision to permanently establish the program long after *direct* funding has elapsed.

LEAP is developing the resources, workshops, and support mechanisms necessary for teachers to grow developmentally in their abilities to use the arts as a part of the everyday teaching methodology. LEAP will:

- maintain support for teacher/artist collaborations;
- create artist workshops and classroom support for small groups of teachers to implement arts learning on their own;
- provide more arts immersion workshops for larger groups to strengthen teachers' capacity and comfort in using the arts; and
- expand and redefine the role of the in-school arts specialists so that they can be more involved in developing integrated lessons in the core curriculum.

Implementing these recommendations will envelop the schools in a supportive environment that will allow the arts to flourish as a catalyst for change and learning.

Finally, LEAP is forming teams at each school to study the long-term impact of our work and what each school individually needs to focus on to sustain the initiative.

Lincoln Park High School Partnership

Anchor Organization:

- Lincoln Park High School (Arts in the City Schools)

School:

- Lincoln Park High School

Arts Organizations:

- Art Encounter
- Hedwig Dances
- Lookingglass Theater
- MPAACT
- Old Town School of Folk Music
- Ms. Betty Sitbon
- Textile Arts Center
- Victory Gardens Theatre

Philosophy:

Lincoln Park High School's vision is to create and maintain an environment where students are empowered to reach their potential as self-directed learners and responsible citizens. The school is committed to the *Total Quality Management* approach of change and continuous improvement. By examining the integration of arts throughout the curriculum, the staff has also reassessed the entire high school curriculum and how it serves the needs of the students. The overall curriculum has been sequenced within each discipline, aligned across the disciplines, and integrated throughout the disciplines. Integrating arts into the curriculum makes learning more active and immediate to the student, and changes the way students, teachers, and parents view knowledge.

Demographics:

Lincoln Park High School has an enrollment of 1,986 students. The two immediate neighborhoods—Lincoln Park and Cabrini Green—sit at opposite ends of the socioeconomic scale. The student population is 44% African American, 20% Latino, 26% White, and 10% Asian and other. Lincoln Park High School has an International Baccalaureate curriculum and a well-respected fine arts department that includes dance, drama, choral, and instrumental music. The school's graduation rate is 66%.

Methodology and Timeline:

Arts learning is integrated into instruction through a variety of strategies:
- The Drama/Language Arts Conflict Resolution Unit reaches freshmen early in the year.
- Freshmen and sophomore students participate in the Dance/Physical Education Program, which includes World Dance and American Dance units.
- All freshmen spend 25 minutes every day in arts training through the Freshman Advisories program.
- Drama units in foreign languages, language arts, and history for freshman, sophomore, and junior classes.
- Visual arts units in math, chemistry, language arts, and foreign languages for freshman, sophomore, and junior/senior classes.
- Music units in history, math, and foreign languages for freshman and sophomore classes.
- The arts/science program includes units in Drama/Biology, Dance/Physics, and Chemistry/Visual Arts.

Teachers will receive training through an artist–teacher-mentoring process. A similar process on a teacher–teacher basis will be used to pass units on within the school.

Tlahui Mexican Fine Arts Center Museum Partnership

Anchor Organization:
- Mexican Fine Arts Center Museum

Schools:

- Jose Clemente Orozco Academy of Fine Arts and Science
- Telpochcalli Elementary School

Arts Organization:

- Mexican Fine Arts Center Museum

Philosophy:

The Tlahui Mexican Fine Arts Center Museum Partnership links the museum with Orozco and Telpochcalli elementary schools in an educational endeavor designed to meet the following goals:

1. Create integrated curricula in which the arts are used as subjects for learn-ing and as pedagogical tools.
2. Establish the schools' curriculum and instruction based on the arts and culture of Mexico and Mexican communities in the United States.

This project is based on the critical need to improve students' educational out-comes at each of the participating schools. Recognizing this need, each school's efforts to improve those outcomes center on the arts and the cultural institutions involved in this project. The arts and culture of Mexico are treated as a bridge to learning about other subject areas and cultures instead of the end point of the cur-riculum. The curriculum is a process of inquiry that uses the students' lives as sub-ject matter.

Demographics:

Students are primarily Mexican-Americans living in the Pilsen area and attending Jose Clemente Orozco Academy or Telpochcalli Elementary School. Telpochcalli (a satellite from Spry Elementary) opened its doors in 1996 with a team of teachers and artists using the teaching methods and curriculum from the first 3 years of the Partnership.

Methodology and Timeline:

Planning.   Planning time will be scheduled throughout the year to ensure maintenance of the co-teaching relationship with artists and to provide necessary assessment of the programs. Mini-intensive sessions allow project leaders to cre-ate strategic assessment methods, develop curricula to strengthen thematic units, and plan for full integration of parents into the program.

Research and Resources.   Much of the work from the mini-intensive ses-sions, as well as the Golden Apple Foundation's Storytelling Workshop, is being in-corporated into the Mexican Curriculum Development Project (MCDP). This teacher resource databank will include background information, research links, and lesson plans under select thematic units. It will also establish links between curricula. Continuing cross-site visits to other CAPE schools will foster potential linkages and facilitate the exchange of ideas and information.

Parental Involvement. Through a new project focusing on the exhibition of student and parent artwork, the Museum's curator will introduce teachers, students, and parents to gallery management. The project will require that all participants learn the steps necessary in administering gallery space, including curatorial preparation and exhibit organization.

One of the Partnership's many parent workshops and seminars will center on strengthening the project's music program. By creating a space for parents to both learn and teach their children the rich musical traditions of their culture, the Partnership further welcomes parents as educational partners and builds an essential bridge to the community.

Pilsen Arts Partnership

Co-Anchors:

- Pros Arts Studio
- John A. Walsh School

School:

- John A. Walsh School

Arts Organization:

- Pros Arts Studio

Community Organizations:

- Casa Aztlan
- Dvorak Park

Philosophy:

The Pilsen Arts Partnership believes that arts integrated curricula are essential for children to develop into productive and successful adults. The Partnership seeks to bring students' everyday experiences and cultural traditions into the classroom while employing the resources and perspectives of the broader community. Teachers function as facilitators of this process, leading to long-term school reform.

Demographics:

Pilsen, historically a port of entry for immigrants, now estimates that 85% of residents are of Mexican descent. The Partnership validates the neighborhood's cultural heritage while providing tools for participation in a global society to both students and their parents. Walsh School has 440 students, covering Grades K to 7, with 30 faculty members, many of whom have been at the school for over 15 years. The student population is 96% Latino. In 50% of the homes, Spanish is the spoken language. Parents are encouraged to support the school and participate in the school's efforts to provide the tools for a bright future.

Methodology and Timeline:

The Pilsen Arts Partnership has had great success in developing active involvement of families and youth in community-based activities. Teachers, artists, parents, and community partners involved with the Partnership will be surveyed to identify key components of the program and skills needed by teachers to continue activities. Arts integrated curriculum activity has been extended to include every classroom from kindergarten through seventh grade. Participating artists work with teachers as mentors to further develop their skills, confidence, and understanding of integrating the arts into the teaching of other curriculum subjects.

South Side Arts Partnerships

Anchor Organization:

- The Hyde Park Art Center

Schools:

- William H. Ray Elementary
- Murray Language Academy

Arts Organizations:

- The Goodman Theatre
- Hyde Park Art Center
- Chicago Children's Choir
- The David and Alfred Smart Museum of Art

Philosophy:

The South Side Arts Partnership seeks to enhance arts literacy and elevate the value of the arts as key disciplines that are taught and integrated within and across the curriculum. The Partnership seeks to redefine the relationships among students, teachers, school staff, artists, parents, and community members by engaging them in planning, implementation, and evaluation of an integrated arts curriculum. The Partnership utilizes the artist as a resource to provide consultation, communication, and documentation to facilitate arts integration in the schools. Recognizing that different students learn through different modalities, teachers develop lessons that include activities related to a variety of art forms (visual arts, music, performing arts, etc.). The program assists students in understanding the importance of the arts across time and culture. In an effort to increase student participation and allow the Partnership greater impact of art integrated activities, the program targets third- to eighth-grade students for participation in program planning, implementation, and evaluation. The schools develop a culture where the arts provide a framework for instruction in all subject areas and welcome the input of teachers, parents, artists, and students.

Demographics:

South Side Arts Partnership's schools are located in Hyde Park on Chicago's South Side. Murray Language Academy is a small K to 8 magnet school of 350 students (75% African American, 20% White) with about 20% from low-income families. William H. Ray Elementary is a K to 8 school of 760 students (59% African American, 27% White, 8% Asian, and 4% Latino) with about 26% from low-income families. Approximately 7% of the students have limited English proficiency. The students of Ray School speak more than 20 different primary languages.

Methodology and Timeline:

Through the leadership of school principals and art specialists, and excited student response, teachers have come to recognize how the arts can contribute to more interesting lessons and give students an opportunity for creative expression:

* *Artist/Teacher Selection Process.*   The project coordinator will attend staff meetings and be available at the schools to talk with teachers about their residency ideas, suggest residency artists, and discuss teacher-integrated units. Teachers will be provided with a chart of what other teachers at their grade level are doing to encourage idea exchanges.

* *Classroom Activities and Teacher/Artist Planning.*   The core of the Partnership's commitment to sustaining arts activity in the classroom is increased artist–teacher–student contact time. Teachers and artists will work together on specialized units of their own choice that speak directly to work being done in the classroom. Partnership leadership firmly believes that changes in teacher behavior are the direct result of classroom experiences with artists.

* *Staff Development/Arts Integration Sharing.* Two staff-development workshops will be given at each school to help teachers gain techniques to integrate the arts into the curriculum on their own. They will also offer an opportunity for teachers to share the work they have done with artists and individually.

* *Teacher Integrated Units.* In a new component to the project, teachers will develop a curriculum unit integrating the arts without the help of an artist. Artists will be made available as advisors and observers to this process, but teachers will take the responsibility for integrating the arts into their own teaching.

West Town Arts Partnership

Co-Anchors:

- Sherwood Conservatory of Music
- Northwestern University Settlement Association

Schools:

- James Otis Elementary School
- Elizabeth Peabody Elementary School
- William H. Wells Community Academy

Arts Organizations:

- Chicago Symphony Orchestra
- The Goodman Theatre
- Mordine Company Dance Theatre
- The Marwen Foundation
- Partners in Mime, Inc.
- Sherwood Conservatory of Music

Community Organization:

- Northwestern University Settlement Association

Philosophy:

The West Town Arts Partnership is dedicated to the development and implementation of multicultural, sequential, arts integrated curricula that encourage students' exploration and discovery of self-identity, cultural identity, and community identity. The Partnership believes that arts integrated curricula can play a significant role in school reform, permanently shifting how schools set goals, plan curricula, deliver and evaluate instruction, and foster learning. The Partnership emphasizes: artistic expression indigenous and relevant to the community; active participation of West Town students, parents, educators, arts organizations, community organizations, and residents; and use of the arts as a tool for nurturing life-long learning.

Demographics:

West Town is a predominantly Latino community on the city's Near Northwest Side. The schools of West Town have historically served children of immigrants and migrants. Partnership schools in West Town experience a mobility rate of up to 40%.

Methodology and Timeline:

- *Establish a permanent resource library at each school.* To assist teachers in continuing arts integrated curriculum work, as well as teach the basics in specific arts discipline areas, the Partnership will gather and compile an organized reference resource housed at each school. The resource will contain the following materials: lesson plans; examples of work; evaluation approaches; unit documentation; "Introduction to the Arts" curricula and resource materials; lists of arts organizations, artists, and community members who have skills and interests in the arts; and other written, video, audio, and visual material.

• *Identify a core of teachers to continue the program.* The Partnership will build on the enthusiastic core of teachers in each school who now regularly use arts integrated approaches in their classrooms. To sustain and increase the number of teachers participating in arts integrated education, the Partnership will empower a committed group of teachers to determine, plan, and implement professional development activities for the schools. Development activities include workshops, classroom exchanges, mentorships, joint planning time, field trips, and curriculum development and refinement.

• *Solidify relationships with current arts partners and develop new relationships to ensure continued arts in the classrooms.* Direct arts services in the classroom will be provided primarily through Americorps program artists. The Partnership will increase the use of community resources and residents in Partnership activities.

Arts Centered Educators (ACEs) Partnership

Anchor Organization:
• Whirlwind Performance Company

Schools:
• Pulaski Community Academy
• Banneker Elementary School

Artists:
• Glenda Baker
• Cynthia Weiss
• Donna Mandel

Community Organizations:
• Coalition of Essential Schools

Philosophy:

Arts Centered Educators (ACEs), a coalition of artists and schools, are working to develop two arts-centered schools in Chicago. Arts-centered schools are more than regular schools with lots of arts going on in them. They are schools in which the arts make inquiry, creativity, and expression central to the learning process. This initiative is as much about school change as it is about arts. This initiative is consciously conceived of as an *organizational change* project.

Demographics:

Banneker Elementary is a South Side neighborhood school serving African-American students, and Pulaski Community Academy is a North Side community academy serving mostly Latino students.

Methodology and Timeline:

At both schools, ACEs will become a school within a school, starting with kindergarten and extending through eighth grade. Education will change from textbook-based to inquiry-based, and curriculum will be created, not just delivered, by ACEs' teachers. Arts-centered, inquiry-based learning will take place in each ACEs classroom at least 10 hours a week. Team teaching between teachers and artists will be the basis for their relationship in the school. This program is time-intensive for artists in the classroom with teachers. Veteran ACEs teachers will become resources for new ACEs teachers. Attention is given to providing sufficient training for students and teachers in the arts disciplines so that the curriculum has integrity in the arts as well as in the other content areas. Curriculum units culminate in exhibitions of student work. ACEs teachers will share arts integrated lessons with nonACEs teachers by "guest" teaching ACEs lessons in "buddy" classes as a way of impacting teachers outside of the ACEs school within the school. Both schools have been piloting Parent and Community involvement activities over the last 2 years. Building on this work, each school will develop full Parent and Community Involvement. The teacher–artist team continues to be the focal point of ACEs' structure. We will continue to fine tune authentic assessment of student learning and continue the co-planned development of arts integrated curriculum organized around "Big Ideas." Each team will come to Whirlwind in September and January to create units through 3-hour planning sessions facilitated by Whirlwind staff. Ten weeks will be allotted for each unit, with an 11th week reserved after each unit for creating documentation. There is a recognized developmental process for teacher involvement in the ACEs project: orientation, immersion, and independence.

Appendix C:
Sample Planning Forms
for Arts Integration

Cape Sample Planning Form #1

Teacher —————————————————————————————

Artist ——————————————————————————————

Unit Name/Topic ————————————————————————

Materials Needed

Work Plan
(Activities for each stage of the integrated curriculum learning cycle)

GETTING STARTED

GOING THROUGH THE CURRICULUM/DOING THE WORK

GOING BEYOND THE CURRICULUM/ASSESSING THE WORK

Cape Sample Planning Form # 2

Teacher _____

Artist _____

Unit Name _____

Organizing Concept/Big Idea and/or Essential Questions

Access Points into the Curriculum
(novel, picture book, skills, process)

Arts Concepts Addressed

Content Area Concepts Addressed

Curriculum Frameworks/Standards Addressed

Projects/Products To Be Created

Culminating Event(s)

Assessment and Reflection Plan

Cape Sample Planning Form #3

A Friendly Guide to using the CAPE Arts Integrated Curriculum Planning and Documentation Form

This form is designed to be used at the beginning of a unit, to help artist/teacher teams plan their work together, and at the end, to document the work accomplished. This form is a useful too to bring to the planning table; it will serve as a worksheet to gather ideas, resources and materials. When documenting the unit, the team can add to the planning form with new information discovered in the course of the work. CAPE has created this form using the expertise and experience of the CAPE partnerships, with special thanks to the Lakeview Education and Arts Partnership (LEAP). We suggest that teachers and artists in your partnership use this form to create future arts integrated curriculum.

How to Fill Out This Form

1. Overview

Briefly describe the intent of this unit in 3–5 sentences. If someone were to read only this narrative, this overview should describe the vibrancy of your work.

2. Big Ideas and Inquiry Questions

Many successful art integrated curricular units are organized around an overarching concept that serves to connect the art and academic content areas. Examples of Big Ideas: *Movement and Migration, Mapping Our Environment, Interdependence in Dance and Science, Perspective and Point-of-View in Historical Conflict, Turning Points and Transformations.*

Inquiry questions, often generated by the students themselves, can also frame a curriculum.
Examples of inquiry questions: *What makes a community hero? From where does hope come? How do we learn to adapt to a new environment?*

Please list the Big Ideas or concepts that connect your art integrated unit, if applicable.

3. Academic Content Area Objectives

List 3–5 learning objectives you have for your students from your classroom curriculum. Example: Students will: *study the components that make up a community.... Understand the causes of the Civil War.... Study the animal and plant life of different habitats.*

4. Arts Content Area Objectives

Integrated lessons are much stronger when art content objectives are clearly articulated. Artists should state the art concepts they plan to teach. Please list 3–5 arts content area objectives you have for this unit. Examples: Students will learn *to use negative and positive shapes in a collage composition ... understand how levels in dance (high, medium & low) are used to create variety ... learn how to adapt a text in the writing of a play.*

5. Social and Critical Thinking Objectives

Please list the social and critical thinking objectives you have for this unit. Example: Students will learn how to: *take on different roles when working in cooperative groups ... to work in peer groups during writer's workshop ... to compare and contrast primary source texts ... to decode popular media.*

6. Key Words and Vocabulary

Please list keywords and vocabulary that students will learn/learned in the course of this unit.

7. Time Frame

Enter the schedule, dates and times of classroom work for this unit.

8. Sequence of Learning Activities

Please list the activities and lessons that made up this unit. Under Access Points—How did you get started? Describe what you used to engage the students in the beginning. An access point can be a field trip, group discussion, a work of art, short story, film, performance, guest speaker, KWL chart or student-generated questions.

In the "Through" section list the variety of hands-on learning activities used in this unit.

9. Assessment

Describe the assessments you used including pre- and posttests, rubrics, journal entries, exit slips, portfolios. Describe assessments used for the integrated project as well as the separate subject areas and art forms if applicable.

Questions 10–13 are self-explanatory.

14. Quotes and Comments

Quotes and comments bring the voice of the participants into the documentation and help make the lessons come alive. Some questions that could be asked of the artists, teachers and students could include: *What did you learn from this arts integrated unit? How did this unit connect to other things you are doing in the classroom? How was this learning experience different? What was the most memorable part of this unit? What would you like to see done differently next time?*
The principal and parents could be asked: *How do you feel that this arts integration project helped the students learn? What should be the role of the arts in schools?*

Thank you for taking the time to carefully document your work. We are developing a wonderfully rich collection of arts integrated curriculum that will benefit our students and colleagues inside CAPE schools and throughout the country.

CAPE Arts Integrated Curriculum Planning and Documentation Form

Title of your Arts Integrated Curriculum Unit:

Created by:

Teacher(s)

Artist(s)

Grade:

School:

Name of Partnership:

Contact Person:

Phone, fax and e-mail address

1. Overview (brief paragraph that describe this unit)

2. Big Ideas and Inquiry Questions (if applicable)

3. Academic Content Area Objectives

4. Arts Content Area Objectives

5. Social and Critical Thinking Objectives

6. Key Words and Vocabulary

7. Time Frame

8. Sequence of Learning Activities
- Into: How will you/did you start your unit? What will be your Access Points?

- Through: What are/were the learning activities in this units?

- Beyond: What will be/was the culminating event and reflection activities?

9. Assessment
What are your plans for teacher assessment and student self-assessment?

10. Resources
Print Materials: list the books, videotapes, and web sites, used in this unit

Human Resources: Field Trips, Interviews

11. Plans for Parent Involvement

12. Materials & Supplies needed for the Art Integrated Unit

13. State Goals and Learning Standards Addressed Documentation

14. Quotes and Comment from participants involved in this Arts Integrated Unit:

Teacher(s)

Artist(s)

Student(s)

Parents(s)

Principal

Documentation of this arts integrated unit can include: examples of student work, preliminary sketches and finished products, photographs and slides that record the process, reflections and exit slips that reveal the students's thought processes in the course of this unit, teacher and student journal entries.

Please attach an example of student's work and/or photos.

Appendix D:
Sample Unit Plans
for Arts Integration

Making Shape Of Our Environment—Primary School: An Arts Integrated Kindergarten Unit

Teacher(s):   Wendee DeSent,
Tricia Rownd,
Kelly Shannon

Artists: Winifred Haun/Dance,
Molly Cranch/Visual Art

Description of Unit:

Making Shapes of our Environment is a month-long integrated kindergarten unit. This unit integrated dance and visual art with math and social studies. The unit was developed by the kindergarten teachers and the two artists over many weeks. The professional artists come into the classroom for five periods per class and team teach with the classroom teacher in their area of expertise (i.e., 5 hours of dance/class and 4 hours of visual art/class) during the month-long period of implementation.

The students combine skills learned in the classroom with dance and visual art to create maps of their environments (bedroom, classroom, and playground). They also learn to read and locate objects on a map.

Classroom Goals:

- Demonstrate a basic understanding of direction, size, shape, and distance relative and absolute location, and other geographic representation.
- Describe the physical environment of neighborhood and local community.
- Identify the shape of objects common to the student's environment.

State Goals:

- Demonstrate knowledge of world geography.
- Use geometric method to analyze, categorize, and draw conclusions about points, lines, planes, and space.
- Understand the sensory element, organizational principals, and ideas expressed in and among the arts.
- Through creating and performing, understand how works of art are produced.

Resources used:

Books:	*The Bee Buzzed By Tar Beach*
Overhead Pictures:	A classroom (looking straight on)
	Same classroom (looking down: a map)
Manipulatives:	Attribute blocks
Art Supplies:	Tempera Paint/Brushes/Paper
	Water Color Pencils

Key Words:

Sharp lines
Smooth lines
Geometric shapes
Free-form shapes
Levels—high, medium, and low

Lesson Outline:

Note: This is a general list of the activities used to teach this unit. My hope is that it gives you enough information to develop your own unit. It is by far no means and exact replica of our unit. You will need to adapt it to your needs.

1. Visual Art—Students are taught painting skills while making a variety of shapes (geometric and freeform) and lines (sharp and smooth).
2. Classroom—Students use attribute blocks to explore shapes.
3. Dance—Students learn how to dance geometric shapes on the floor. They also explore the dance space. How many big steps across the floor and how many little steps across the floor?
4. Classroom—Read the story *The Bee Buzzed By*. This story illustrates perspectives. It shows the same environment from a straight-on look and an overhead look. Help student discover which perspective is the way a map is drawn.
5. Classroom—Two overhead pictures of a classroom are used to show two perspectives of a classroom. The same classroom is shown as pictures and a map view. A detailed discussion takes place to discover the differences shape objects look like from each perspective.

6. Classroom—An activity to reinforce the transparency discussion. The teacher chooses a small area of the classroom and draws a map of that area. The teacher invites students to locate things that are pointed to. The teacher also asks the students to place objects in a space by pointing to the designated location on the map.

7. Classroom—Shape Hunt—The class will take a walk around the school to discover shapes in the environment. Include in the discussion the differences shape objects take from different perspective.

8. Visual Art—Students will paint shapes and lines in specific locations on the paper. "Paint a smooth line going across the paper," "paint a freeform shape on top of the line."

9. Dance—Students dance shapes and others guess them. Students learn to dance straight, smooth, and sharp lines.

10. Classroom—Creating a classroom map. (This activity may take several days.)
   Part One: As a group, students generate a list of things they want to include in their classroom map. The teacher will write down the object with the shape and color of the object (i.e., garbage can).
   Part Two: Create paper cut outs to match the objects. Don't forget to consider scale.
   Part Three: Help students glue the object on a large piece of paper where they belong to create the map. We found the students liked to keep adding details to the map.

11. Visual Art—Students create a picture using craypas. By looking at a specific area of three classrooms, they draw pictures of what they see. Try to choose an area that has a lot of shapes and levels.

12. Dance—Students will dance a simple floor plan as a group. They will design a plan and take turns dancing it. They are told to start with a shape, move to another area of the room, and dance another shape.

13. Classroom Field Trip—In Chicago, we like to go to the John Hancock building with our classes to look at the city from high level.

14. Classroom—read *Tar Beach*; discuss the different perspectives in the book.

15. Classroom—Students are asked to map their bedrooms. (overhead view) This must be explained well so parents understand.

16. Dance—Students create and dance individual floor plans to dance themselves.

17. Classroom—Mapping the playground. In pairs, students are given a piece of paper with two objects drawn in the correct place and need to complete the map.

18. Visual Art—Students sketch with pencils and a city block outside. We choose an area with houses with a lot of shapes.

19. Visual Art—Students add color to their drawings with watercolor pencils.

20. Dance—Students complete dancing their floor plan and music is added. We have several students dance at one time.

Describe Assessments You Used:

A. For Integrated Project—Students had to look at a map and get a specific item from a specific place. They also had to return the item to another specific place that was pointed to on the map.

B. For subject areas/art forms involved—The visual artist had the students paint a picture with specific directions. She used a rubric to grade it.

Comments from teacher(s) involved:

Question: What did you learn from getting involved in this arts integration project? What are the next steps? What would you do differently next time?

We found that the students were able to learn very difficult material through integrating the arts. It made things make much better sense. We are currently working on creating more assessments. It is a never-ending process. We are in our third year of implementing, and we are still improving it.

Comments from artist(s) involved:

Question: What did you learn from getting involved in this arts integration project? What are your next steps? What would you do differently next time?

We found it helpful to ask the teachers for insights on the best way to handle the classes. The teachers must participate for the lessons to be successful.

Comments from parent(s) involved:

A portion of a note from a parent during this unit: "*What a great project. Jake knew exactly how to approach the medium level concept and seemed to understand the differences from other levels. He told me about ovals and rectangles and explained that his race car bed was a free form shape. This is a thorough process and appreciation never taught to me. Great Job! Keep up the creativity you are teaching parents too.*"

Mayan Inca Aztec Cultures—
Elementary/Middle School

Drama Integration with Language Arts, Social Studies, Art
For Grades 4 to 6
Developed by Martha Cerda (Ogden School) and Jean Parisi (Pros Arts Studio)

Day 1:

Discuss drama journal. Students will need to keep record of what we do each day for drama and how they feel about what they are doing for each day.

Discuss history of Native Americans (previously studied) and their migration routes from China to the New World.
Trace routes on the world map. Have students do this.
Trace both routes—northern through the Bering Strait and southern island hopping to South America.

Discuss timeline of when each culture thrived.
Make class time line of events in history including these.

Maya	3114 BC–1500 AD
Aztec	900 AD–1520 AD
Inca	400AD–1532 AD

Discuss reasons that this culture ended so abruptly at approximately the same time (European, mainly Spanish conquest after discovery of New World–1492).

Day 2:

Introduce maps of Central America and South America for students. Tell them that they will be making a large project, a Mayan book called a *codex*, and they will have to keep all materials in their portfolios until the entire book is completed and ready to bind in an accordion book.
Together (teacher using large group map), have students label bodies of water, surrounding continents, countries.
Students need to make a key for each map to show where each culture lived.
Label Yucatan Peninsula, Valley of Mexico, Chichén Itzá, Tenochititlán, Andes Mountains, and Gulf of Mexico.

Days 3 and 4:

Discuss climate zones and possible crops, jobs, homes, and food, for all three ancient cultures based on the climate zones. (Predict)
Show cooperative learning groups large envelopes with puzzle inside.
Explain how to complete project.
Model process for puzzles:

1. Put puzzle together as a group.
2. Check puzzle with smaller duplicate picture in envelope.
3. Decide as a group what colors to use for each part of the puzzle.
4. Gather materials to color puzzle.

5. Each group member colors two sections of the puzzle, keeping in mind which colors the other members are using.
6. When finished, group assembles puzzle and pastes to a large sheet of construction paper.
7. Mount the puzzles on the bulletin board. Cut out the labels that explain the puzzle pieces.
8. Tack labels to the bulletin board and connect to their parts of the puzzle with string.
9. Add pictures of people belonging to each culture.

Days 5, 6, and 7:

Give students Maya, Aztec, and Inca charts.
Each cooperative group looks up information for its own group from books in the classroom library and bulletin board puzzles.
Share information on the board. Each group presents its own chart.
Students fill out their own charts from information gathered by each group.

Day 8:

Students should already have been working in drama on being expressive and dramatizing stories, situations, and characters.
Discuss expressiveness in reading.
> What is it?
> What does it sound like?
> What does it not sound like?
> How can you be expressive? What are specific things to do? Not do?

Preview *Papagayo* by having students look at picture on cover.
Students write prediction paragraphs:
> Who is the main character? What kind of personality does the main character have?
> What is the conflict or problem in the story?
> How is the conflict or problem solved?

Homework: List the events of the story in sequential order.
> Tell what happened briefly.

Days 9 and 10:

Have students share their predictions and events.
Have some students act out their stories.

Day 11:

Read *Papagayo* to children.
Discuss main events and characters and how to dramatize them.
Have different students act out different characters and/or events from the story.

Day 12:

Introduce *Flame of Peace*, an Aztec story.
Give background and history.
Read it to the children.

Discuss characters and conflict.
Read it again.
Record main events.

Days 13 and 14:
Start writing scene script with children.
Each student writes own copy on recycled paper.
List props, characters, action, and setting for each scene.

Days 15 to 29:
Tryouts and selection of characters.
Jean Parisi works with children from different scenes.
Marty Cerda works with children doing costume design.
      Students paint Aztec designs on tunics (narrow cotton sheets with hole cut out for head, hang on shoulders).
      Students make own props for their own scenes and help others.
> Use suggestions from the teacher's guide.
> White cardboard bones tied together, wrapping paper rolls with spear points of paper, balled up paper for rocks, cut paper torches, streamers for wind, but cloth for the river, brown cloth for the road

Students design program and flyer.

Reading should include *People of the Corn*, *The Woman Who Outshone the Sun*, and *The Hummingbird King* as a quiet time during the day.
If multiple copies are available, use with reading groups.
Performance of *Flame of Peace* for parents and other students.

Day 30:
Introduce students to art projects within the codex.
1. Mayan mask to be done in mosaic style using holes punched from green (jade) and blue (turquoise) sheets of paper.
2. Aztec calendars—yearly—to be colored and cut carefully using lots of red (blood).
3. Color Mayan eagle and select color for the front cover (to be laminated).
4. Inca sun god to be colored and mounted on gold or silver foil paper.

These projects need to be completed in class time and during time allowed for project work.
Give students deadline for completion of projects and binding of codixes.
Things to remember:
> Be realistic:
> > about how much can be accomplished in the allotted time.
> > about what your goals are—process or product.
> Students can do a lot more than you think.
> Double up on characters if there are a lot of kids. There can be twins instead of just one main character, and so on.
> Make time to reflect on project.

References/Resources

Baquedaro, E. (1999). *Aztec, Inca, and Maya.* New York: Eyewitness Books.

Chrisp, P. (1999). *The Maya.* New York: Raintree/SteckVaughn.

Gerson, M.-J. (1995). *People of the corn: A Mayan Story.* New York: Little Brown and Co.

Lattimore, D. N. (1991). *The flame of peace: A tale of the Aztecs.* New York: HarperCollins.

Martinez, A. C. (1991). *The woman who outshone the sun.* New York: Children's Press.

McDermott, G. (1992). *Papagayo.* New York: Harcourt Brace.

McKissack, P. (1985). *The Inca.* New York: Children's Press.

Palacios, A. (1993). *The hummingbird king: A Guatemalan legend.* New York: Troll Associates.

Strohl, M., & Schneck, S. (1996). *Mayas, Aztecs, Incas: Cooperative learning activities.* New York: Scholastic Trade.

How to Read Codex

In Ancient Mexico—that is to say, before the arrival of the Spanish conquistadors—their lived the Aztecs or, as they called themselves, *Mexica*. They spoke *Nahuatl*—a language that many people in Mexico still speak today. Of the *Mexica*, there were many artists that dedicated their time to making books. These *tlacuilos* (scribes) drew their histories on paper made from the bark of trees, which the *Mexica* called *Amatl*. Histories were also written on strips of deerskin.

What were these books like?

Each book was made up of a long strip of paper folded like an accordion. With each fold you had one page. Each of these books is called a codex or *tonalmatl*.

What kind of things were recorded in these codixes?

Some were about history and religion, and others dealt with administrative matters.

The *Mexica* wrote stories using pictographs, glyphs, or hieroglyphs instead of words. In other words, they used pictures to communicate ideas. To read a codex is to read pictures. The *Mexica* would open up the long strip of paper and begin to read pictures, starting from the right side of the codex and moving toward the left. Part of this text was translated from Spanish. Como Leer un Codices by Esther Jacob.

The Flame of Peace: An Aztec Story

Long ago in the Aztec capital city of Tenochtitlan, there lived a boy named Two Flint, his father named Five Eagle, and his mother named One Flower. One day Two Flint was fishing in the river by the marketplace. He caught many fish. As he turned to leave, he saw two warriors with battle flags approaching the marketplace. He also saw Emperor Itzcoatal himself approaching the market.

The next day, Five Eagle stood in front of the temple alter with the other ambassadors. They all had gifts to offer Tezozmoc during the Twenty Days of Talking. For 20 days and 20 nights, Two Flint searched the distant mountains for a sign of his father and the other ambassadors. On the twentieth day, Two Flint saw the ambassadors coming toward the city.

Later, at home, Two Flint and One Flower talked sadly about the coming war.

As he slept, Two Flint dreamed of Lady Morning Star.

The next morning, Two Flint left to search for Lady Morning Star and the flame of peace. At the same time, Emperor Itzoatal led his warriors on the opposite road to battle the Tezozomoc's warriors.

Late in the morning, Two Flint came to a crossroads where the first of nine evil demons awaited him.

Two Flint watched as Lady Wind blew Lord River out of his bed.

Then Lady Wind blew Two Flint down the Hill of the Star.

The voice grumbled, but Lord Volcano destroyed Lord Earthquake with his lava rocks.

Two Flint was trapped. Suddenly a cool wisp of air tricked over Two Flint's feet. He followed the air to another opening and with terror saw Lady Smoking Mirror.

Two Flint quickly made a stone statue of himself.

Two Flint ran to the top on the Hill of the Star. There Lady Morning Star waited Two Flint.

Two Flint entered the city calling to the people as he ran to the temple with the Flame of Peace. He placed the new flame on the alter.

The warriors of Itzcoatal and Tezozomoc threw down their spears and embraced friends. Deep inside the temple, the glow of a single fire burned brightly. From that day on, there was peace.

Jazz Poetry/Antebellum Period In U.S. History— High School

Reginald Lawrence—Drama Artist, Impact Theater
Kyle Westbrook, U.S. History Teacher, Lincoln Park High School
(Lessons A and B teachers in Lesson Outline)

Department/Class—Social Sciences–African-American History
Arts Areas—Theatre/Music
Suggested Grades—10 to 12
Number of Class Sessions—7 to 10

Course Objectives–African-American History
1. Demonstrate decision-making skills in real-life historical situations.
2. Recognize events and circumstances surrounding the Antebellum Period of U.S. history
3. Create a narrative first-person poem utilizing historical facts and trends of the Antebellum Period.

Art Form Objectives–Drama/Music
1. Demonstrate the behavioral skills necessary to create and perform drama
2. Write a character profile using four aspects of character development and utilize them in performance with the established dramatic context.
3. Write a scene (monologue, poem) using setting, character, and language appropriate to historical context.

Activity Descriptions
Lesson #1 Introduction and overview of Jazz Poetry by teacher and artist. Introduce Tempo, Tone, and Subject as the basic elements of performance poetry. Activity: Artist performs improvisational jazz poetry to allow students to manipulate the three basic elements.

Lesson A Teacher explores "subject" and "personal voice" utilizing writing prompts about the historical period and the concept of regionalism.

Lesson #2 Introduction to character deconstruction and reconstruction exercises utilizing three component model (Sociological, Psychological, and Physiological). Homework: Create a character profile utilizing traits as identified in character reconstruction.

Lesson B Teacher explores Character and Personal Voice utilizing varied societal factors.

Lesson #3 Introduction to focus and personal voice/characterization exercises through student-directed role-playing utilizing stage sculpture. Activity: In small groups, students select phrases from a hat and must perform them silently, with direction from a student director. On completion, each member must define his or her character using the three-component model. Homework: Continuation of character work. Students utilize the Character Profile to create a complete Character Biography.

Lesson #4 Continuation of Lesson #3. Homework: Continuation of character work. Students utilize Character Biography to create a complete Character Monologue/Poem.

Lesson C Students complete their poems effectively using Tone, Tempo, and Subject.

Lessons #5 and #6 Musicians compose original score for each student's poem while students perform for their classmates.

Lesson # 7 Student performances

Lesson #8 Classroom evaluation

Arts in the City Schools Student Evaluation Recording FormUnit Evaluation

(Used with Jazz Poetry Unit—Lincoln Park High School)

Teacher _____

Department _____

Artist _____

Arts Organization _____

Name of Unit _____

1. I found the material in this unit very interesting.
   Strongly Disagree   Strongly Agree
   1   2   3   4   5

2. I did new activities during this unit that I've never done before.
   Strongly Disagree   Strongly Agree
   1   2   3   4   5

3. I found these activities exciting.
   Strongly Disagree   Strongly Agree
   1   2   3   4   5

4. These activities helped me learn the material.
   Strongly Disagree   Strongly Agree
   1   2   3   4   5

5. The arts skills I learned during this unit can help me learn the material in my class through the rest of the year.
   Strongly Disagree   Strongly Agree
   1   2   3   4   5

6. I understand the connections between the arts skills and the academic material.
   Strongly Disagree   Strongly Agree
   1   2   3   4   5

7. I would be interested in having another unit like this one in my class.
   Strongly Disagree   Strongly Agree
   1   2   3   4   5

8. I see how the ideas we discussed and explored in this unit are relevant to my life.
   Strongly Disagree   Strongly Agree
   1   2   3   4   5

9. During this unit I learned new things about other students in the classroom.
   Strongly Disagree   Strongly Agree
   1   2   3   4   5

Improvisational Comedy For Learning Foreign Language—High School

Created in the Lincoln Park High School
Arts in the City School Partnership
by French Teacher Maureen Breen and Musician/
Playwright Ralph Covert of Lookingglass Theater

Overview:

High school students are taught improvisational sketch comedy skills as a way to develop strong conversational foreign language skills. Students demonstrate their skills through performances that serve as final exams.

Inquiry: How does one "think on one's feet" in a foreign language?

Classroom Goals:

Foreign Language: Students will perform improvised comedy sketches in French. Students will incorporate specific vocabulary and grammar skills into their scenes, and use their French language skills in a flexible manner. Students will demonstrate the ability to comprehend and respond appropriately using their French, manipulating the language to meet their communication goals. As a result of this unit, students will (a) understand oral communication in French, (b) interact in French in a variety of settings, and (c) use French to present information, concepts, and ideas for a variety of purposes and in a variety of settings.

Theatre: Students will perform their sketches incorporating appropriate drama skills, such as the use of their Actor's Tools (mind, body, and voice), maintaining an open-stage picture, and projecting their voices. Students will incorporate improvisation skills, such as supporting their scene partners, remaining in character, building and heightening their scene partners' ideas, and working as a team to create and perform improvisational comedy scenes. As a result of this unit, students will (a) analyze a work for technical elements of acting, (b) analyze a work for technical elements of playwriting and scene structure, (c) demonstrate skills used in the creation and performance of theater, and (d) demonstrate the behavioral skills necessary to learn and contribute productively as individuals and as members of a group.

Key Vocabulary:

Improvisation
Stage picture
Character
Concentration

Focus
Articulation
Pronunciation

DAY-BY-DAY LESSON PLANS:

Day 1:

Introduction: Discussion of the relationship between improvisation and foreign language use, and how much more able one is to summon up a foreign language when there is a need for it (for example, when Ralph was in France and was very hungry).

Warm-up: Concentration and group responsiveness exercise: "Zip Zap Zop." Students are in a circle; by using eye contact and clapping their hands toward another player, they pass the words *zip*, *zap*, and *zop* back and forth around the circle.

> **Key lessons:** Paying attention, being engaged, getting loose, and communicating the idea: "Hey, you're next."

> **Discussion:** What did this exercise ask of you to do it well? How does this relate to learning a foreign language?

Activity #2: Mirror exercise.

Students pair up and mirror each others' movements as if in a mirror. Emphasis is placed on being quiet and focused, and on neither student leading or following all the time, but on sharing the process.

> **Key lessons:** Paying attention, being engaged, knowing your intent, physically listening.

> **Discussion:** How was this communication? What limits were placed on communication?

Activity #3: Circle conjugation game.

Students return to the circle as in "Zip Zap Zop" and play a similar game using French words. For instance, they may conjugate *avoir* or list colors or any other vocabulary or grammar category.

> **Discussion:** How was this harder? Why is it more fun? What level of language knowledge does it require?

> **Outcome:** Students will understand that language exists to facilitate communication – that there is a difference between learning the French language and communicating in French. Communicating is the goal.

Day 2:

Warm-up: Students circulate freely through the space, not making any contact with each other. Next step: Students are asked to make eye contact as they pass each other. Next step: Students are asked to each create their own nonverbal signature and greet each other using their own unique gesture. Next step: Students are asked to exchange gestures, taking on the other person's gestures and letting go of their own, then taking on the next one that is exchanged, and so on.

Discussion: How many gestures did you go through? How is this communication?

Key lessons: Loosening up, establishing the expectation of appropriate behavior in a nondesk-bound activity, encouraging creative expression.

Activity #2: Creating an ideal space.

Ask the students to find their own place on the floor anywhere in the classroom. Let them know that they need to be comfortable. Dim the lights. Ask the students to close their eyes and go to their own personal ideal place. Ask them to experience the place in as rich detail as they can, using as many of their senses as they can and to enjoy being there. After about 4 minutes, give them a warning that they have a minute or so to come back, and to return to the class and open their eyes when they're back. Ask students to share the details of their ideal spaces, encouraging them to elaborate on specific details and sense memories.

Next, ask the class to choose one of their classmate's ideal places and create it as a group. Let them know they can be anything they want, be it a breeze, a sound, a person, an object, or whatever. Ask them to do the exercise in complete silence without planning what they intend to be. Repeat this exercise several times—you will find the students becoming capable of pulling a scene together very quickly by the second or third example. Then ask them to add sound effects.

The next step is adding a story line—each specific step of the story needs to be suggested by the student, acknowledged by the teacher/artist, and acted by a student within the scene. For instance, the teacher says, "Okay, what happens next?" A student calls out, "The mailman arrives!" The teacher says, "Okay, I need a mailman." Several students volunteer. The teacher says, "Susan is the mailman." Susan stops being a tree, becomes the mailman, and knocks on the door. The teacher says, "Okay, what happens next?" And so on. Even when students make absurd suggestions like "The mailman is hit by an asteroid," incorporate the suggestion and then ask, "Okay, what happens next?" Students learn very quickly that suggestions that don't move the action forward aren't much fun.

Discussion: What actor's tools did you use to create these scenes (mind, body, voice)? How do these relate to foreign language use?

Key lessons: A deeper understanding of the students as people from the ideal spaces they share, a reinforcement of the idea that this is a very different but very fun way of concentrating on schoolwork, and an awareness of the actor's tools.

Day 3:

Warm-up: Bouncing the voice off the walls.
Each student says his or her name loudly and quietly, listening for the very quiet slap-back from the walls that tells them their voices are not loud enough to fill the room.

Discussion: The volume you would project your voice at in a conversational situation is different than the volume you would use in front of a group. Bouncing your voice off the walls gives you a helpful measure of whether your voice is loud enough to fill a room.

Outcome: Understanding of the importance of projecting your voice, and how to mea   sure when you are doing so.

Activity #2: Basic improv in English.

The class plays a game of "freeze tag," where two students act out an improvised scene; when another student says "Freeze," they freeze. The new student taps one of the other two on the shoulder and starts a new scene based only on the body positions of the students. For instance, the first scene may be a guy buying a car, and reaching out his hand to take the car-keys, and the new scene may start with him reaching out his hand to shake hands.

Discussion: When did the scenes work best? When did the scenes not work so well? What could you do to improve your scenes? Question both the students doing the scenes as well as the students do the scenes. This encourages them to both analyze their scenes as well as to put their observations into practice.

Outcome: Understanding of the fundamental principles of improv: supporting your partners, paying attention, flexibility.

Day 4:

Activity: Improv in English:

Call the students up in groups of two and have them create improvised scenes in English. Discuss with them the basic rules of improv, using examples from scenes they are creating.

Key lessons: Cheat your body to the audience (keeping an open stage picture), bounce your voice off the walls (proper volume for performance), match and heighten the absurdity and imagination of your partner (students need to be encouraged to support each others' ideas, and flourish when allowed to), always support your stage partner (this builds deep teamwork as they realize that when they are on stage with a partner they have only each other to rely on), never say "no" to you stage partner's choices, and do not use preconceived ideas, but be open to what actually happens.

Discussion: What worked in this scene and why? What limited it? What could you/they have done differently?

Madame Breen created the following reminders to reinforce theatre skills:

1. Using the acrostic **"C-O-M-E-D-Y"**:
   Cheat your body to the audience!
   Off the wall your voice must bounce!
   Match and heighten the absurdity and imagination of your partner!
   Everyone needs a supportive partner—be one!
   Do not use preconceived ideas.
   Yes, not No, is the word to use!

2. Use the phrase "Be Very Marvelous" to remember the actor's tools:
Body
Voice
Mind

Days 5 and 6:
Same as Day 4, making sure all the students get a chance to participate and learn.

Day 7:
Transition into doing improvisations in French. Students will be intimidated at first, but will gain confidence as they succeed.

Discussion: What makes this more difficult? The lack of fluency in French makes the ideas less creative; the students are forced to think about what they can say, not what they want to say. The rhythm of the scenes is slower and less spontaneous, and so on.

Outcomes: Students learn that when improvising in French, the basic improv skills are even more important (e.g., it is very important for your scene partner to speak clearly and loudly). Students gain confidence in their ability to combine improv and French, but realize it is a big challenge.

Day 8:

Assessments: The test.
Students are assigned general outlines of scenes and specific usage requirements, and are allowed 5 minutes to review or research the vocabulary and grammar they will use and sketch out a general outline of their scene. Students do not have time to script or memorize their scene, and so are forced to do it using their improv skills and using their internalized French knowledge. Being allowed to prepare a general outline and specific vocabulary and grammar allows them to enter the scene confident of where they are going and to focus on having fun, being creative, and using their French in an active and flexible manner.
Students are graded using the following rubric created by Madame Breen and Ralph Covert:
Excellent—3
Good—2
Needs Improvement—1
No Effort—0

Drama Skills:
1. Focus, concentration, staying in character
2. Supporting partner/s
3. Sufficient volume

4. Facing audience, open stage picture

French Skills:
1. Language easy to understand: articulation, pronunciation
2. Use of new vocabulary
3. Six full sentence in French per actor
4. Scene performed in French from start to finish

5. Starting performance within 30 seconds of being called

6. Fun factor

5. Appropriate level of difficulty (grammar, etc.)

Grammar (correctness)

7. Title given in French

8. Scene ending dramatic and clear ("La Fin")

Scoring Guide:
38–36 = A
35–34 = B
33–32 = C
31–29 = D
28 and below = F

Comment from teacher: "*I was surprised and delighted to see that many students who normally do not actively participate in class shone during this unit, and demonstrated real incorporation of conversational French skills. Who'd have thought I'd have students actually looking forward to their final French exam?*"

Physics in Motion—High School

Lincoln Park High School and Hedwig Dances
Teacher: Ed Metzl
Artist: Peter Sciscioli

Unit Lesson Plans

Day 1:

A. Introduce myself, learn students' names.

B. Set objectives for the course and for today's class. This will include distribution of the Assessment Grid to each of the students and a brief discussion on grading. Concepts for today's class will be listed on the board.

C. Lead students through a warm-up that covers the following concepts:
    1. Center of gravity in the body
    2. Naming of different muscle groups and parts of the spine
    3. Pendulum/swinging (at arm and hip joints)
    4. Gravitational and electromagnetic forces and their application to movement
    5. Axial and locomotor motion

D. Students will perform a series of going-across-the-floor exercises. Concepts to be explored include:
    1. Axial vs. locomotor motion
       Example: Using the center of gravity in our bodies, we bounce in place (axial motion) and then exert a force to move our centers through space by pushing off our back legs (locomotor motion).
    2. Average velocity: $v = d/t$
       Example: Setting up Point A and Point B in the room, we can measure the distance and the time it takes to either walk, run, or do our movement phrase explained earlier to calculate velocity.
    3. Acceleration: $a = v/t$
       Example: If we were to add Point C in the room, existing on the same line as AB, we could calculate acceleration when a student increases his or her velocity between Points A and C.
    4. Gravitational and electromagnetic forces
       Example: Have students experience gravitational forces by leaning forward and at the last minute letting their feet keep them from falling on their faces. Have students experience electromagnetic forces by discussing the pathways that messages from the brain must take to reach the muscles and produce movement. Experience as a group how we are able to flex, extend, squeeze, and exert our muscles in a variety of ways. Combining these abilities is what produces movement or dance.

Day 2:

A. Review concepts from Day 1 and their application to movement:
    1. Center of gravity in the body

      2. Axial vs. locomotor motion
      3. Average velocity: v=d/t
      4. Acceleration: a=v/t
      5. Gravitational and electromagnetic forces

B. Lead students through similar warm-up to Day 1

C. Exploration of Newton's Laws of Motion
      1. First Law: An object with no net force acting on it remains at rest or moves with constant velocity in a straight line.
      Example: standing still or falling through the universe.
      2. Second Law: The acceleration of a body is directly proportional to the net force acting on it and inversely proportional to its mass.
      Example: F=ma (measured in Newtons), so a smaller body will accelerate faster than a larger body if each has an equal force. Have students find a partner and experience what level of force is required to push their partners across the room (walking then running).
      3. Third Law: When one object exerts a force on a second object, the second object exerts a force on the first that is equal in magnitude but opposite in direction.
      Example: Facing their partners, students press the palms of their hands together with their partners'. Next have them step away from each other as far as they can, using the force exerted between themselves to balance each other. They should eventually be able to create a triangle with the floor as one side.

D. Friction: the force that opposes the motion between two surfaces that are in contact. All surfaces are essentially rough, and, when in contact, particles from each bond electromagnetically.
      1. Static friction: the force that opposes the motion when two objects are not in relative motion.
      2. Sliding friction: the force between objects in relative motion.
      Example: Have one person sit on the floor. Have his partner hold him beneath his arms and experience the force required to start him across the floor (static friction) and the force required to keep him in motion (sliding friction).

E. Terminal velocity: constant velocity of an object when it is falling through space, and the net force is equal to zero. Air resistance/drag force is the force acting upward on an object, whereas gravity is the force working downward. Altering the shape of the object can alter the drag force, and thus affect acceleration.
      Example: A skydiver opens a parachute to increase drag force and thus reduces velocity. Have students alter the shape of their bodies from big to small by doing sit spins; as they create a smaller shape that moves through space, their velocity has the ability to increase.

Day 3:

A. Review concepts from Day 2 and their application to movement:
      1. Newton's Laws of Motion
      2. Friction: static vs. sliding
      3. Terminal velocity

B. Lead students through similar warm-up to Day 2.
C. Physical concepts to be explored in movement in an outdoor atmosphere:
    1. Gravitational forces on an inclined plane.
       Example: Have students run or roll down a hill, emphasizing the point at which each student feels as if he or she is "falling through space," or experiencing constant velocity where acceleration equals zero.
    2. Centripetal acceleration: $a_c = v^2/r$ Always points toward the center of the circle and is directly proportional to the square of the speed (v) and inversely proportional to the radius of the circle (r).
       Example: Have students work with a partner. Holding on to each other's wrists, have them lean away from each other and then start to accelerate in a circle by moving their legs to one side. As they increase speed and reach a constant, they will feel the exertion of force toward the middle of the circle.
    3. Torque: the product of the force and the lever arm (the perpendicular distance from the axis of rotation to a line along which the force acts). Torque explains the start, stop, or change in direction for objects in circular motion.
       Example: Have students experience torque by doing the prior exercise with only one arm (decreases speed), by having one partner exert a force in the opposite direction of rotation (will stop the motion), and by letting go (other partner will travel in a straight line).
    4. Combination of Newton's Second and Third Laws
       Example: Have students play tug of war, explaining that the force exerted on the rope must increase to accelerate the rope (and the opposing team) toward the direction of greater force. When Newton's Third Law is at work, the teams will be equal.

Day 4:

A. Review concepts from Day 3 and their application to movement:
    1. Gravitational forces on inclined plane
    2. Centripetal acceleration
    3. Torque
    4. Newton's Second and Third Laws
B. Application of activities from Day 3 to subsequent mathematical formulas:
    1. How do we calculate our acceleration down an ideal inclined plane?
       Example: $a = F/m = W(\sin\ theta)/m$. Since W=mg, the m cancels out, and we are left with a=g(sine theta). Therefore, every student will accelerate down an ideal inclined plane at the same rate regardless of his or her weight.
    2. How do we calculate our individual centripetal acceleration?
       Example: $a_c = v^2/r$ or $a_c = 4\pi^2 r/T^2$. r in this case is approximately the length of one arm (for the exercise listed for Day 3). Since our arm spans are approximately our height, r=1/2 of our individual heights. T in this case is the period, or time it takes for us to complete the circle one time. In this case, T=.25s. Have each student calculate their centripetal acceleration using the prior guidelines and record the solution in their notebook entries.

3. Look at a diagram that explains how torque works.

C. Show students video segments from three selected dances. During the first segment, point out and illustrate which physical concepts are being shown in the movement, and ask what other concepts students see. For the second and third segment, have students list or describe which concepts they see. These can include anything covered in our group warm-ups, in our class activities, or from their knowledge of physics as a whole.

D. Have students fill out student evaluation forms and turn in notebook entries.

Filling the Empty Stage: Improvising and Playwriting to Enhance Literary Learning— High School

Jackie Murphy—Drama Artist
Ken Mularski—Teacher
Diane Fashingbauer—Teacher

Steps for Setting the Stage for Discussion, Writing, and Improvisation

Reading Aloud

The first step is reading aloud a selected poem. Choose volunteers and reassure them that you know it is a cold reading. They will have already heard you read it once. (Your reading should be clear, but it should not be so dramatic and powerful that it suggests it is the only way the poem could be read.)

After the reading, ask the class what emotions were evident in the voices of the characters. This is the first phase of establishing student as character, and the necessity of listening to the tone, pace, and emphasis in the voices of the readers. Listening is the important skill. The reading should be done twice. Inevitably there is a difference in the readings, and the class is on its way to accepting the possibility of more than one interpretation.

Preparing for Playwriting

For example, the situation and emotions suggested in the poem, *Mother to Son*, are intriguing to the students. This attraction to the characters becomes a point of entry for further exploration.

1. Scan all possible situations that are suggested in the poem:
   - Who is giving advice to whom? (*Mother to daughter, grandfather to grandson, brother to sister*)
   - What conflict caused the situation? (*School problems, peer pressure, etc.*)
   - What is the attitude of the person giving advice? (*Caring, angry, desperate, etc.*)
   - What is the attitude of the person hearing the advice? (*Wanting to listen, not wanting the advice, etc.*)
   - Where could this be taking place? (*In the dining room, living room, kitchen*)

It is important to get an array of possibilities out into the open before they begin to write. It is also important that every child feels his or her image is as valid as anyone else's.

2. Advise everyone that it is evident that there are many instances to consider; however, they must now select a moment they see clearly and focus on that moment.

3. Direct them to freeze this moment and frame it by answering the following questions (Answers must be written so that the details come to life in the scene written as well as in the improvisation):
   - Who are the characters?
   - How old are they?
   - Where do you see the scene taking place? Inside? Outside?
   - What time is it?
   - Are there objects you see or sounds you hear?
   - What is the immediate problem—the action that is causing the conflict?
   - Describe each character's mood, attitude, state of mind.
4. Now turn and face the front of the room and tell the class to imagine the empty stage. Then ask them to write down the words: *When the curtain opens* … The students should fill in the details of what they see on the stage and what the characters are doing.
5. Once they have written the details of a particular moment that they have seen clearly, they are ready to listen to the voices of the characters. Ask them to write down who says the first line. This can be done in play form. A quick example on the board will usually suffice. With a first line written, they have begun their play. Tell them to listen to the tone of voice in the first line and then write the response by the other character. Give them 3 to 5 minutes.

Improvisation

When the writing is finished, ask for volunteers to read their scenes aloud. Usually I stop after three readings and ask the students to donate their scripts to the class. This is the moment that we begin to explore possibilities, alternatives, and consequences that arise from the words of the students. Improvisation in this style is the writing process live—the Socratic method applied to the words of the students. When we have finished, we have entered the motives, fears, determinations, and hesitations of a variety of fictional characters in conflict.

Appendix E: Assessing Arts Integration by Looking at What Students Know and Are Able To Do

An Evaluation Instrument for CAPE Partnerships

INCREASING STUDENT CAPACITY—A CAPE GOAL

CAPE is providing initiative-wide assessment instruments and professional development to assist individual Partnerships in assessing student outcomes. The areas named below (a–g) have been named by the Department of Labor as necessary for success in the 21st century. They also serve as useful indicators for CAPE. They are yardsticks for Partnerships to plan, measure, and assess their growth and development. Each indicator must be addressed in terms of age of children, grade level, and degree of experience with arts integration. *They are guidelines, not mandates*. Remember, these are skills identified as necessary for success in a complex 21st century. We assume that you will also be assessing what students know through assessments in content areas and art forms. We hope that some of these assessments will integrate the art form(s) and the content fields that you are exploring.

You, your team or grade level, or entire school may decide to focus on several indicators in this evaluation at a time, rather than all of them at once. You may use them as focus points for conversations among teachers and artists. Clearly, some projects lend themselves more to one indicator than to another. They are meant to help Partnerships work toward useful outcomes for students. *No one arts integration project can accomplish all outcomes*. The indicators can also be used to look at projects and set goals over time in the Partnership. CAPE requests that you complete at least two of these evaluation instruments per year.

Choose one project or one unit to focus on for this evaluation. Please type responses wherever possible.

What is the title for your arts integrated project or unit?

Teachers/Artists/Grade Levels involved:

School/Arts Partnership:

Arts integration involves one or more arts areas. List *arts goals/standards* you used for this project.

Dance	Drama	Media Arts	Music	Visual Arts

Arts integration usually involves the following four basic skills. Note how this occurred by listing *goals/standards* you used in each area.

Reading	Writing
Speaking	Listening

Arts integration may involve one of the following basic content areas. List *goals/standards* you used for this project.

Mathematics	Science	Social Studies

Now use the space below to indicate how you see this various areas ***integrating*** in this arts integration project. What did the arts integration process look like? How did the basic skills, content areas, and art forms intersect and interact? Draw, graph, outline …

These skills (a–g) have been named by the U.S. Department of Labor as essential for life and work in the 21st century. They also reflect many of CAPE's goals for meaningful arts integration. Use this evaluation instrument as a way to evaluate progress and set new goals for the arts in your school.

a) **Resources**: students can organize space and time effectively.

Using a scale of 0 to 5 (5 = *very much*, 0 = *not at all*), during arts integration, to what extent did your students:
___ Do independent research?
___ Help to plan how large projects were divided into daily or weekly assignments?
___ Demonstrate time management skills?
___ Participate in ranking or prioritizing tasks within an arts integrated unit or project?
___ Participate in planning room use and organization of materials needed for arts integration?

In your classroom work with arts integration, were there any surprises in students' uses of space, time, and resource materials?

Comment:

b) **Interpersonal skills**: Students can negotiate with others to solve problems and reach decisions; work comfortably with other students from diverse backgrounds; work well both individually and in teams.

Using a scale of 0 to 5 (5 = *very much*, 0 = *not at all*), during arts integration:
___ Did students work in small groups?
___ Did students have the opportunity to teach each other?
___ Did students work independently without adult help?
___ Did boys and girls work together?
___ Did each group member in a group project make a contribution?
___ Did leadership rotate in small groups?
___ Did group members divide up tasks?
___ Did students use artists and teachers as resources for problem solving?
___ Did students appropriately change or adapt assignments?

In your classroom work with arts integration, were there any surprises when students worked in groups?

Comment:

c) **Information**: Students can demonstrate what they know effectively orally, in writing, and through diverse art forms. If a unit is integrated, students probably have the opportunity to convey information *in more than one way and in more than one medium.*

In the arts integrated unit/project, did students: (check all that apply)
___ Demonstrate learning through exhibition of artwork?
___ Demonstrate learning through performance?
___ Demonstrate learning through writing?
___ Demonstrate learning through speaking?
___ Have choice in how they demonstrated learning?

Comment:

d) **Self-management**: Students are able to anticipate consequences and monitor and correct their own behavior.

Using a scale of 0 to 5 (5 = *very much*, 0 = *not at all*), during arts integration:
___ Were most students attentive and listening to the adults?
___ Were most students attentive and listening to each other?
___ Did most students demonstrate an awareness of personal space?
___ Did most students, in a dance or drama unit, understand how movement is to be undertaken in the class? Can they describe that?
___ Did most students understand how arts materials are to be used in the class? Can they describe that?
___ Did most students monitor their own behavior?
___ Did students have the opportunity to discuss behavior norms?
___ Did students help to design rules for behavior?
___ Were there any surprises regarding students' self-management during the arts integrated project/unit?

Comment:

e) **Technology**: Students are able to use new technology to develop and represent their learning through the arts.

___ During arts integration, was technology used as a tool for: (check all that apply)
___ Acquiring information/doing research? *Tech.Tools Used:*
___ Documenting the unit/project? Word processing
___ Collaborating/communicating with others? Internet
___ Making art? scanner

___ Exhibiting? graphic design
___ Performing? video
___ Assessing? Getting feedback?spreadsheet
___ other (explain)

f) Thinking skills: Students demonstrate capacity in creative thinking, making decisions, solving problems, imaging, knowing how to learn, and reasoning.

Using a scale of 0 to 5 (5 = *very much*, 0 = *not at all*), during arts integration, did students:
___ Generate new ideas?
___ Have choices to make between paths; have options in terms of product and process?
___ Recognize problems and implement plans of action to solve them?
___ Organize information?
___ Find or discover parallels or connections between content areas and arts forms?
___ Have the opportunity to talk about *how* not just *what* they are learning?
___ Were there any surprises in how students learned to think, solve problems, and reason during the arts integration?

g) Personal qualities: Students demonstrate individual responsibility, self-esteem, sociability, and integrity.

Using a scale of 0 to 5 (5 = *very much*, 0 = *not at all*), during arts integration, did you see evidence that students:
___ Persevered in order to achieve goals?
___ Demonstrated belief in their own self-worth?
___ Participated in self-evaluation?
___ Chose ethical courses of action that required honesty?

Comment:

Final Reflections:

What went well during this arts integration unit?

What will you work on and/or do differently next time?

What do you think were the key ideas/themes/learnings that
students gained from this particular arts integration project?

What did you as adults learn?

Feel free to attach any artifacts, samples of student work, curriculum plans, photos, or
assessments that you think clarify what this arts integration project was about.

Persons who contributed to this Increasing Student Capacity evaluation:

_____

_____

_____

Date: _____

Appendix F:
CAPE Checklists:
Strategies for Effective
Arts Integration

Criteria for Effective Partnerships

One of the primary issues that arts education and curriculum development initiatives such as CAPE confront is how to plan and document innovative curricular work in a way that is DETAILED enough to be useful to other teachers, but is also FLEXIBLE enough to capture the originality and vitality of the work in action. The goal is to create living, breathing curriculum. Planning and documentation should be GENERATIVE, not PRESCRIPTIVE or PROSCRIPTIVE.

The CAPE web site has tried to address this dilemma by distilling the principles that have consistently emerged in CAPE's most exciting practice. As you will see in the curriculum examples on the web site, the most effective curricular work developed by the CAPE Partnerships consistently exhibits the following strategies:

___ Clear identification of arts content, academic content, and learning skills that will be developed by the arts integrated curricular work

___ Identification of primary research and inquiry questions

___ Identification of a variety of hands-on approaches to generating and representing new knowledge

___ A clear understanding of how hands-on activities connect to applied analytical thinking

___ An expectation that students will draw on field research from sources outside the school

___ Articulated assessment methodologies

___ Opportunities for students to reflect on their work with their peers

___ Opportunities for students to make presentations about their new knowledge

___ Opportunities for students to teach what they have learned to others

___ Strategies for engaging parents and community

___ A clear and productive relationship between the activities of the partnership, principal leadership, and the larger vision of curriculum development and school improvement at each school.

___ Regularly scheduled partnership planning and professional development time for teachers as well as opportunities for teachers to present their new strategies to their peers and to develop leadership skills.

___ Parents and parent organizations have a clear commitment to and involvement in the work of the partnership.

___ Significant contact and on-going collaboration between artists and teachers.

___ Clear evidence of increased teacher capacity to develop and implement new teaching strategies as a result of their work with the partnership, as well as internalization of arts skills.

___ Clear evidence of new and productive collaborations between teachers as a result of their work with the partnership (peer mentoring projects, team teaching, co-planned cross-class curricular projects, etc).

___ Clear evidence of innovative, rigorous teaching strategies that actively engage students in their own learning. This will include participatory and hands-on learning as well as reflection and analysis.

___ Cultural diversity in artistic content and representation, combining respect for the culture and ethnicity of the students being served with access to the arts of other cultures.

___ Clear evidence of rigorous formative self-assessment and on-going planning as a key characteristic of all partnership activities.

___ Clear evidence of effectively spreading the program equitably.

___ Clear evidence of effective planning to sustain the partnership beyond CAPE support (such as identifying teacher leaders to maintain integrated units, collaborative planning time scheduled for in-school arts specialists, commitment of school dollars to on-going artist fees, etc.)

Note that these are behavioral indicators—that teachers, artists, administrators, parents, or students could document for accountability purposes, but more importantly, for planning purposes.

The CAPE web site can be accessed at: *www.capeweb.org* or at: *http://capeweb.interliant.com*.

Appendix G:
Scope and Sequence
Sample: Orozco School

Seventh-Grade Arts Integrated Social Studies Curriculum—The Formation of Our Nations

Units/Goals/Quarter	Q1 Olmec	Q1 Teotihuacan	Q1 Middle Ages	Q2 Day of the Dead
Social Studies	First Americans and Early Civilization in Mexico	Development of classical civilization in Valley of Mexico and relation of man to environment	Influence of Church, Feudal System, and economic influence of Crusades, Signing of Magna Carta	Combining of European and indigenous traditions in Mexico
Art	Olmec head drawing—use mathematical formula and symbols to show values of Olmec culture	(P) Painted fresco mural fragment—use of multimedia, symbols, repetitive design	Illuminated Manuscripts —calligraphy—writing as an art form	(P) Mask making. Use of symbolic forms of life and death— participation in Day of Dead Parade
Language Arts	Write a historical fiction using knowledge of Olmec life	Students write a didactic card with key historical facts and interpretation of nature symbols	Students will read Robin Hood— elements of fiction and legends	One page reflection paper on meaning of Day of the Dead
Student Learning	Students construct meaning	Students construct meaning through understanding and using symbols	Students work in collaborative groups—RobinHood drama	Students collaborate on learning activities— Students construct meaning.
Assessment	Rubric— teacher/student	1. Rubric for art project student/teacher	1. Texts related objective test 2. Dramatization of Robin Hood	1. Rubric for art project teacher/ student 2. Student reflection paper.
Social Studies State Goals/ CAS	State 16/CAS A	State 17/CAS A&C State 18/CAS B	State 14/CAS D State 15/CAS A	State 18/CAS A
Resources	To See A World Text/Video/ Handouts/ Overhead	Video, handouts, teacher-made video and slides, resource books	To See A Word Text	Museum visit, video, guest artist

Social Studies	Accomplishments of Maya Civilization in Meso America	Development and achievement of Renaissance. Spread of Renaissance through Europe	Aztec rise to power, empire, market system, religious beliefs, and accomplishments	Unification of Spain, development of empire, and Colombian exchange
Art	(P) May Temple Drawing—use of value/ shading with charcoal and two-point perspective	Pencil drawing of the Mona Lisa using perspective in the background	(P) Codex—write a creation myth using Aztec glyphs and images	No visual art component
Language Arts	Read and Outline The Maya Book	Read in class Romeo and Juliet	Read the Aztec Book and learn about beliefs, myths and heroes of Aztec culture	Read The Captive— influence of Spain in Americas and characterization
Student Learning	Directed observation of objects and the environment/use inquiry to understand past and present events	Students are producers	Develop interpersonal skills and use cultural symbols to construct meaning	Define and clarify problems and issues
Assessment	1. Rubric teacher/student 2. Objective Test on Maya Book	Object/Essay Test Performance scenes from Romeo and Juliet	1. Rubric for art project teacher/student 2. Text related objective test	Object/essay test
Social Studies State Goals/CAS	State 16 CAS A,B,C	State 15/CAS A State 16/CAS-A	State 16/CAS B	State 14 CAS D State 15 CAS A
Resources	The Maya trade book, In Search of Maya Video, slides,handout	To See A World Text/Video	The Aztec Trade Book – 500 Nations Video Tape	To See A World Text, 1492 – Conquest of Paradise Video Tape

continued on next page

Seventh Grade Arte Integrated Social Studies Curriculum – The Formation of Our Nations   (continued)

Units/Goals/Quarter	Q3 Colonial Mexico	Q4 Colonial American (U.S.)	Q4 U.S. Independence	Q4 U.S. Constitution
Social Studies	Spanish colonization of the Americas, introduction of Spanish culture and effects on indigenous population	French and English colonization of areas that became the United States	The creation of modern democracies form colonial foundations	Foundations of United States democracy, separation and balance of power, individual rights
Art	(P) Retablos (painted picture depicting family miracle)—portraiture, figure drawing, and color	No visual art component	(P) Timeline / use computer program to create an illustrated timeline of events studied	Timeline project continued
Language Arts	Research family stories and write a narrative for Retablo painting	Read Witch of Blackbird Pond	Perform a dialogue depicting conflict between colonies and mother country	In groups write an interpretation of section of Bill of Rights and present to the class
Student Learning	Express family history, and appreciate Mexican culture form cultural blending		Evaluate and judge information related political problem	Students act as teachers and interpret benefits of various constitution amendments
Assessment	1. Rubric for art project teacher student 2. Text-related test	Text-related test	1. Text-related test 2. Rubric for art based project/teacher student	U.S. Constitution Test
Social Studies State Goals/CAS	State 15 CAS C State 16 CAS A	State Goal 14 CAS C&D	State 14/CAS A,B,C State 15 CAS A,B,C	State 14/ CAS A,B,C,D
Resources	Video of Retablos, guest artist, To See A Word Text, Our U.S. History	Our U.S. History, videos – The Pilgrim, Jamestown, Last of Mohicans	Our U.S. History Text and videos	Our U.S. History, Constitution Book, and Video on U.S. Government

Note. Red = Indigenous Americans, blue = Europe Origins, purple = blending or European and indigenous traditions or emerging North American nations, (P) = arts-based project.
Appendix H: Three Approaches to Evaluating and Interpreting Progress/Success With Your Partnership
(Adapted from Stringer, E. T., 1996. *Action research: A handbook for practitioners* Thousand Oaks, CA: Sage.)

Appendix H:
Three Approaches
to Evaluating
and Interpreting
Progress/Success
With Your Partnership

Approach 1: Ask Interpretive Questions

A. Who was involved?
    Who was influential?
    Who else was significant?
    Who has resources?
    Who was cooperative?
    Who started?
    Who joined later?
    Who is still not involved?
    Who_____ ?

B. What was our focus?
    What were the major events?
    What were the main purposes?
    What were the failures?
    What were the interests of people involved?
    What did we learn?
    What _____ ?

C. How did we get started?
    How did we sustain the activity?
    How were decisions made?
    How were resources used?
    How much influence did various participants have?
    How were students involved in the planning?
    How _____ ?

D. Where were resources found?
   Where did most activities happen?
   Where did culminating activities happen?
   Where did people meet, plan, work?
   Where _____ ?

E. When were events planned during the year?
   When was leadership needed?
   When did problems occur?
   When did people meet?
   When were students involved in the planning?
   When _____ ?

F. Why did we begin this partnership?
   Why did it continue?
   Why do we want to continue from here?
   Why _____ ?

Approach 2: Partnership Review

- Vision and Mission
     Overarching/general purpose
     Ways in which the partnership enacts its vision
- Goals and Objectives
     How the partnership seeks to achieve its purposes
     Outcomes the partnership is seeking
- Structure of the Partnership
     Roles
     Responsibilities
     Resources
     Rules/procedures
- Operation
     Each person's roles and responsibilities
     Tasks and responsibilities not clearly assigned
     Gaps
     Barriers
     Factors hindering
     Successes
     Factors contributing to success
- Problems, Issues, Concerns

Approach 3: Concept Mapping

Draw/Diagram the partnership as a series of concentric circles or as a continuum timeline. Who are the participants and when have they been involved? How can progress be seen in the time that has elapsed? What is the central concept and how can we illustrate its evolution?

(Adapted from Stringer, E. T., 1996. *Action research: A handbook for practitioners.* Thousand Oaks, CA: Sage.)

Appendix I:
Key Questions
for Partnerships

First Set of Key Questions—
When partners are thinking about a new partnership:

Do I need any help to:
Solve a problem?
Meet specific student or member needs?
Develop, influence, or implement a plan, policy, or mandate?
Build better community relations?
Better use an available resource?
Take advantage of an opportunity?
What do I need?
Who could help me?
How could I help them?
What are my limits to working with them?

Second Set of Key Questions—
When partners have decided to collaborate:

What are our shared goals?
Who are we trying to help?
What are our specific objectives?
Who will make fundamental decisions for the partnership?
How much will this cost?
Where will we get the funds?
How will we operate?
How will we know if we are succeeding?

Third Set of Key Questions—
As the partnership matures:

How are we doing?
Do we need to:
Recruit new partners?
Adjust our projects?
Revise our goals or objectives?

(Adapted from Dreeszen, C., Aprill, A., & Deasy, R. 1999. *Learning partnerships: Improving learning in schools with arts partners in the community.* Washington, DC: Arts Education Partnership/Council of Chief State School Officers: The entire document is available online at http://aep-arts.org.)

Appendix J: Contributors— All who were interviewed, submitted writing, photographs, units, and lesson plans

(We know we may have missed a few names below, but ... we thank all of you!!

1. Ahlman, Angelica
2. Alexopoulas, Constantine
3. Alvarez, Myrna
4. Amon, Connie
5. Anderson, Wendy
6. Arnold, Greta
7. Arzate, Mitzy
8. Avalos, Olga
9. Baker, Glenda
10. Bartozyk, Jan
11. Bernard, Dianne
12. Bernard, Trenisean
13. Beyer, Patti Kelly
14. Bowden, Tiffany
15. Breen, Maureen
16. Brooks, Sharlean
17. Brown, Abena Joan
18. Burnette, Forian
19. Bucsi, Andrea Federle
20. Bustamente, Sarah
21. Calderon, Eric
22. Capers, Ethel
23. Carlson, Sandy
24. Carroll, William
25. Casey, Anne
26. Casper, Elizabeth
27. Castro, Rodolfo
28. Cathey, Paul
29. Catterall, James
30. Cerda, Martha
31. Chaloff, Lissa
32. Chan, Samantha
33. Chico, Anne
34. Chong-Hinojosa, Gabriela E.
35. Clayton, Dr. Ronald
36. Cobb, Mary
37. Coleman, Harriet
38. Conde, Katherine
39. Contro, Antonia
40. Cook, Terry
41. Cooper, Ashley
42. Cornelis, Darlene
43. Cornelis, Polly
44. Cortez, Martha
45. Covert, Ralph
46. Crabill, Ellen
47. Cruz, Ivan Bello
48. Da Silva, Aandraya
49. Daniels, Harvey
50. Dawkins, Ernest
51. Dawson, Kay
52. Deckert, Diane
53. Dee, Jim
54. De los Reyes, Rebecca
55. Delgado, Guillermo
56. DeSent, Wendee
57. Diehl, Deb
58. Dillon, Samantha
59. Doolas, Rosemary
60. Drogmueller, Karen
61. Dunne, Margie
62. Economou, Maria
63. Emmons, Lynette
64. Engel, Cyd
65. England, Chanita
66. Erickson, Karen
67. Erling, Susana
68. Escobar, Jose

69. Ewing, Eve
70. Extract, Lon
71. Fashingbauer, Diane
72. Fields, Cydney
73. Fitzgerald, Denise
74. Flatley, David
75. Flores, Laura
76. Floros, Theodore
77. Franklin, Logan
78. Fratto, Francesco
79. Fratto, Ruth
80. Gausselin, Patti
81. Geldermann, Nancy
82. Gonzales, Abi
83. Goulding, Laura
84. Gray, Harry
85. Gray, Joan
86. Gregory, Shannece
87. Gressou, Morine
88. Grigg, Kendall
89. Grisham, Esther
90. Guan, Sandy
91. Guerra, Marina
92. Gunning, Aron
93. Hall, Lauren
94. Hallenberg, Ann
95. Halter, Jacob
96. Hardman, Cheryl
97. Hernandez, Maria
98. Hinojosa, Gabriela Chong
99. Hinton, Bettye R.
100. Hogg, Grethel
101. Hooper, Lansana, Emily
102. Hoover, Mary
103. Huante, Lydia
104. Hughes, Phelida
105. James, Joslyn Guillotte
106. James, Tara S.
107. Jensen, Jennifer
108. Jimenez, Irma
109. Jirasek, Rita Arias
110. Johnson, Jamila
111. Jones, Theresa
112. Juarez, Genevieve
113. Kelly, Marge
114. Kerwin, Joellen
115. Kersnar, David
116. Kidd, Laura
117. Kincaid, Susan
118. Kopoulos, Dani
119. Kranicke, Michelle
120. Kuykendoll, Charles
121. Lad, Matthew
122. Lam, Annie
123. Lamey, Doug
124. Lammie, Carol
125. Landrum, Carol
126. Larson, Mike
127. Laville, Tamara
128. Lawrence, Reginald
129. LeMoine, Andre
130. Lewis, Donna
131. Lewis, Felipe
132. Lieber, Esther
133. Lowe, Amy
134. Maldonado, Jeff
135. Maltese, Kathleen
136. Mandel, Donna
137. Manderschied, Ron
138. Martin, Kathleen
139. Martinez, Patricia
140. Mason, Lisa Harris
141. Maude, Karen
142. Maugeri, Frank
143. Mawrence, Sandra
144. Mayer, Elizabeth
145. McDonough, Nancy
146. McGrady, Conor
147. McGrath, Katherine
148. Mendoza, Irene
149. Metzl, Edward
150. Micsko, Tim
151. Micula, Adrian
152. Mondragon, Kristina
153. Moore, Charles Michael
154. Moreno, Mari Carmen
155. Mosley, Richard
156. Mui, Daniel
157. Mularski, Ken
158. Murphy, Jackie
159. Murphy, Pat
160. Mutua, Jason
161. Nakayama, Margo
162. Nambo, Alfredo
163. Nangle, Eleanor
164. Navarro, Carol
165. Nieciak, John
166. Nixon, Rachel
167. Ogada, Sheba
168. Oliveri, Sonja
169. Oquendo, Carlton
170. Osorio, Erik
171. Overstreet, Kaja
172. Parisi, Jean
173. Park, Thomas
174. Passman, Roger
175. Pedrote, Carlos
176. Pekin, Donna
177. Pfeiffer, Angelia
178. Pino, Ed
179. Pinski, Daniel
180. Pinski, Joanna
181. Pitchford-Jolly, Marva
182. Pointer, Leonia
183. Port, Soloman
184. Pratt, Shanetta
185. Price, Alice
186. Price, Ramon
187. Pospishil, Marilyn
188. Pruitt, Lara
189. Ramey, Sarah
190. Raymond, Debbie
191. Raymond, Dominick
192. Richards, Bob
193. Rikoski, Rick
194. Riley, Pat
195. Rivera, Edith
196. Robinson, Ken
197. Robinson, Nina
198. Robinson, Robin
199. Robles, Elena
200. Roche, Erin
201. Rodriguez-Giles, Tatiana
202. Rojek, Michaeline
203. Romaniu, Natalya
204. Ronzio, Johnathan

205. Ronzio, Maryann
206. Rownd, Tricia
207. Rusk, Patricia
208. Ryan, Ryna
209. Sacre, Antoni
210. Salas, Eduardo Angulo
211. Salerno, Kim
212. Salgado, Diego
213. Samuel, Jackie
214. Sanders, Dorothy
215. Santas, Brian
216. Savato, William
217. Schilling, Marie
218. Schlichting, Rich
219. Schlick, Hardy
220. Schmidt, Mary Lou
221. Sciscioli, Peter
222. Searcy, Deidre
223. Shabu, Kwabena
224. Shigley, Scott
225. Shupe, Sue
226. Sidwell, Sydney
227. Sigman, Mary Tracy
228. Sikkema, Scott
229. Skydell, Eleanor
230. Socoloff, Miriam
231. Sollmon-St. John, Laura
232. Steele, Tammy
233. Stover, Margaret
234. Strauss, Ben
235. Strong, Thelma
236. Sullivan, Monica
237. Sydney, Lisa
238. Taylor, Jim
239. Terrassa, Jackie
240. Tinajero, Fernando
241. Torre, Detra
242. Townsend, Rene
243. Tran, Khoa
244. Trinder, Vicki
245. Tritschler, Ellen
246. Turbov, Victoria
247. Twichell, Charles
248. Twill, Michael
249. Urschel, Beverly
250. Usloga, Andrea
251. Valenzuela, Lourdes
252. Vaske, Virginia
253. Vena, Joanne
254. Vinson, Andrea
255. Vivas, Elizabeth Chase
256. Vivas, Gerardo
257. Waldorf, Lynn
258. Walton, Rochel
259. Washington, Carolyn
260. Watkins, Barbara Eason
261. Weaver, Patricia
262. Weaver, Susan
263. Westbrook, Kyle
264. White, Colin
265. White, David
266. Widegrin, Carol
267. Williams, Nancy Wright
268. Williams, Noelle
269. Williams, Shenethe
270. Wise, Dennis
271. Witzl, Tamara
272. Ziegler, Maryellen

CAPE Principals and their schools

Louis J. Agassiz Elementary School—Gail D. Ward

John L. Audubon Elementary School—Nereida Bonilla

Benjamin Banneker Elementay School—Rufus Brown

James Blaine Elementary School—Gladys Vaccarezza

Charles S. Brownell Elementary School—George S. Huff

Nathaniel Hawthorne Scholastic Academy—Sandra J. Mawrence

Robert Healy School—Analila Chico

Lakeview High School—Scott Feaman

Lincoln Park High School—Janis Todd

James McCosh Elementary School—Barbara Eason-Watkins

Metro/Crane High School—George E. Frey

Phillip Murray Language Academy—Virginia Vaske

William B. Ogden School—Kenneth Staral

Isabelle C. O'Keeffe Elementary School—Gloria D. Baker

Jose Clemente Orozco Academy of Fine Arts—Rebecca de los Reyes

James Otis Elementary School—James Cosme

Parkside Academy—Dr. Burgess L. Gardner

Ravenswood Elementary School—Joy Donovan

Elizabeth P. Peabody Elementary School—Mary Ellen Mongoven

Casmir Pulaski Community Academy—Robert Alexander

William H. Ray School—Cydney Fields

Mark Sheridan Math and Science Academy—Jerome Sheppard

Telpochcalli School—Tamara Witzl

John A. Walsh School—Dr. Ronald Clayton

William E. Wells Community Academy—Carmen C. Martinez

Appendix K: Resources, Web Sites, and Materials

SELECTED BOOKS

Teaching in Arts Partnership Classrooms

Albers, P., & Murphy, S. (2000). *Telling pieces: Art as literacy in middle school classes.* Mahwah, NJ: Lawrence Erlbaum Associates.

Blecher, S., & Jaffee, K.(1995). *Weaving in the arts.* Portsmouth, NH: Heinemann.

Buchwald, E., & Roston, R. (Eds.). (1991). *Mixed voices: Contemporary poems about music.* Minneapolis, MN: Milkweed Editions.

Cahan, S., & Kocur, Z (1996). *Contemporary art and multicultural education.* New York: Routledge.

Calkins, L. (1994). *The art of teaching writing.* Portsmouth, NH: Heinemann.

Carnegie Hall. (1999). *LinkUp! 1998–1999: The composer's world from sketch to score.* New York: Author.

Cecil, N. L., & Lauritzen, P. (1994) *Literacy and the arts for the integrated classroom.* New York: Longman.

Chancer, J., & Rester-Zodrow, G. (1997). *Moon journals: Writing, art and inquiry through focused nature study.* Portsmouth, NH: Heinemann.

Cohen, E., & Gainer, R. (1995). *Art—Another language for learning.* Portsmouth, NH: Heinemann.

Daniels, H., & Bizar, M. (1998). *Methods that matter: Six structures for best practice classrooms.* York, ME: Stenhouse Publishers.

Edwards, C., Gandini, L., & Forman, G. (1993). *The hundred languages of children: The Reggio Emilia approach to early childhood education.* Norwood, NJ: Ablex.

Ernst, K. (1994). *Picturing learning: Artists and writers in the classroom.* Portsmouth, NH: Heinemann.

Ernst, K. (1997). *A teacher's sketch journal: Observations on learning and teaching.* Portsmouth, NH: Heinemann.

Gallas, K. (1994). *The languages of learning: How children talk, write, dance, draw, and sing their understanding of the world.* New York: Teachers College Press.

Garoian, C. R. (1999). *Performing pedagogy: Toward an art of politics.* Albany: State University of New York Press.

Goldberg, M. R., & Phillips, A. (1992). *Arts as education.* Cambridge, MA: Harvard Educational Review.

Gridley, M. C. (1997). *Jazz styles: History and analysis* (6th ed.). Upper Saddle River, NJ: Prentice-Hall.

Heinig, R. B. (1992). *Improvisation with favorite tales: Integrating drama into the reading/writing classroom.* Portsmouth, NH: Heinemann.

Hindley, J. (1996). *In the company of children.* York, ME: Stenhouse Publishers.

Hubbard, R. (1996). *A workshop of the possible: Nurturing children's creative development.* York, ME: Stenhouse Publishers.

Jenoure, T. (2000). *Navigators: African-American musicians, dancers, and visual artists in academe.* Albany: State University of New York Press.

Lane, B. (1993). *After THE END: Teaching and learning creative revision.* Portsmouth, NH: Heinemann.

Laughlin, M. K., & Street, T.P. (1992). *Literature-based art & music.* Phoenix, AZ: Oryx Press.

Marzan, J. (1997). *Luna, luna: Creative writing ideas from Spanish, Latin American, and Latino Literature.* New York: Teachers & Writers Collaborative.

Ohanian, S. (1992). *Garbaga pizza, patchwork quilts, and math magic.* New York: W.H. Freeman.

Robinson, G. (1995). *Sketch-books: Explore and store.* Portsmouth, NH: Heinemann.

Selwyn, D. (1993). *Living history in the classroom: Integrative arts activities for making social studies meaningful.* Zephyr Press.

Sobel, D. (1998). *Mapmaking with children: Sense of place education for the elementary years.* Portsmouth, NH: Heinemann.

Whitin, P. (1996). *Sketching stories, stretching minds: Responding visually to literature.* Portsmouth, NH: Heinemann.

School Improvement and the Arts Resources

Fiske, E. B. (1999). *Champions of change: The impact of the arts on learning.* The Arts Education Partnership, The President's Committee on the Arts and Humanities. Funded by the GE Fund and the John D. & Catherine T. MacArthur Foundation.

National Assembly of State Arts Agencies. *Eloquent Evidence: Arts at the Core of Learning.* 1029 Vermont Avenue NW / Washington, DC 20005.

President's Committee on the Arts and the Humanities. *Creative America.* 1100 Pennsylvania Avenue NW / Washington, DC 20506.

Remer, J. (1996). *Beyond enrichment: Building effective arts partnerships with schools and your community.* New York: American Council for the Arts.

Remer, J. (1990). *Changing schools through the arts.* New York: American Council for The Arts.

Wilson, B. (1997). *The quiet evolution: Changing the face of arts education.* Los Angeles: Getty Education Institute.

Negotiation With Community Resources

Cousins, E., & Rodgers, M. (Ed.). (1995). *Fieldwork: An expeditionary learning outward bound reader*. Virginia: New American Schools Development Corporation.

Dreeszen, C. (1991). *Intersections: Community arts and education collaboration*. Amherst, MA: Arts Extension Service.

Fisher, R., & Ury, W. (1991). *Getting to yes: Negotiating agreement without giving in*. New York: Penguin Books.

Fullan, M. (1993). *Change forces: Probing the depths of educational reform*. Mississauga, Ontario: Falmer Press.

Holl, M.G., & Jones, P. d'A. (1995). *Ethnic Chicago: A multicultural portrait* (4th ed.). Grand Rapids, MI: William B. Eerdmans.

Trend, D. (1992). *Cultural pedagoge: Art/Education/Politics*. New York: Bergin & Garvey.

Children's and Adolescent Literature and Music Integration

Bunting, E. (1994). *Smoky night*. New York: Harcourt, Brace.

Clement, G. (1999). *The great poochini*. Vancouver: Groundwood Books.

Cole, J., & Calemenson, S. (1990). *Miss Mary Mack and other children's street rhymes*. New York: Beech Tree Books.

Cole, J. (1989). *Anna banana: 101 jump-rope rhymes*. New York: Beech Tree Books.

Collier, J. L. (1994). *The jazz kid*. New York: Puffin Books.

Diller, H. (1996). *Big band sound*. Honesdale, PA: Boyds Mill Press.

Downing, J. (1991). *Mozart tonight*. New York: Bradbury Press.

Isadora, R. (1979). *Ben's trumpet*. New York: Mulberry Books.

Kuskin, K. (1982). *The philharmonic gets dressed*. New York: HarperCollins.

Martin, B. (1994). *The maestro plays*. New York: Henry Holt.

Mora, P. (1994). *Listen to the desert/Oye al Desierto*. New York: Clarion.

Near, H. (1993). *The great peace march*. New York: Henry Holt.

Olaleye, I. (1995). *The distant talking drum: Poems from Nigeria*. Honesdale, PA: Wordsong Press.

Oram, H., Davis, C., & Kitamura, S. (1993). *The creepy crawly song book*. New York: Farrar, Straus & Giroux.

Seeger, P. (1986). *Abiyoyo*. New York: MacMillan.

Shange, N. (1994). *I live in music*. New York: Stewart, Tabori, & Chang.

Stemple, A. (1992). *Jane Yolen's Mother Goose songbook*. Honesdale, PA: Boyds Mill Press.

Tomlinson, T. (1997). *Dancing through the shadows*. New York: DK.

Weik, M. H. (1993). *The jazz man*. New York: Aladdin Books.

Winter, J. (1988). *Follow the drinking gourd*. New York: Alfred A. Knopf.

Wolff, V. E. (1991). *The Mozart season*. New York: Henry Holt.

Yolen, J. (Ed.). (1992). *Street rhymes around the world*. Honesdale, PA: Wordsong Press.

Yorinks, A. (1988). *Bravo Minski*. New York: Farrar, Straus & Giroux.

WEB SITES

Chicago Arts Partnerships in Education: *www.capeweb.org*

Orozco School: *www.orozco.cps.k12.il.us*

Carnegie Hall: *education@carnegiehall.org*

Goals 2000 Arts Education Partnership: *http://aep-arts.org*

Very Special Arts/Start with the Arts: *www.vsarts.org*

Galef Institute: Different Ways of Knowing: *www.dwoknet.lgalef.org*

Wolf Trap Institute for Early Learning Through the Arts: *www.wolf-trap.org/institute*

Smithsonian Early Enrichment Center: *www.si.edu/organiza/centers/seec*

Learning to Read Through the Arts: *bcob@worldnet.att.net*

Arts Education Partnership: *http://aep-arts.org*

ArtsEdge: *http://artsedge.kennedy-center.org*

Coming Up Taller: *http://www.cominguptaller.org*

ArtsEdNet: *http://222.artsednet.getty.edu*

Arts for Learning: *www.arts4learning.com*

American Alliance for Theatre and Education: *www.aate.com*

American Music Conference: *www.amc-music.com*

Educational Theatre Association: *www.etassoc.org*

Music Educators National Conference: *www.menc.org*

National Art Education Association: *www.naea-reston.org*

National Endowment for the Arts: *http://arts.endow.gov*

National Dance Association: *www.aahperd.org/nda/nda.html*

Heinemann Publications (numerous books on arts and learning): *www.heinemann.com*

Appendix L:
State Arts
Agency Directory

For more information about arts and education resources in your state and community, contact the Arts in Education Coordinator at your state's arts agency.

Alabama State Council on the Arts
(334)242-4076/FAX(334)240-3269

Alaska State Council on the Arts
(907)269-6610/FAX(907)269-6601

American Samoa Council on Culture, Arts, and Humanities
(684)633-4347/FAX(684)633-2059

Arizona Commission on the Arts
(602)255-5882/FAX(602)256-0282

Arkansas Arts Council
(501)324-9770/FAX(501)324-9154

California Arts Council
(916)322-6555/FAX(916)322-6575

Colorado Council on the Arts
(303)894-2617/FAX(303)894-2615

Connecticut Commission on the Arts
(860)566-4770/FAX(860)566-6462

DC Commission on the Arts & Humanities
(202)724-5613/FAX(202)727-4135

Delaware Division of the Arts
(302)577-8278/FAX(302)577-6561

Florida Division of Cultural Affairs
(850)487-2980/FAX(850)922-5259

Georgia Council for the Arts
(404)685-2787/FAX(404)685-2788

Guam Council on the Arts & Humanities Agency
(671)475-2242/3(CAHA)/FAX(671)472-ART1(2781)

Mainland Contact for Guam Council
(202)624-3670/FAX(202)624-3679

Hawaii State Foundation on Culture and the Arts
(808)586-0300/FAX(808)586-0308

Idaho Commission on the Arts
(208)334-2119/FAX(208)334-2488

Illinois Arts Council
(312)814-6750/FAX(312)814-1471

Indiana Arts Commission
(317)232-1268/FAX(317)232-5595

Iowa Arts Council
(515)281-445 I/FAX(515)242-6498

Kansas Arts Commission
(785)296-3-335/FAX(785)296-4989

Kentucky Arts Council
(502)564-3757/FAX(502)564-2839

Louisiana Division of the Arts
(504)342-8180/FAX(504)342-8173

Maine Arts Commission
(207)287-2724/FAX(207)287-2335

Maryland State Arts Council
(410)767-6555/FAX(410)333-1062

Massachusetts Cultural Council
(617)727-3668/FAX(617)727-0044

Michigan Council for Arts and Cultural Affairs
(313)256-3731/FAX(313)256-3781

Minnesota State Arts Board
(612)215-1600/FAX(612)215-1602

Mississippi Arts Commission
(601)359-6030 or 6040/FAX(601)359-6008

Montana Arts Council
(406)444-6430/FAX(406)444-6548

Nebraska Arts Council
(402)595-2122/FAX(402)595-2334

Nevada State Council on the Arts
(702)687-6680/FAX(702)687-6688

New Hampshire State Council on the Arts
(603)271-2789/FAX(603)271-3584

New Jersey State Council on the Arts
(609)292-6130/FAX(609)989-1440

New Mexico Arts
(505)827-6490/FAX(505)827-6043

New York State Council on the Arts
(212)387-7000/FAX(212)387-7164

North Carolina Arts Council
(919)733-2821/FAX(919)733-4834

North Dakota Council on the Arts
(701)328-3954/FAX(701)328-3963

Commonwealth Council for Arts and Culture (Northern Mariana Islands)
(011)(670)322-9982 or 9983/FAX(0l1)(670)322-9028

Mainland Contact (Northern Mariana Islands)
(202)673-5869/FAX(202)673-5873

Ohio Arts Council
(614)466-2613/FAX(614)466-4494

Oklahoma Arts Council
(405)521-2931/FAX(405)521-6418

Oregon Arts Commission
(503)986-0087/FAX(503)986-0260

Pennsylvania Council on the Arts
(717)787-6883/FAX(717)783-2538

Institute of Puerto Rican Culture
(787)725-5137/FAX(787)724-8393

Rhode Island State Council on the Arts
(401)222-3880/FAX(401)521-1351

South Carolina Arts Commission
(803)734-8696/FAX(803)734-8526

South Dakota Arts Council
(605)773-3131/FAX(605)773-6962

Tennessee Arts Commission
(615)741-1701/FAX(615)741-8559

Texas Commission on the Arts
(512)463-5535/FAX(512)475-2699

Utah Arts Council
(801)236-7555/FAX(801)236-7556

Vermont Arts Council
(802)828-3291/FAX(802)828-3363

Virgin Islands Council on the Arts
(340)774-5984/FAX(340)774-6206

Virginia Commission for the Arts
(804)225-3132/FAX(804)225-4327

Washington State Arts Commission
(360)753-3860/FAX(360)586-5351

West Virginia Commission on the Arts
(304)558-0240/FAX(304)558-2779

Wisconsin Arts Board
(608)266-0190/FAX(608)267-0380

Wyoming Arts Council
(307)777-7742/FAX(307)777-5499

Author Index

Subject Index

Printed in the USA/Agawam, MA
August 22, 2013

579221.002